Building Kingdom Communities

An environmentally friendly book printed and bound in England by
www.printondemand-worldwide.com

http://www.fast-print.net/bookshop

BUILDING KINGDOM COMMUNITIES
WITH THE DIACONATE AS A NEW ORDER OF MISSION
Copyright © David Clark 2016

A catalogue record for this book is available from the British Library

ISBN 978-178456-311-0

First Published 2016 by
Fast-Print Publishing of Peterborough, England.

Building Kingdom Communities
with the diaconate
as a new order of mission

David Clark

Contents

To Sue Jackson
former Warden of the Methodist Diaconal Order
who warmly welcomed me as a colleague

Introduction

'For such a time as this'

The purpose of this book is to set out the case for the renewal of the diaconate as an order of mission called to facilitate the transformation of a fragmented society and world through the gifts of the kingdom community.

This Introduction is being written on Holocaust Memorial Day. It is a day commemorating the liberation of Auschwitz-Birkenau, the largest of the Nazi death camps which in the Second World War witnessed the extermination of over a million people, ninety per cent of whom were Jews. The remainder of the twentieth-century saw a world struggling to ensure that the holocaust never happened again. There was encouragement, with the emergence of the European Union and the collapse of the Berlin Wall in 1989. Five years ago this month saw the first signs of the Arab Spring with an uprising in Tunisia and protests in Tahrir Square in Egypt. Hopes were high for the democratization of at least some countries in the Middle East.

Yet, as so often happens in human history, those forces which appear to offer a new beginning are all too soon eclipsed by others which remind us how fragile are our attempts to build community. September 2001 witnessed the assault on the Twin Towers in New York, the destruction of which fanned the flames of war in Afghanistan and led to the invasion of Iraq with its tragic aftermath. We now know that the Arab Spring, far from heralding a new era of justice and peace, has led to reactionary oppression and hugely destructive conflicts in Syria and other Arab nations. As al-Qaeda has faded, so ISIS has moved centre-stage.

Since 2008, Europe, which for many decades had forged a new solidarity, has been set back by deep economic problems. And now the huge influx of refugees from a war-torn Syria and elsewhere is seeing the barricades going up once again, a retreat into xenophobia and the vilification of incomers, all threatening the coherence of the European Union itself. These and other crises worldwide demonstrate that the quest to create a brotherhood and sisterhood of humankind will be at the top of the political and religious agenda for a very long time.

'For such a time as this'

In 1998, the Anglican House of Bishops set up a working party with the above title to explore the potential of 'a renewed diaconate in the Church of England'. The report was given this title because the working party believed that a new form of diaconate would enable the church to meet the challenges facing it at 'a decisive moment in God's time' (p. 1). Today that 'decisive moment in God's time' faces the church with the immense task of helping to transform a fragmented and fractious world into a global community.

That moment also faces the church in the West with a deep crisis of confidence created not only by a drastic decline in membership but also by the increasing number of people stating openly that they no longer regard Christian faith as credible. Consequently if there were ever a time when the church should be exploring every conceivable way in which to engage in more meaningful ways with society and world, the present is such a moment.

A renewed diaconate as an order of mission

We believe that *For such a time as this* was correct in stating that a renewed diaconate is essential if the church is to be equipped to pursue its mission in a relevant and effective way in today's world. However, we go further and argue that any renewed diaconate needs to assume the form of an order of mission. This books sets out the case for that conclusion.

It is our contention that such a development would help to bring the resources of Christian faith to bear more fully on the demanding task of enabling humankind to live in justice and peace and as a global community of communities. It would also enable the church to fulfil its calling as a movement offering life, liberation, love and learning, later described as the gifts of the kingdom community, as well as an institution ensuring the resilience and continuity of its own life as a community of faith.

At the same time, it is essential that the creation of a renewed diaconate as an order of mission is complemented by presbyters becoming an order of continuity. Ensuring continuity is no secondary calling. Just as a diaconal order of mission must be committed to the transformation of society and world through the gifts of the kingdom community, so a presbyteral order of continuity has to be responsible for the ongoing transformation of the church through those same gifts.

Diaconal leadership in a changing world

In the life of the church, the diaconate has had a long and influential history even though the role of deacon has undergone many changes over the centuries. For a considerable period in the life of the Western church the diaconate virtually disappeared. However it re-emerged in a number of forms. First, a tradition had early on taken root that those ordained into the ministry of the church should be given the title of deacon for a brief period before they were ordained to the priesthood. Secondly, a number of post-reformation churches ascribed the title of deacon to lay people holding a largely administrative role in the life of the local church. In the early nineteenth century, the name deaconess or deacon was given to those, mainly lay women, who formed associations of one kind or another to minister to the sick, poor or marginalized, especially in the emerging urban conurbations. Finally, in the twentieth century came a reaffirmation of the permanent or distinctive diaconate, most conspicuous within the Roman Catholic Church after Vatican II, designated a ministry in its own right.

Two facts of particular relevance to this book can be gleaned from the history of the diaconate. The first is its deep embeddedness in the leadership of the church from the days of the early church. The second is the diversity of forms it has taken and thus its ability to adapt to the pressing needs of church and world at different times and in different places. It is these two attributes that make the diaconate a form of ministry exceptionally well suited to enable the church to engage in mission in a way that remains true to the gospel yet meets the needs of this day and age.

Half a loaf

Despite the hopes of those involved, what emerges from *For such a time as this*, and other reports on the same issue from the Church of England, Roman Catholic Church and Methodist Church[1], is a great

---

[1] In particular the following reports: Anglican (*For such a time as this. A renewed diaconate in the Church of England,* 2001 and *The Distinctive Diaconate*, Diocese of Salisbury, 2003); Roman Catholic (*From the Diakonia of Christ to the Diakonia of*

deal of confusion as to the form and function of a renewed diaconate. Furthermore, the governing bodies of the denominations concerned greeted these reports with faint praise and little has changed since their publication. A much bolder and more far-sighted vision is needed. This book offers such a vision and describes ways in which it might be made a reality.

A communal theology and ecclesiology

Any re-appraisal of how the church can communicate the gospel in more meaningful and imaginative ways to a world in search of community and to a disbelieving or, even more challenging, apathetic public, has to begin with a realistic theology of mission and an ecclesiology founded on that theology. Therefore, before we can grasp the significance of a renewed diaconate as an order of mission, a foundational theology and ecclesiology must be put into place.

The argument we put forward in this book is that any theology that is meaningful 'for such a time as this' must be a theology of community. Because such a theology needs to be grounded in the images of Trinity and kingdom, it will be a theology of the *kingdom* community offering to a fragmented society and world the gifts of life, liberation, love and learning. We also argue that an ecclesiology able to hold its own in the future must be founded on a communal theology, with the church recognized as the servant of the kingdom community and therefore a *diaconal* or servant church.

Servant leadership

If a theology of the kingdom community and the church as the servant of that community are at the heart of the Christian message, then another vital issue is the kind of leadership required to enable the diaconal church to fulfil its calling. Does the nature of ordained leadership currently in place help or hinder the church as it seeks to equip itself 'for such a time as this'?

The contention of this book is that, as it exists today, the model of leadership within an inherited church still largely shaped by Christendom, is inadequate for this task. The threefold form of

---

the Apostles, 2003); and Methodist (*What is a Deacon?* Methodist Conference, 2004).

ordained ministry (deacon, presbyter or priest[1] and bishop), as interpreted at present, results in a hierarchical and outmoded understanding of leadership. Furthermore, the office of deacon is still treated as a transitional and fleeting phase in the life of the priest or, if permanent, as a role subordinate to that of presbyter or priest. The creation of a renewed diaconate as an order of mission requires deacons to be given a standing equal to that of priests or presbyters and their ministry to be acknowledged as complementary not secondary to the latter.

The layout and origins of the material

In **Part 1** the parameters of a theology and spirituality of the kingdom community as the foundations on which the ecclesiology of the diaconal church is based are set out. The hall-marks of the diaconal church, in particular the primary place of the laity within it, are explored. The roles of deacon, presbyter and bishop are described in the context of servant leadership. Finally, we look at the meaning of mission as the discernment of the gifts of the kingdom community and at methods of intervention shaped by such discernment.

In **Part 2** the role of the deacon past and present, and some of the factors which could help the emergence of a renewed diaconate, are described. It is argued that the next phase in the development of servant leadership should be the formation of a renewed diaconate as an order of mission, with presbyters becoming an order of continuity. A profile of both of these orders is offered.

In **Part 3** we have selected an existing church and diaconal order to explore how the latter might develop as an order of mission and, in the process, give impetus to a church seeking to develop as a movement committed to the building of kingdom communities. In this context, we have chosen the Methodist Church in Britain because it has the advantage of already embodying many characteristics of the diaconal church, and the Methodist Diaconal Order, because it has important attributes which would be a great asset in its development as an order of mission. Finally, we explore a number of changes which would need to take place within

---

[1] Throughout this book we use the term presbyter rather than priest as the former applies to the most common form of ordained leadership across most denominations in Britain. However, it is recognized that in the public realm, at least in the West, it is the term priest which is normative.

Methodism for the developments suggested above to become a reality.

Most of the material in this book is drawn from my own writing over the past ten years. The chapters are arranged to facilitate the development of the models of the diaconal church and of a renewed diaconate as an order of mission, and not in date order. Thus a brief preamble is given at the beginning of each chapter to indicate why it has been placed where it is and when it was first published.

Because the chapters are not in date order, there is here and there some repetition. Thus where essential minimal editing of the original text has taken place to remove anomalies or dated material. More important, however, is for the reader to note that my understanding of the nature of a renewed diaconate has developed over the decade during which these chapters were written. Only in later chapters, written specifically for this publication, does the explicit designation of the diaconate as an order of mission appear. This is not because the concept of the diaconate as an order of mission has been an afterthought but because my earlier reflections have been leading to that conclusion, though not in such a definitive way as more recently.

One other development in the text needs to be mentioned. In the material published some years ago, my belief was that the key role for the deacon within a renewed diaconate should be that of community educator, that is helping the laity to understanding the foundations of and to equip them for the practice of kingdom community building. My conviction that deacons should be primarily educators and enablers of the laity, the church's primary resource for mission, remains very strong. However, more recently I have come to acknowledge that, when operating in situations where the church is weak or non-existent, deacons may sometimes need to take a more directive approach and employ a number of other roles associated with servant leadership, as indicated in the chapters concerned.

David Clark
Bakewell
January 2016

Part 1
The kingdom community and the diaconal church

1. Community or chaos?

Preamble

If mission is to be 'transforming', as David Bosch (1991) claims in his classic work on that subject, then the church must have a vision of what transformation means in order to make that vision a reality. We believe that such a vision includes what it is for men and women to become fully human. However, becoming fully human is not simply an individual concern. The humanity of any one of us is inseparably linked to the humanity of all of us. Thus 'transforming mission' must always indicate how human beings can be equipped and empowered to live together as a community, from the local to global scale.

In subsequent chapters we explore the meaning of community, employing the concept of 'the kingdom community' to inform, enrich and empower our vision. First, however, we need to come to grips with some of the factors which make the building of the world as a community, in practice a global community of communities, such a difficult undertaking. There is of course always the insecurity and self-centredness of human beings to take into account. But there are also more objective factors impinging on the quest for community peculiar to the day and age in which we live. In this chapter we explore the relatively recent phenomenon of a mobile world so that we can address how the church might more effectively shape its 'transforming mission' to the needs of our time.

The material for this chapter was developed in a number of papers, most recently published in 2005 as an introduction to *Breaking the Mould of Christendom*[1]. Thus many of the examples and references are to that period. However, the chapter concerned is reprinted here because the challenge that a civilization on the move presents to the quest for community is as relevant today as it has ever been.

Introduction

'In retrospect the millennium marked only a moment in time. It was the events of 11 September that marked a turning point in history,

---

[1] Clark (2005: second printing, 2014) *Breaking the Mould of Christendom* (pp. 3-12).

where we confront the dangers of the future and assess the choices facing humankind.' Thus Tony Blair began his speech to the Labour Party Conference in Brighton in October 2001.

We begin this new millennium facing the age-old problems of poverty, homelessness and disease. It is a sobering thought, as Glover (1999) graphically reminds us, that the twentieth century was one which witnessed more people perish in wars than any other in human history. The new millennium, however, sees endemic problems assuming new forms, and fresh challenges to the sustainability of human civilization taking centre-stage.

Conventional wars have become ever more dangerous not least 'because technology makes them a threat to the survival of the whole species' (p. 41). Virulent diseases, such as HIV/AIDS and SARS, appear on the scene just as others are apparently vanquished. Our small and fragile planet is now faced with an exploding world population and the destruction of a life-sustaining environment, matters which caused previous generations little concern (*Two-thirds of world's resources 'used up'*, Guardian, 30/3/05). And the emergence of international terrorism, allied to the proliferation of weapons of mass destruction, means that no corner of the globe can any longer regard itself as a safe haven.

Yet these self-evident threats to the survival of human civilization remain 'presenting problems.' Their resolution is possible only if we put at the top of our agenda the fundamental issue of how we can affirm the riches of our common humanity and work together in pursuit of the common good. It is not the dangers outlined above which threaten our world most profoundly, but the breakdown of community. As Tony Blair put it in his Brighton address (Blair, 2001): 'To-day the threat is chaos. (Our response must be) the power of community'. But why is 'the power of community' so difficult to harness?

A civilization on the move

My grandfather worked as a booking clerk on the Great Western Railway. Though associated with transport all his life, he never left England, either for work or for pleasure. In a life of over ninety years, he lived entirely in middle England – Ludlow, Birmingham and Nottingham. My father, who was over a hundred when he died, also lived in middle England. However, his work as the first personnel manager for a large pharmaceutical company often took him to the continent and occasionally, by sea, to the USA. As a boy, an army officer, a student, a Methodist minister, a college lecturer and now retired, I have already lived in eleven different locations from London to the Lake District and have travelled around four continents. Our son is married to an American girl and now works for a research institute of international fame in Seattle. His three children hold passports for several countries. The story of my own family, as well as that of many others, shows that over only a few generations 'mobility' has transformed human life in a quite dramatic way. If this were merely physical movement then perhaps the world would have changed more slowly. But alongside spatial mobility has gone cognitive, cultural and social mobility.

My mother was a remarkable correspondent, so much so that we always said that a logo of pen and paper should have been her epitaph. I have produced many thousands of words, but it was not that long ago that I replaced my battered typewriter with a lap-top. Our son lives by the computer and the Internet. He accesses the web daily as a matter of course and his emails constantly traverse the globe. His three children operate the new technology with total ease and immense competence.

We have well and truly entered what Drucker calls 'the knowledge society' (1993, p. 2). This not only means that 'information is power' for each and every one, but that many billions of people now have instant access to worldwide contacts and global experiences. Such 'cognitive mobility' has profound implications for the creation and sustaining of community at every level on human civilization from the local to the global.

Spatial and cognitive mobility bring with them 'cultural mobility'. It may not be entirely true that 'You can always tell a Brummie by the shamrock in his turban', but from my experience of living for many years in Birmingham I can empathize with that sentiment. Cultures are in transition more rapidly than ever before because people, spatially and cognitively, are on the move. Mobility means the emergence of pluralism. Mobility and pluralism together are bringing into being a new era, call it 'post-modern' or what you will.

Spatial, cognitive and cultural mobility go hand-in-hand with 'social mobility'. The latter indicates the way in which the traditional class and caste structures of human society, though still tenacious, are being slowly eroded. Here education is playing a crucial role. Old hierarchies, secular and religious, are being challenged as the 'layman' becomes increasingly well-informed, and knowledge and expertise are made available to all. Status and privileged founded on birth or tradition have by no means disappeared, but are giving way to a more open world in which 'equal opportunity' is regarded as an entitlement.

Centrifugal and centripetal forces

Mobility, in the forms we have described, gives impetus to two powerful forces now impinging on every society worldwide. They have been present throughout human history, but where they were once limited or latent, they are now global and manifest. One such force is *centrifugal*. It dislodges people, their beliefs, values and relationships, from traditional foundations, and thrusts them outwards into a bewildering 'cosmopolitan' world (Merton, 1957, pp. 387-420). The other force, often arising as a reaction to it, is *centripetal*. Here people are impelled inwards in an attempt to retain or reclaim their physical and human roots, their common heritage and a distinctive identity.

Centrifugal and centripetal forces are essential for the future viability of human life on this planet. But they also have the potential to destroy it. Thus the most critical task facing humankind as it enters a new millennium is discovering forms of community that can enable these two forces to become complementary, not mutually destructive. It is a task that is a central concern of this book.

'Moving out'

Centrifugal forces at work in our world are shifting people around spatially, cognitively, culturally and socially and in unprecedented ways. There is no doubt that the resulting transformation of human relationships is hugely creative.

We are now aware, as never before, how the rest of the world lives. Many people will remember for years what they were doing when news of the 9/11 attacks on the World Trade Centre in New York reached them, whether they be American or Arab, English or Indian, German or Japanese. Knowledge of those who suffer through human violence or natural disaster is now an immediate and worldwide experience.

'Moving out' means that opportunities to share knowledge, skills, ideas, values and beliefs are now available, not just to the rich and powerful but to billions of people across the globe. Our generation has access to a storehouse of human resources past and present like no generation before it. From finance to films, from cooking to sport, from architecture to wildlife, from fashion to property, all now constitute a worldwide 'exchange and mart'.

These centrifugal forces currently at work also bring massively enhanced opportunities for scientific and technological innovation and change. Medical skills, commercial experience, engineering know-how, information technology expertise, together with many other scientific and technical resources, can be passed around the globe at immense speed. The potential benefits from such advances promise a vastly enhanced quality of life for millions of people in every continent.

'Moving out' is also a phenomenon that offers the possibility of a more humane and responsible international ethic for economic and political affairs. Organizations such as the United Nations and the Commonwealth, however much they may fail in practice, symbolize a growing global commitment to human rights, social well-being and ecological stewardship. And alongside the international search for a just and sustainable world order, there now exists the myriad 'special issue' groups, from Amnesty International to Green Peace, themselves networking widely.

'Moving out' brings immense enrichment to our quality of life worldwide. But it is about far more than 'enrichment'; it is about the preservation of life on earth. Economically, politically and ecologically, the centrifugal forces at work today offer us the means to make human interdependence a reality and to create a world working for the common good. Daunting as the challenge is, we have the means to get our human act together for the sake of future generations.

However, there is a problem. The centrifugal forces at work on our civilization today also contain within them the seeds of disaster and chaos. The misuse or mishandling of nuclear power or biological expertise and the ecological collapse of our planet through pollution or the wasteful use of finite resources can only be overcome if we discover new forms of community that will enable us together to work for the common good. Yet, the very mobility that brings us such benefits also disconnects people from their territorial, mental, cultural and social roots and profoundly weakens those human bonds that previously held life together (Bauman, 2001, pp. 39-49). Two words sum up the shaking of our communal foundations: *'anonymity'* and *'amorality'*.

Anonymity and amorality

Anonymity

Our cosmopolitan society is one in which we now relate to people through role rather than personal relationships. Typically, I do not want to know the life-history of the mechanic who services my car, of the assessor who deals with my insurance claim or even of my local newsagent. In a society of such immense numbers and variety, we cannot cope with more than a handful of intimate and ongoing relationships. This is why ' bureaucracy' is essential; effective organizations can no longer operate on the basis of interpersonal affinities that get in the way of the job to be done.

Such anonymity can be a liberating experience, as young people leaving home to study or work elsewhere know full well. Yet it can also be exploited in the quest for unaccountable power and material gain, a response which Bauman calls 'the secession of the successful' (2001, pp.50-57). However, anonymity remains a high-risk gamble even for members of 'the globe-trotting elite' as Bauman acknowledges (p.113), with loneliness, isolation and loss of identity also stalking them. 'The homeless mind', as Berger (1973) calls this loss of our moorings, or getting lost in 'the lonely crowd' as Riesman describes it (1950), can be a hugely destructive phenomenon. Such anonymity can bring an acute sense of alienation from the real world of people and increase the threat of communal chaos, individually and collectively,

Centrifugal forces foster anonymity, or what Beck (1992) calls 'individualization', at all societal levels. The demise of the extended family in the Western world, the emergence of 'organization man' (Whyte, 1956) who must be trained in the art of constant uprooting, and the huge rise in the number of migrant workers across the world, are but indicators of forces steadily affecting us all and weakening sustainable personal relationships. 'Moving out' may bring us a great enhancement of choice, but increasing exposure to insecurity and isolation are also part of the package.

Amorality

Hand-in-hand with anonymity goes the problem of amorality. Mobility of mind and culture are key factors in the emergence of 'the vertigo of relativity' as Berger terms it (1980, p.9). 'Never before', he states, 'has "the pluralization of meaning and values" (been) experienced as massively by as many people' (p. 58).

Among the first to have to come to terms with an increasingly relativistic and amoral world have been the great religious traditions. Their claims to embody codes of ethics based on ultimate values are now openly exposed to questioning and are often summarily dismissed. But into the vacuum come other mechanisms of social control, economic and political, that have little interest in the well-being of humanity.

Amorality has been given an immense boost by the emergence of 'the market' as a core ideology in the shaping of human affairs. The credibility of the market rests on the assumption that it is ethically neutral and that it lifts economics out of the realm of contested values onto firm and universally reliable ground. In reality, the market attempts to raise amorality to the status of a virtue. The problem is that amorality has a good deal in common with what Emile Durkheim (1951) calls 'anomie', a state of normlessness wherein the roles and rules sustaining human relationships and giving people a sense of identity and purpose collapse. Durkheim found that the consequences could be the destruction of our social moorings and, not infrequently, suicide. Today, amorality lies at the heart of the threat to identity and meaning experienced not only by individuals, but also by ethnic, religious and social groupings whose values have hitherto been rooted in a common heritage and cohesive cultural tradition.

The centrifugal forces now affecting our world have much to commend them: a new openness and enrichment of experience, greater choice, the chance to learn from one another and share resources, and the hope of tackling critical global problems with at least some chance of success. The wizardry of modern technology offers us a unique opportunity to build a new worldwide community and human civilization. 'Massification', the coming of a universal culture, it is argued, is not to be feared but welcomed as the harbinger of a new 'global embrace' which can overcome the barriers of 'both space and time' (Mcluhan, 1973, p. 11). And if such a global community is not yet in place, at least we seem to be well on the way to it, as seen in the emergence of new identities which cross national boundaries and derive from shared interests rooted in our experience of being cosmopolitan citizens (Isin and Wood, 1999).

However, centrifugal forces have their dark side. They threaten to atomize relationships, create anonymity, promote amorality and destroy cultural identity and destroy those shared values that have previously given meaning and purpose to life. No wonder, therefore, that many people are now seeking to discover or re-discover forms of community that can hold together a world that seems to be rapidly fragmenting.

'Moving in'

It will come as no surprise, therefore, that opposing these centrifugal forces are *centripetal forces* resisting dispersal and disintegration. The quest for community is as much about depth as about breadth. It is an inward as well as an outward journey.

There are many signs of an ongoing search for human relationships that can give us a renewed sense of community. A vital aspect of this is an attempt to retrieve 'human scale' relationships. It is a quest seen in the explosion of communes in the 1960s on both sides of the Atlantic, the growth of the human potential movement and its many forms of group therapy, the vast expansion of 'special interest' associations and support groups, political, professional and leisure (Wuthnow, 1994), the emergence of what Drucker (1993, pp. 152-61) calls 'citizenship through the social sector' (the latter made up of 'autonomous community organizations'), as well as the 'escape' from cities in the West into towns and villages. All are indicators that we need the human group as an essential building block in any new world order.

However, the search for community also goes on at societal level. Many communities are born out of 'moving in' (or 'moving back') in order to recover a common heritage that has been latent or suppressed. So, following the collapse of colonialism, we have the attempted resurrection of historic cultures such as those of the Indians in North America, the Maoris in New Zealand, the

Aborigines in Australia, as well as many tribal cultures in Africa. Cultural retrenchment in places such as Canada, Kurdistan and the old Russian states, which Ignatieff (1993) describes as the resurgence of 'blood and belonging', also features here. Renewing bonds of this kind can bring a powerful sense of community.

However, as with centrifugal forces, centripetal forces have their dark side. If fragmentation threatens to be the cost of 'moving out', fundamentalism and exclusivity can be the consequences of 'moving in'. The quest for community can become circumscribed by rigid boundaries which foster paranoia by persuading those engaged in such a quest that beyond their own group or clan lies a hostile world

The destructiveness of 'moving in' is evident not only where there is poverty, marginalization, or deprivation, but also wealth, privilege or good fortune. There is just as great a danger of élite and articulate groupings who have attained a 'culture of contentment' (Galbraith, 1992) carving out for themselves impenetrable niches in order to secure their status and ensure their influence, as there is of alienated and vulnerable groups becoming ghettos or sects. 'The "community" the former seek stands for a burglar-free and stranger-proof "safe-environment"... "Community" (in their case) stands for isolation, separation, protective walls and guarded gates', states Bauman (2001, p. 114).

Even more destructive of our common humanity is the kind of 'moving in' which takes history with it and locks collectives into an anachronistic tribalism in the name of past glories or defeats. The Afrikaner in South Africa and the Jew in Palestine, for example, have frequently championed the concept of 'the chosen people' and 'the promised land' in a way that has brought bitter conflict and suffering to millions. Protestants and Catholics in Northern Ireland have for many years entrenched themselves in a past as degrading as it was glorious. The horrors of the conflict between Serb, Croat and Moslem in the former Yugoslavia and acts of terrorism perpetrated by al-Qaida (and now ISIS) further underline the human cost of a quest for community which becomes historically or culturally myopic.

Most calamitous of all has been that 'moving in' which has led to a peculiarly twentieth century form of communal incest, the totalitarian state. Such states are rooted in the power of 'community' which, when turned in on itself, has corrupted nations absolutely the more absolute it has become. Totalitarianism has taken a diversity of forms, imperialism, fascism, Stalinism, Maoism. All have proved how easy it is for genocide to triumph over humanity. More recently there are those, such as Philip Jenkins (2002), who are warning us that a confrontation between Islam and 'the coming of global Christianity' in the form of 'the next Christendom' may be the next threat to the future of human civilization. Centripetal as well as centrifugal forces can turn community into chaos.

The quest for community

> Universalism is destroying the particularity needed to nourish it; particularity, especially in the political order, is threatening the universalism needed for human survival, not just for progress. Can the two be reconciled?
>
> (Charles Davis, 1994, pp. 133-4)

Where, then do we go from here in our search for forms of community that can prevent the annihilation of humankind? The challenge is by no means a new one, but, as recent events have shown, it is even more urgent than when George Simpson summed it up some eighty years ago (1937, p. 39):

> The challenge facing humankind is that of communalizing those who are in conflict. That is a large problem. It is the problem of carrying over the ideal of the primary or face-to-face group which is most easily communalized, to the larger group, and ultimately to nations and international action. What is needed is a return to the ideals of the primary group in such a shape and so adjusted as to be capable of application to cosmopolitan conditions. Otherwise, a sort of return to the communal womb is being urged, a nostalgia for the infantile.

It is a sentiment echoed in more recent times by Vaclav Havel when he was President of Czechoslovakia (September, 1990): 'We must not be ashamed that we are capable of love, friendship, solidarity, sympathy and tolerance but just the opposite', he wrote. 'We must set these fundamental dimensions of our humanity free from their "private exile" and accept them as the only genuine starting point of meaningful human community.'

'Community', writes Parker Palmer (1987, p. 15) 'means more than the comfort of souls. It means, and has always meant, the survival of the species.' And the 'survival of the species' is now what we are about. 'At no other time has the keen search for common humanity, and a practice that follows...been as imperative and urgent at it is now', writes Bauman (2001, p. 140). The momentous choice before us is community or chaos

A global community

The survival and flourishing of human civilization in the millennium ahead requires a compelling vision of the power of community. 'Without a vision the people perish', warns Proverbs (29:18), a word of wisdom as true today as it was when written.

The first task before us is a global commitment to share our visions. This means our being open to listen to and to learn from one another. The kind of communities we now need are those that recognize and utilize the experience, insights and resources of each and every member, whilst being open to learn from and draw on the experience of other communities. 'The real community of man, in the midst of all the self-contradictory simulacra of community', writes Bloom (1988, p. 381), in his attack on *The Closing of the American Mind*, 'is the community of those who seek the truth, of the potential knowers, that is, in principle, of all men to the extent they desire to know'. 'And to the extent they desire to learn', we would add.

If human civilization is to survive, the quest for community is one in which all of us must be involved. Every human collective from the smallest group to the largest institution needs to play its part. The consequences of our attempts to build community will have profound implications for the home and the neighbourhood, the school, the hospital, the world of business and commerce, for law and order, for local and national government and, not least, for religious institutions such as the church. There really is 'no alternative'. The choice is community or chaos.

2. A theology of the kingdom community

Preamble

If the quest for community is now at the top of the political agenda, the gospel for today's world must be the contribution that Christian faith has to make to the deepest meaning of community and to the art of community building. Like any understanding of mission, that gospel needs firm theological foundations. This chapter, therefore, sets out a theology of community. However, because it is a theology intimately bound up with the kingdom, we call it a theology of the kingdom community.

The theology offered in this chapter has been honed over many years. It is published in its latest form, that which appeared in *The Kingdom at Work Project* in 2014[1]. In that publication, the theology of community described laid the foundations for an exploration of the nature of mission in the world of work. However, because a communal theology applies to every aspect of the church's engagement with society and world, it is just as relevant here.

The future

The Future, as Al Gore (2013) impressively surveys it, presents humankind with as daunting a task as we have ever faced. At the top of the agenda are issues concerning how to preserve the natural resources of planet earth, manage the destructive consequences of climate change, resolve the problems of an exploding global population, overcome new endemic diseases and handle nuclear power responsibly. Along with these immediate challenges, there is the ever-present task of lifting billions out of poverty and hunger and of creating a just and peaceful world.

Humankind also enters a new century facing the task of achieving economic sustainability and social justice. The demise of communism, and the apparent triumph of capitalism, is not proving to be the end-game which many predicted. The collapse of the banking system in 2008, revelations of malpractice within the

---

[1] Clark (2014) *The Kingdom at Work Project* (pp. 35-53).

financial markets then and since, and the rising tide of unemployment in many countries, has re-opened the debate as to what sort of economic model can sustain the well-being of humanity in the century ahead.

To these issues must be added a digital revolution which is creating exciting new possibilities and challenges for humankind and profoundly changing the way in which people relate to one another. This raises many questions as to how human beings, from the family to the nation and beyond, can build and sustain relationships of an enduring and creative kind.

Furthermore, humankind is attempting to address this massive agenda in the context of a world which has relatively recently experienced what Charles Taylor calls 'the great disembedding' (2007, pp.146-58, 270-95). 'Disembedding' refers to the processes of privatization (the individualization of life and its meaning), of societalization (where large and impersonal collectives take over from local and interpersonal ones) and of rationalization (where naturalistic and scientific interpretations of reality displace religious and the spiritual ones). Disembedding is a phenomenon which has led to the creation of an increasingly functional and individualistic understanding of human existence, one in which 'the ontological relations that bound the physical, the political, and the cosmic together no longer hold' (Ward, 2009, p. 229).

None of these challenges can be addressed effectively unless we recognize that the survival of human civilization is dependent upon our creating a world which learns to live together. Thus the building of community, from the local to the global, is an issue of paramount importance.

The meaning of community

Unfortunately, the word 'community', like aerosol, has been sprayed onto so many human activities to try and give them a pleasant aroma – community development, community care, community health, community policing, community newspapers, community schools, community businesses, the European Economic Community itself – that it has come to mean all things to all people and thus little to anyone. This casual use of the concept of community has led to what Boswell (1990) calls 'a gigantic omission' (p. 3). It is an omission of which we need to be acutely aware and speedily address if any kind of global order is to come out of potential chaos. To appreciate the full implications of this 'omission' we must explore the potential of community to bring good or ill.

Many linguistic usages of the concept conceal rather than reveal the dynamic nature of community. For example:

> - the power of community appears as very weak when the word is used to refer to some vague *human collective* described as '*the* community'.

> - its power is also minimal when the concept is used to describe a human collective situated in an ill-defined form of *place* - such as 'a suburban community' or 'a rural community'.

> - its power increases when the word is used to describe a human collective drawn together by *shared interests* - such as 'a mining community' or 'a school community'.

> - its power is even greater when the concept is used to describe those *relationships* characterizing a human collective connected by kinship or cultural bonds - such as 'the extended family' or 'a Moslem community'.

However, for the power of community to reveal its full potential, attention must be focused first and foremost on communal *feelings*. This happens when a phrase such as *a sense of community* is employed. This offers an understanding of community founded on the passions and power that *feelings* generate. What, then, are the feelings which give particular dynamism to 'a sense of community'?

MacIver and Page (1950, pp. 291-296; see also Clark, 2005, pp. 16-18) call such feelings 'community sentiments'. They identify three such sentiments as of paramount importance. Here we build on their work. The first essential communal feeling or sentiment is **a sense of security**, where security refers to adequate physical and material well-being, as well as freedom from the fear of natural forces or human agencies which might threaten life or limb.

The second essential feeling is **a sense of significance**. This is the sentiment which is engendered when people feel they have a role to play, formal or informal, which carries public recognition and/or which offers personal fulfilment.

The third essential feeling is *a sense of solidarity*. This is the sentiment experienced when people feel that they belong to and are an integral part of some human collective.

We would argue that a fourth essential communal characteristic should be added here, that of **socialization**. This is the process of induction whereby, beginning with the family, members of human collectives are nurtured, instructed and trained within a particular culture that gives human collectives associated with it clear boundaries and a distinctive identity (Clark, 2005, pp. 34-35).

These four fundamental *sociological* communal components we term **the 4Ss**. When such communal feelings are strong and socialization intense, those concerned will experience a strong sense of community; when they are weak, their sense of community will also be weak.

The communal dilemma

All human beings need to experience a sense of community within a bounded human collective before they are able to experience similar sentiments within larger and more open ones. The problem is that human collectives often remain bounded, self-protective and exclusive. Such insulation is so commonplace that it can be called the default condition of all societies (Clark, 2005, pp. 18-20). For fear of weakening their sense of security, significance and solidarity, people become victims of cognitive, geographic, social or cultural exclusivity. They remain closed to any experience that is not familiar and seems to threaten their established way of life. This faces a world which needs to become a global community of communities with the difficulty of resolving what we call 'the communal dilemma'.

This dilemma is typified by human collectives (especially those with a very strong sense of community) which remain insular and exclusive, and normatively suspicious of and hostile towards other human collectives. As David Jenkins (1976) puts it: 'That by which we identify ourselves and gain our sense of identity, significance and belonging is also that by which we dehumanize others' (pp. 14-16). In more recent history, such exclusive communal collectives have been exemplified by groups (such as the Ku Klux Klan), by movements (like al-Qaida and ISIS), as well as by entire nations (Nazi Germany and Mao's China).

It is this propensity for human collectives to strengthen their sense of community at the expense of others which presents humankind with *the communal dilemma - the problem human collectives face when needing to become increasingly open to one another without undermining or weakening their own sense of community or that of others*. Unless the communal dilemma is resolved we will never be able to create a global community of communities. The power of community will then, at best, go to waste and, at worst, become incestuous, exclusive and ultimately destroy us. McFadyen (1990) recognizes this problem when he comments: 'Given that so much of our present social and political situation can be described as a reversal of the values of true community, our situation is one of immense seriousness and urgency' (p. 270).

Trinity and kingdom

Breaking the stranglehold of the communal dilemma

Breaking the stranglehold of the communal dilemma is an immensely difficult task. Even when we are aware of the dire consequences of that dilemma and wish to resolve it, we still need an understanding of the tools needed to address such a challenging a task.

Learning as education

The key to breaking the grip of the communal dilemma lies in moving beyond the constraints of socialization. It is imperative that humankind acquires the motivation and the ability to question the assumption that the culture into which one has been socialized is the only possible source of one's communal identity. We have to learn how to build positive communal relationships not only with those with whom we have a cultural affinity but with strangers and even enemies. This necessitates us going beyond an experience of learning shaped by nurture, instruction and training, and becoming open to learning as education in its fullest and richest sense.

Only learning as openness to new vistas can offer us experiences that question the received wisdom into which we have been socialized, enable us to gain a deeper understanding of what it means to be human and engage with life as a journey of discovery (Clark, 2005, pp. 32-7). It is only a shift from closed to open learning, that which genuine education should be all about, that can offer us the opportunity to break the stranglehold of the communal dilemma,

16

enable us to become 'dialogue-partners' (McFadyen, p. 269) with the wider world and make possible the creation of a global community of communities.

Argyris and Schön (1978) refer to learning of this kind as 'double-loop' learning. It brings experiences which expand our conceptual frame of reference to identify and then challenge those underlying assumptions that maintain exclusive goals, values and convictions. Argyris and Schön see double-loop learning as the antithesis of 'single-loop learning', or closed learning, which never questions deeply embedded social and cultural assumptions.

Peter Hawkins (1991) goes even further (pp.172-187). He is convinced that we can have an experience and discover the art of what he calls 'triple-loop learning', learning that is even more open-ended than double-loop learning. Hawkins argues that if we want to resolve the communal dilemma, double-loop learning has limitations because it remains conditioned by an implicit 'philosophy of effectiveness' emanating from a competitive and dominating materialistic market-place culture. He believes that the most important questions arise out of our being engaged in a form of learning, triple-loop learning, which requires that the learner faces up to his or her mortality and the issues of life's meaning and purpose. Hawkins also claims that triple-loop learning opens our eyes to envisaging not only our own planet but the entire cosmos as a physical, communal and spiritual whole, and to the importance of discovering our place within it.

We interpret Hawkins as talking about learning as a journey of *spiritual* discovery. We see such learning as not only a human endeavour but as a divine gift through which we are privileged to grasp something of the purposes of God in creation and redemption. Triple-loop learning, as we understand it, is inspired and informed by revelation and discernment.

By helping us to move beyond closed human collectives held captive by the communal dilemma, double-loop learning and, if we follow Hawkins, triple-loop learning in particular, open up a theological vision of community greater than that encompassed by the 4Ss on their own, the sociological dimension of community, though a sense of security, significance and solidarity, and the process of socialization, remain the experiential foundations for any deeper meaning of community.

17

Symbolic universes

A vision of community in its fullest and richest sense is always informed by some kind of 'symbolic universe', a nexus of all-embracing values and the beliefs from which these are derived (Berger and Luckmann, 1984). At their best, symbolic universes present a vision of community which is open not closed, inclusive not exclusive, universal and not circumscribed by culture, race, gender or nationality.

Symbolic universes are clearly manifest within the world's great religions. As a symbolic universe, Christian faith offers us two dynamic communal images, that of the Trinity and that of the kingdom of God. Both embody a vision of community as an open, inclusive and universal phenomenon. Both build on the 4Ss, a sense of security, significance, solidarity and the process of socialization - but go much further. Both embrace a triple-loop, a cosmic vision of community and offer the power to make that vision a reality.

We maintain that this transformative vision of community embraces four universal and inclusive gifts of grace; ***the gifts of life, of liberation, of love and of learning*** (*Diagram 1*). We call these gifts ***the 4Ls***.[1] The first three gifts, life, liberation and love, build on the experiences of security, significance and solidarity respectively but add a radically new dimension to them. The fourth gift, learning as education, builds on the process of socialization but goes a great deal further. It inspires, informs and guides our spiritual journey of discovery and is paramount in enabling us to break the stranglehold of the communal dilemma.

---

[1] In the context of Methodist theology, these gifts are the heart of the gift of 'communal holiness' described in Chapter 11.

Diagram 1
The gifts of the kingdom community

To begin to understand the full meaning and implications of these four communal gifts, it is to the images of the Trinity and the kingdom that attention must be given. The Trinity portrays the essence and interdependence of the 4Ls; the image of the kingdom illustrates how these gifts are grounded in everyday living, with the life and teaching of Christ as the supreme exemplification of this grounding.

The Trinity

Alastair McFadyen (1990, p. 166) writes:

> The conditions of fallen human interaction are such that expectation, love, hope and trust are continually disappointed. The hope of reaching a genuine mutuality of understanding can be sustained by faith neither in oneself nor in the other, much less in mutual trustworthiness, but only in the empowering co-inherence of Father, Son and Spirit - that is, in God as the one hoped for.

'The full beauty of Trinitarian grace can only be discerned when human beings live and work together in community' writes Bakhtin (in Cunningham, 1998, pp. 155-164). The Trinity, above all religious images, embodies the divine gifts of life, liberation, love and learning. It is no surprise, therefore, that these four gifts reveal the essence of community at its zenith. They are gifts offered by 'a holy community of Persons' (Ecclestone, 1975, p. 112), distinctive gifts yet intimately and dynamically interrelated.

The first Person of the Trinity, God as Creator, Provider and Sustainer, offers us *the gift of life*. It is a gift which gives far greater depth and much greater strength to any sense of security we may experience, the first of the 4Ss. The gift of life embraces the power and glory of the whole created universe and offers humankind, as Fox (1994) contends, a part in ' "the Great Work" of creation itself' (p. 61). It is a gift which reminds us that our lives and our destiny are intimately linked to the preservation and sustainability of the planet. The gift of life also promises human flourishing. 'The glory of God is man fully alive', as Irenaeus puts it.

The gift of life embraces *a sense of security*. However, it also offers us such gifts as:

> *vitality and energy;*
> *health and healing;*
> *enjoyment and well-being;*
> *beauty, awe and wonder;*
> *reverence and respect;*
> *vision and inspiration.*

Our response might be that of *adoration, gratitude and devotion*. It should also include:

> *thanksgiving and celebration;*
> *delight and pleasure;*
> *fun and laughter;*
> *generosity and munificence;*
> *responsibility for the preservation of life;*
> *the fight against ugliness, squalor and disease;*
> *concern for all those materially and physically in need;*
> *faithful stewardship of the earth's resources.*

The second Person of the Trinity, Christ as Redeemer and Liberator, offers us *the gift of liberation*. As a gift which affirms that we are not only of human but of divine worth, it greatly deepens and enriches our sense of significance, the second of the 4Ss.

The gift of liberation is so unexpected and unwarranted because the assurance of our divine worth comes to a world which, in Spufford's (2012) words, has 'a crack in everything' (pp. 24-53). More often than not, responsible for the creation and perpetuation of that crack, as Spufford frankly describes it, is 'the human propensity to fuck things up' (p. 27). We may strive to build a world which is a global community of communities, but time and again we end up with a world which is unjust, divided and inhuman.

Accessing the gift of liberation depends on our recognition and acceptance of 'what God has wrought in us and not what we deserve'. On a personal level, it is a gift which liberates us *from* whatever destroys the divine image within us and *for* the service of One 'whose service is perfect freedom'. However, as the Old Testament and New Testament indicate, from the Exodus ('Let my people go!' - Exodus 5:1; 7:16; 8:1, 20; 9:1, 13; 10:3) to the promise of a new Jerusalem (Rev 3:12; 21:2), the gift of liberation also has a corporate dimension. It offers human collectives the means and the power to break free *from* the destructive forces of a 'cracked' world, be those forces political, social or economic, and *for* the task of building a just and peaceful global community of communities.

The gift of liberation embraces *a sense of significance*. However, it also offers such gifts as:

> *affirmation;*
> *forgiveness and renewal;*
> *joy;*
> *self-confidence and fulfilment;*
> *courage.*

On a personal level, our response might include:

> *the affirmation of others;*
> *the forgiveness and restoration of others;*
> *humility;*
> *gratitude and thanksgiving.*

On a collective level, our response might include:

> *the pursuit of justice and peace;*
> *the empowering of the powerless;*
> *the inclusion of the marginalized.*

The third Person of the Trinity, the Holy Spirit as Unifier, Reconciler and Comforter offers us **the gift of love** (*agape*). 'Love is the cosmic energy that flames from the constellations and is concealed in the abyss of the atom: is whispered by the Holy Spirit in the heart and placarded before men's eyes on the Cross', writes Bishop Lumsden Barkway (1953, p. 23). The gift of love promises humankind a profound experience of interdependence and togetherness which transcends the forces of fragmentation, conflict and division. By inviting us to enter into 'the fellowship (or unity) of the Holy Spirit', the Spirit not only gives depth and strength to any sense of solidarity, the third of the 4Ss, but goes far beyond that experience. That invitation requires of us a readiness to place the two great commandments, love of God and love of our neighbour, at the very heart of what is means to be human, for ourselves, our families, our society and our world.

The gift of love embraces *a sense of solidarity*. However, it also offers us the gifts of:

> *compassion and kindness;*
> *honesty and integrity;*
> *empathy and reconciliation;*
> *fellowship and friendship;*
> *belonging and unity.*

Our response might include:

> *trust and loyalty;*
> *generosity and kindness;*
> *caring and hospitality;*
> *respect and courtesy;*
> *sharing and co-operation.*

The Trinity also offers us **the gift of learning**, that is, learning as a journey of *spiritual* discovery. As a holy or whole community, the Trinity is open not closed, inclusive not exclusive, universal not circumscribed. It is the supreme exemplification of the learning community (Clark, 2005, pp. 37-40). The gift of learning embraces the fourth of the 4Ss, socialization, which includes nurture, instruction and training. However, it breaks the stranglehold of what we have called single-loop forms of learning, not least nurture, and involves us in an educational engagement with life and experience which is truly open. It inspires, energizes and guides us on a journey of spiritual discovery enlightened by revelation and informed by discernment. It is a gift which enables us to break the fetters of the communal dilemma.

The gift of learning begins with socialization, the fourth of the 4Ss. However, it goes far beyond the latter and embraces the gifts of:

> *curiosity;*
> *revelation;*
> *discernment and insight;*
> *imagination;*
> *wisdom.*

Our response might include:

> *openness and eagerness to widen out experience;*
> *dialogue and debate;*
> *inquiry and questioning;*
> *listening and reflection;*
> *perseverance and life-long engagement.*

The Trinity embraces the gifts of life, liberation, love and learning within *a dynamic and holy, or living and holistic learning community*. In a Methodist context, we have elsewhere[1] described these four gifts as integral components of 'the gift of communal holiness' or wholeness (Clark, 2010, pp. 172-82). They are gifts of grace offered in order that humankind might become one: whole individuals, families, neighbourhoods, workplaces, cities and nations, all contributing to the emergence of one world and 'the integrity of creation'. As Elliott puts it (1985), 'The good news of social and individual wholeness is cosmic in its extent' (p. 120).

The four gifts of the kingdom, as with the Persons of the Trinity, are distinctive communal dimensions of an integral whole. Where one exists, others will inevitably be present. Their attributes overlap and often merge. However, we identify these four gifts' particular contribution to the communal whole in order that the depth and richness of that whole can be recognized.

The kingdom

The second great communal image, the kingdom, lies at the very heart of Christ's life and teaching. If it was so central to the ministry of Christ, it can be no less so for us today. Elliott (1985) believes that 'the kingdom implies the transformation of human society – its politics, its economics, (and) its personal, group, institutional and international relationships... (The kingdom is about) the real potential of the whole created order for the fullness of life in community' (p. 1). Hendrik Kraemer writes (1958), the kingdom is 'the order of

---

[1] See Chapter 11.

existence for which the whole world unconsciously yearns' (p. 171). Thus we neglect what Ecclestone (1975) refers to as 'the great tidal wave of His oncoming kingdom' (p. 125) at great cost.

The kingdom is an image supremely personified in the life and teaching of Christ. As Lesslie Newbigin (1980) puts it: 'The presence of the Kingdom is the presence of Jesus himself' (p. 19). His ministry manifests the gifts of life, liberation, love and learning, all attributes of the Trinity, and earths them in everyday human experiences and happenings.

The gift of life is revealed in the dynamic power of the tiny mustard seed (Mt 4:30-2), the leaven (Mt 13:33) and the seed growing unnoticed (Mk 4:26-9). 'The kingdom depends on the invisible but unstoppable processes of God', Elliott observes (1985, p. 88). We are offered a gift which enables us not only to live life but to live it 'abundantly', here and hereafter (Jn 10:10 and 11:25).

The gift of liberation on a personal level brings liberation *from* self, sin and failure, a gift earthed in Christ's call to repentance (Mk 1:15), offering the assurance that all things work together for good for those who put God's kingdom first (Mt 6:33). Collectively, it is a gift bringing 'good news to the poor... release to the captives... recovery of sight to the blind... and liberty (for) those who are oppressed' (Lk 4:18). Individually, it is gift about liberation *for* the redemption of others, as witnessed in the parable of the king who forgave his servant's debts (Mt 18:23-5). Collectively, it is a call to strive *for* liberty, justice and peace (Mt 5:6, 9 and 10).

The image of the kingdom grounds *the gift of love* in everyday life. The kingdom is inherited by any who, even if unconsciously, become channels of the gift of love: by feeding the hungry, giving water to the thirsty, offering hospitality to the stranger, providing clothes for the naked, visiting the sick or befriending the prisoner (Mt 25:34-6). The gift of love is exemplified by the counter-cultural generosity of the owner in the parable of the labourers in the vineyard (Mt 20:1-16). It is a gift which embraces everyone, as witnessed in the story of the great banquet (Lk 14:16-24).

The ministry of Christ gives profound meaning to *the gift of learning*. He repeatedly referred to the latter as a spiritual journey of the utmost importance (Mt 6:33). He taught that learning is a gift which requires discernment and wisdom (Mk 4:11). He stressed that learning what membership of the kingdom entails is a life-long task which rules out those who put their hand to the plough and then look back (Lk 9:62).

The gifts of the kingdom, life, liberation, love and learning, are offered to all, righteous and unrighteous, just and unjust alike (Mt 22:2-10). Thus the kingdom is *an inclusive and universal,* indeed *cosmic kingdom* (Elliott, 1985, p. 120).

Though the fullness of 'the kingdom is not yet evident and therefore remains indistinct, nevertheless it persists, perdures' (Ward, 2009, p. 171). At the same time, the gifts of the kingdom are 'an index of the mysterious – that is, the sacramental excess that invests the everyday realities of things' (p. 170). Or, as Elliott puts it, the gifts of the kingdom are about 'changing water into wine', the transformation of the ordinary into the extraordinary (1985, p. 99).

An upside-down kingdom

The gifts of the kingdom are not innocuous gifts because Christ overturns accepted standards. 'He does put down the mighty from their seats, and raise up the humble and meek' states Newbigin (1958, p. 19). Christ gives 'priority in the announcement of the kingdom to the poor, the outcasts, the marginal, the "little ones," the sick, the despised and rejected - the *sinned-against...* (The harshest words of judgement are addressed) to the strong, the arrogant, the pious, the self-righteous, the supposed owners of the kingdom', writes Arias (1984, p. 79). If the gifts of the kingdom are brought to bear on the life of society, they inevitably clash with those forces which encourage greed and the exploitation of the planet, foster injustice and violence, debase and devalue compassion, condone ignorance and promote indoctrination. Because of this, to live in accordance with the gifts of the kingdom is a very costly endeavour. It is to take up the cross on behalf of the King (Mk 8:34-5).

The kingdom community

The kingdom is about a Sovereign whose rule extends throughout the created universe. It embraces those who, Christian or otherwise, have come to treasure the Trinity's gifts of life, liberation, love and learning, and have committed themselves to making those gifts manifest. Thus the kingdom is not only about a Sovereign, however important, it points to *a divinely ordained and ordered community*. We call this 'the kingdom community' (Clark, 1987, 2005, pp. 13-53; Snyder, 1991, pp. 145-156).

The kingdom community, through its universal and inclusive gifts of life, liberation, love and learning, becomes the supreme expression of and model for all forms of human community. Because these gifts are embodied in the Trinity (its communal essence) and the kingdom (its communal practice), essence and practice come together in a unique and exemplary way.

The gifts of the kingdom community embody the offer of transformational grace to a world that all too often makes a mess of things because it ignores or refuses the divine generosity. 'As long as we imagine that the world can be changed by our activities, our good works, our energy, we substitute our effort for the power of God. That is as ineffective as it is blasphemous... Our power to transform the world is God's power', writes Elliott (1985, pp.19, 20). Evelyn Underhill (1953) reflects on the unique nature of the kingdom community as follows (p. 58):

> What we look for... is not (an earthly) Utopia, but for something which is given from beyond: Emmanuel, God with us, the whole creation won from rebellion and consecrated to the creative purposes of Christ. This means something far more drastic than the triumph of international justice and good social conditions. It means the transfiguration of the natural order by the supernatural; by the Eternal Charity. Though we achieve social justice, liberty, peace itself, though we give our bodies to be burned for these admirable causes, if we lack charity we are nothing. For the Kingdom is the Holy, not the moral; the Beautiful not the correct; the Perfect not the adequate; Charity not law.

The gifts of the kingdom community are indispensable. The endemic problem is that we are still operating with an impoverished understanding of the nature and power of community. That understanding remains captive to social, economic and sometimes religious myths which can never bring us salvation. If the communal transformation of humankind is to become a reality, then a new communal vision, that of the kingdom community is needed. 'Without (such) a vision the people perish' (Proverbs 29:18). This means that *for the transformation of society and world to become a reality,* secular as well as religious collectives need to become communities transformed by the kingdom community's gifts of, life, liberation, love and learning.

Diagram 2 sets out the key components of the kingdom community.

Diagram 2
The kingdom community

A theology of community

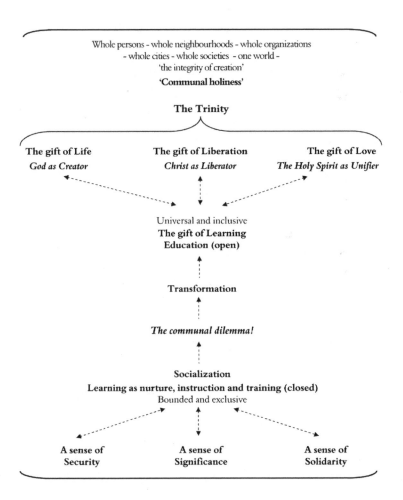

A sociology of community

A theology of the kingdom community is an essential foundation for the Christian's attempt to further the transformation of society and world. However, theology offers only one frame of reference. To promote and empower action, a theology of the kingdom community needs to be complemented by a spirituality of that community.

3. A spirituality of the kingdom community

Preamble

Theology needs spirituality to enrich and empower it. For too long a spirituality captive to insular denominationalism has strengthened the divisions of the church and impoverished spirituality. In this chapter we show that drawing on the spiritual resources found in a number of different denominations can reveal the immense riches of a spirituality of the kingdom community. It is a spirituality which is omnipresent, empowering, transformative and profoundly sacramental in nature.

This chapter first appeared in *The Kingdom at Work Project*[1]. I argued there that a spirituality of the kingdom community is essential for empowering mission within the world of work. However, it is a spirituality which is applicable to every field of mission.

Introduction

Any spirituality of the kingdom community without a theology of the kingdom to give it form and purpose is rudderless. However, a theology of the kingdom community without a spirituality of the kingdom community to empower and earth it remains a dead letter.

How does a spirituality of the kingdom community enable us to become more effective in building a society and world transformed by the gifts of the kingdom community? In Chapter 2 we offered a theology of the kingdom community founded on the image of the Trinity, and its inclusive gifts of life, liberation, love and learning, made manifest and earthed through the universal presence of the kingdom community. In Chapter 3, we seek to show how these gifts are expressed through four major forms of spirituality: *Celtic (the gift of life)*, *Ignatian (the gift of liberation)*, *Methodist (the gift of love)* and *Quaker (the gift of learning)*. Each of these spiritualities can be seen as having a particular affinity with the gift indicated, though all embrace other gifts of the kingdom community in a less explicit way. All offer the Christian essential resources for mission.

---

[1] Clark (2014) *The Kingdom at Work Project* (pp. 61-76).

A spirituality of the gifts of the kingdom community

A Trinitarian Reality

'Spirituality is concerned with seeking out what is real in life', writes Alan Ecclestone (1999, p. 36). Evelyn Underhill (1937) gives the search for what is real a spiritual orientation when, in her classic meditation on *The Spiritual Life,* she quotes the words of Augustine: 'God is the only Reality, and we are only real in so far as we are in His order and He in us' (p. 122). *It is the quest to engage with, learn from and share with others our experience of Reality that gives meaning and purpose to the engagement of Christians with the world.*

We have identified the Reality on which a theology of the kingdom community is founded as that of the Trinity. The same holds true for a spirituality of the kingdom community. In this context **Celtic spirituality** has a great deal to offer us. The Celtic spiritual tradition is grounded in 'a profound awareness and belief in the Holy Trinity... (It) sees all relationships as inherently reflecting our being made in the image of a relation-based Triune God in whom we live and move and have our being' (Timothy Joyce in Esther de Waal, 2001, p. viii). For Celtic Christianity, the Trinity was an intensely personal *and* corporate reality. The Celts lived and worked at ease with a deep awareness of and an intimate relationship with the Trinity, in one evening prayer, God, Son and Holy Spirit being invoked as 'the Three of my love' (de Waal, 1996, p. 85). For the Celts, 'It is always to the Three-as-One that prayer is made' but also 'prayer which sees the Godhead in its cosmic context' (de Waal.1996, p. 44).

Celtic spirituality and the gift of life

Elliott in his book *Praying the Kingdom* (1985) notes that 'Many of Jesus' *acts* (his italics) are prophetic demonstrations of the new life, the new quality of life, that the Kingdom offers' (p. 93). It is perhaps **Celtic spirituality** which once again has most fully grasped the all-embracing power of the divine gift of life and the beneficence and generosity of God as Creator.

The Celts had a profound awareness of 'the great God of life, the Father of all living' (de Waal, 1996, p. 85). 'O Lord and God of life' and 'O Father everlasting and God of life' (p. 175) are typical of the ways God is addressed in Celtic literature. The Celts believed that 'the very nature of God is to create and that the entire universe is in some senses an overflowing of his being,' writes Ian Bradley (1993, p. 68).

'The God whom they (the Celts) worshipped was not conceived primarily as the Lord of history... but rather as the Lord of Creation, the one who revealed himself most fully and characteristically in the wonders and splendours of the natural world' (Bradley, p. 52). He was described as 'the Craftsman of the Heavens' (de Waal, p. 170). 'Understand the creation if you wish to know the Creator... For those who wish to know the great deep must first review the natural world,' said Saint Columbanus (p. 59).

To the Celtic saints 'human life is contained within, and unfolds within, the dimension of the eternal' (p. 160). Thus rising each morning from sleep to the responsibilities of daily life was always a kind of resurrection:

> Thanks to Thee, O God, that I have risen to-day,
> To the rising of this life itself;
> May it be to Thine own glory, O God of every gift... (de Waal, p. 175).

The Celts also experienced a providential rhythm to life in the changing seasons which for them represented 'the alternation of opposites: light and dark, warmth and cold, life and death' (p. 54). 'The dark and light are themselves symbols of the Celtic refusal to deny darkness, pain, suffering and yet exult in rejoicing, celebration, in the fullness and goodness of life,' states Esther de Waal (p. 2). Although nature was recognized as often cruel, menacing and uncertain, Celtic Christianity was sustained by a belief in the power of 'light in darkness, hope in despair, life in death' (p. 106).

'When life is seen as the gift of God praise and thanksgiving is inevitable', writes Esther de Waal (p. 177). Euros Bowen, a modern Welsh poet, reflecting the Celtic tradition, speaks of a 'sense of unity with all creation, both human and non-human, that transcends time and space and brings the whole world together as participants in the singing of one great hymn of praise' (p. 173). Alexander Carmichael, the famous collector of Celtic prayers, provides many examples of this profound sense of gratitude for the gift of life. For example:

Thanks be to Thee, Jesus Christ
Who brought'st me up from last night,
To the gladsome light of this day,
To win everlasting life for my soul,
Through the blood Thou didst shed for me.
Praise be to Thee, O God, for ever,
For the blessings Thou didst bestow on me -
My food, my speech, my work, my health… (p. 16)

and

I believe, O God of all gods,
That Thou are the eternal Father of life…
I am giving Thee worship with my whole life,
I am giving Thee assent with my whole power,
I am giving Thee praise with my whole tongue,
I am giving Thee honour with my whole utterance. (pp. 176-177)

The Celts believed that they were co-workers with God the Creator. 'Everything they touched, every tool they handled, was done with respect and reverence; every activity performed with a sense of the presence of God, indeed done in partnership with him' (de Waal, p. 70).

Ignatian spirituality and the gift of liberation

The Celts had a genuine awareness of a fallen and fearful world. For them 'creation (came) with pain' (p. 59). How could it be otherwise when they were subjected to the destructiveness and unpredictability of the natural elements, as well as to the violence of marauding invaders? It is no surprise, therefore, that the cross was at the heart of their faith, a sign and symbol of the triumph of light over darkness, good over evil. 'In a Celtic cross we see that great round O, the circle of the globe itself, held in tension by the two arms of the cross – creation and redemption together' (de Waal. 1996, p. 125). 'There is no divide here between this world and the next. Heaven and earth are interconnected and interacting' (de Waal, 2001, p. xxvi). At the same time, theirs was a belief in 'Christ as liberator and enabler, rather than judge and reprover' (Bradley, 1993, p. 61).

Nevertheless, it is to **Ignatian spirituality** that it is particularly helpful to turn to enrich our understanding of the meaning of the gift of liberation, a spirituality forged within the more complex world of the sixteenth century. In 1548, well before he founded the Society of Jesus, the Jesuits, Ignatius Loyola drew up his *Spiritual Exercises* which are today as widely a used spiritual resource as at any time in history. At the heart of the *Exercises* is his experience as an ex-soldier who, increasingly aware of his own failures, 'wrestled with God and won emancipation at tremendous cost' (Brodrick, 1942, p. 20). Behind its many rules, annotations and additions is the experience of 'the survivor of a grim battlefield, a war-torn veteran, stiff-jointed indeed, but wise beyond the fashion of many more graceful counsellors' (p. 20). Ignatius believed the Christian to be engaged in a life or death struggle with what he called 'the enemy' (*Spiritual Exercises*, para. 350, p. 106).

For Ignatius, therefore, the Christian life was a journey from captivity to liberty. His Exercises start with a wholehearted acknowledgement of sin and the need for repentance. The first 'week' of the Exercises begins with meditations on the themes of death, judgment and hell, which bring 'the soul through its valley of troubling to Christ, its door of hope' (p. 23). Thereafter, the life of Christ (whom in relation to a theology of the kingdom community is called 'the Liberator') forms the entire content of the *Exercises*. At the end of the fourth 'week', the *Exercises* are meant to lead those engaged in them to 'rejoice in the great joy and gladness of Christ our Lord', 'to call to mind and think about those things which cause happiness, gladness, and spiritual joy, such as final glory' and, in a more everyday context, 'to make use of the light and pleasures of the seasons' (*Spiritual Exercises*, para. 229, p. 67).

Ignatius believed that his *Exercises* should lead to a definitive choice between good and evil. The purpose of the *Exercises* is 'the overcoming of self and the ordering or one's life on the basis of a decision made in freedom from any disordered attachment' (para. 21, p. 11). He sees the Christian as needing to be liberated from feelings which distract, in order to be able to engage in 'effective not affective love'.

Nevertheless, liberation is not an end in itself. In the fourth 'week' of the *Exercises* these memorable words appear:

> *Take Lord and receive all my liberty* (our italics), my memory, my understanding and my entire will, all that I have and possess. You gave it all to me; to you I return it. All is yours, dispose of it

entirely according to your will. Give me only love of you, together with your grace for that is enough for me. (para. 234, p. 68)

In more recent years, a much shorter version of the *Exercises* has emerged in the form of the *Examen of Conscience*. This is meant to be a regular review of how the participant is living out the Christian life. It has two aspects – the *Particular Examen* (often undertaken in the middle of the day) which focuses on some detrimental practice or habit which needs to be changed; and the *General Examen* (undertaken at the end of the day) which reviews the day's doings in the context of thanksgiving, forgiveness, renewal and commitment.

However, a qualification must be made in taking the *Spiritual Exercises* and the *Examen* as exemplifying a spirituality reflecting the kingdom community's gift of liberation. Although retreatants are exhorted to put love into action (para. 230, p. 68), the *Exercises* and *Examen* are essentially individualistic in nature. The gift of liberation, and any spirituality associated with it, is treated very much as a personal matter. In contrast, a theology of the kingdom community is not only about the liberation of the individual but the redemption of the whole creation (Romans 8:18-25). It thus concerns the liberation of all human collectives from the local to the global.

Methodist spirituality and the gift of love

All four of the spiritualities we are considering are closely associated with the kingdom community's gift of love. However, it is **Methodist spirituality** which, as fully as any, manifests the passion which empowers this particular gift. In the early twentieth century, Fitzgerald (1903) summarized the mission statement of the early Methodists in the words: 'All need to be saved, all can be saved, all can know that they are saved and all can be saved to the uttermost'. This affirmation, which in the language of Methodism brings a 'heart-warming' experience of the all-embracing love of God, has become something of a Methodist mantra. The phrase 'saved to the uttermost' represents Wesley's conviction that the goal of the Christian life was a state of sanctification or holiness, a state which he also described as one of 'Christian perfection' or 'perfect love,' writes Gordon Wakefield (1999, p. 24). It was this 'emphasis on holiness as perfect love (which) gave Methodist spirituality its own distinctive character' (*Called to Love and Praise* (1999, 4.3.19).

In what has come to be regarded as a classic exposition of Methodist faith and practice, *Called to Love and Praise* (note the title) (1999, 4.3.10), John Wesley's words in *A Plain Account of Genuine Christianity*, written in 1753, are quoted as being at the heart of a Methodist spirituality grounded in the love of God.

> Above all, remembering that God is love, he (the Christian) is conformed to the same likeness. He is full of love to his neighbour: of universal love, not confined to one sect or party, not restrained to those who are allied to him by blood or recommended by nearness of place. Neither does he love those only that love him, or that are endeared to him by intimacy of acquaintance. But his love resembles that of him whose mercy is over all works.

For Wesley the outworking of the gift of love in the life of the Christian was 'the work of the Holy Spirit, whom Christ has sent to transform us into his (Christ's) likeness' (Williams, 1960, p. 100). The Spirit within gave the Christian the assurance of sins forgiven, and the power and passion to live out their liberation by witnessing to the transforming nature of the love of God, an experience Wesley described as a 'religion of the heart'. A hymn of Charles Wesley illustrates this heart-warming religion (*Singing the Faith*, 2011, 564):

> O thou who camest from above
> the pure celestial fire to impart,
> kindle a flame of sacred love
> on the mean altar of my heart!
>
> There let it for thy glory burn
> with inextinguishable blaze,
> and trembling to its source return
> in humble prayer and fervent praise.

Methodist spirituality grounded the gift of love in what Methodism came to call 'fellowship'. 'Fellowship was the spiritual cement of early Methodism…' (*Called to Love and Praise*, 1999, 4.2.14). It was given distinctive expression within small groups known as bands and classes (Martyn Atkins, 2010, p. 28). Though bands, for the particularly devout, and classes for all other members declined in number during the nineteenth century (Munsey Turner, 2005, p. 52), the experience of fellowship within Sunday Schools, women's meetings, the Wesley Guild movement and, in the twentieth century, a multitude of youth clubs and university societies, took their place and remained at the heart of what it meant to be a Methodist.

Methodist worship, with its focus on the exhortatory sermon and '*Singing the Faith*' (2011), also nurtured and deepened an experience of fellowship rooted in the gift of love. Methodism's *Hymns and Psalms* (1983), until 2011 its official hymnbook, retained a section on 'Fellowship' including many hymns of Charles Wesley with verses such as:

> He builds us build each other up;
> And, gathered into one,
> To our high calling's glorious hope
> We hand in hand go on.
> The gift which he on one bestows,
> We all delight to prove;
> The grace through every vessel flows,
> In purest streams of love. (753)

Methodism also demonstrates loving commitment to the divine fellowship of the Trinity in its annual Covenant Service which includes the following vow:

> I am no longer my own, but thine.
> Put me to what thou wilt, rank me with whom thou wilt:
> put me to doing, put me to suffering;
> let me employed for thee or laid aside for thee;
> exalted for thee or brought low for thee…
> And now, glorious and blessed God, Father, Son and Holy Spirit,
> Thou art mine and I am thine. So be it.
> And the covenant which I have made on earth,
> let it be ratified in heaven.

However, for Methodism, 'holiness was never understood as an individualistic affair. In Wesley's own words, "the gospel of Christ knows no religion but social: no holiness but social holiness" ' (*Called to Love and* Praise, 1999, 4.3.9). In the nineteenth century, love for one's neighbour came increasingly to be focused on the preaching and practice of the 'social gospel'. This was manifest in the so-called 'Forward Movement' when, towards the end of that century, over a hundred Methodist 'central halls' were built to address the needs of the destitute and needy within the inner city. At that time Methodism also exercised a vigorous campaign against the social evils of drinking and gambling. A century later, from 1983 to 1996, Methodism was still actively engaged in a programme entitled 'Mission alongside the poor'.

Methodism's passionate witness to the kingdom community's gift of love, to the latter's power to change lives, to the importance of fellowship in making that gift manifest and to its expression through an ongoing concern to create a world founded on social and economic justice, remain an important contribution to a spirituality of the kingdom community concerned with the transformation of society and world.

Quaker spirituality and the gift of learning

Judith Jenner, then a tutor in Quaker Studies at Woodbrooke Quaker Study Centre, Birmingham, writes (2008): 'The Society of Friends exemplifies what it means to be a learning community, with deep roots in the kingdom community' (p. 147).

Life as a learning community is a vital aspect of **Quaker spirituality** and is well documented in their 'bible', *Quaker Faith and Practice* (QFP) (2005). The latter has two main sections. The first is *Advices and Queries*. Jenner describes these as 'the ground from which our faith and life spring and (which) are fundamental in shaping the Society of Friends as a learning community' (p. 150). The second part of *Quaker Faith and Practice* is by far the longer. It contains personal reflections recorded over many centuries intended to help Quakers discover what it means to live out their faith in daily life, as well as major sections on how the Society of Friends should conduct its internal business. Here we focus on *Advices and Queries*.

'The Religious Society of Friends is rooted in Christianity and has always found inspiration in the life and teaching of Jesus' (QFP, 1.02.4). Thus Quakers continue to be prompted to consider how Jesus is speaking to them and whether they are following his example of love in action (1.02.4). However, for Quakers, 'Christianity is not a notion but a way' (1.02.2).

Advices and Queries places Quaker worship at the heart of what it means to be a learning community. It states: 'As Friends we commit ourselves to a way of worship which allows God to teach and transform us. We have found corporately that the Spirit, if rightly followed, will lead us into truth, unity and love' (1.01). Quakers are urged to let worship and everyday life enrich one another (1.02.1).

The life and work of the Society of Friends, is rooted in the conviction that Quakers are called to a life-long journey of spiritual discovery.

> Be aware of the spirit of God at work in the ordinary experience of your daily life. Spiritual learning continues throughout life, and often in unexpected ways. There is inspiration to be found all around us, in the natural world, in the sciences and arts, in our work and friendships, in our sorrows as well as in our joys (1.02.7).

For Quakers, learning requires the discipline of being open to 'God whose Light shows us our darkness and brings us to new life' (1.02). It is a 'Light that is in all of us' and a *Light to Live By* (Ambler, 2002). Thus we need to 'take time to learn about other people's experiences of the Light' (*Advices and* Queries, 1.02.7). This means a readiness to 'respect that of God in everyone' and to 'listen patiently and seek the truth which other people's opinions may contain' (1.02.17). *Advices and Queries* prompts Quakers to respect the wide diversity of people who make up their Society and to 'foster the spirit of mutual understanding and forgiveness which (their) discipleship asks of (them)' (1.02.22).

Being prepared to question hitherto unquestioned assumptions is an essential aspect of the spirituality of the Society of Friends as a learning community. Quakers are urged to 'appreciate that doubt and questioning can... lead to spiritual growth and to greater awareness' of the Light (1.02.7). Such questioning is not to be undertaken in a critical or aggressive spirit, but by joining with others 'in expectant waiting' (1.02.8). Those involved are to 'think it possible that (they) may be mistaken' and 'listen patiently and seek the truth which other people's opinions may contain' (1.02.17).

Quakers believe that their life as a learning community should bear fruit in the way they conduct their internal business, especially in the way they approach decision-making. In that process, they should 'wait patiently for divine guidance' as to 'the right way' rather than 'seek a majority decision (or even consensus' (1.02.14).

Quakers' experience as a learning community must be manifest in daily life. *Advices and Queries* urges them to 'live adventurously' and let their lives speak for themselves. Quakers should 'seek to understand the causes of injustice, social unrest and fear'. Their learning needs to 'bear witness to the humanity of all people' and help create 'a just and compassionate society' (1.02.33). Living simply (1.02.41), temperance (1.02.40), a loving home life (1.02.26), integrity in business (1.02.37), working for peace (1.02.31 and 32) and concern for the planet (1.02. 42) are all manifestations of their commitment to be constantly 'in the light walking and abiding' (1.01).

Attributes of a spirituality of the kingdom community

Inclusive and universal

A spirituality of the kingdom community is an inclusive and universal spirituality. It is underpinned by the conviction that the gifts of the kingdom community are latent within every person. Ian Bradley writes that 'in finding God's presence in everybody and everything, however high and however lowly, Celtic Christianity... found the most fundamental reasons for loving and serving others' (1993, p. 50). Methodist spirituality likewise is rooted in the conviction that God's love, as 'prevenient grace', is available to all ('All can be saved') and not just to the chosen few (Colin Williams, 1960, pp. 39-46). Both Celtic and Methodist spirituality reflect the heart of Quaker spirituality that 'the Light of the Christ-like God shines in every person' (*Quaker Faith and Practice*, 2005, 26.65). In particular, the gifts of the kingdom community are on offer to the poor, marginalized and vulnerable. 'For the Kingdom is for them first... (It is) the triumph of the last over the first, of the humble over the proud, the ordinary over the exotic' (Elliott, 1985, p. 28).

A spirituality of the kingdom community reminds us of our inherent interdependence. Esther de Waal notes that 'Celtic spirituality is corporate spirituality with a deep sense of connectedness to the earth itself and the natural elements, to the human family, not only the present immediate family... but the extended family as it stretches back in time through many generations' (1996, p. 39). Richard Andrew (1999) argues that Methodism too has what he calls 'a catholic vision (which)... entails embracing the unity of *all* humanity' (p.22). Meg Maslin, a Quaker, comments: 'Personality, sex, race, culture and experience are God's gifts. We need one another and differences shared become enrichments, not reasons to be afraid, to dominate or condemn' (*QFP*, 23.33).

A spirituality of the kingdom community transcends human divides. Celtic spirituality regards women and men as whole persons and many of their prayers place body, mind and spirit under God's protection. Methodist hymnology sees God's grace as transcending every social division. From Charles Wesley's pen:

> Thy sovereign grace to all extends,
> Immense and unconfined;
> From age to age it never ends;
> It reaches all mankind.
>
> Throughout the world its breadth is known,
> Wide as infinity;
> So wide it never passed by one,
> Or it has passed by me. (*Hymns and Psalms*, 46)

A spirituality of the kingdom community recognizes no sacred-secular dualism. The Celts believed that God was present throughout the whole of creation. Even so, 'there (was) no blurring of the distinction between Creator and created, no worship of nature for its own sake but rather a wonderful sense of the whole creation as a theophany – a marvellous revelation of the goodness and wonder and creativity of God' (Bradley, 1993, p. 35). Ignatian spirituality operates on the premise of 'finding God in all things', hence Jesuits have always been active in the arts, literature and science. In 1989, a group of Quaker scientists wrote that 'science and religion have much in common. They are communal activities and involve a search for some greater truth' (*QFP* 26.24).

A transformational spirituality

Because a spirituality of the kingdom community which is inclusive and universal faces a world that remains exclusive and divided, it inevitably takes on the character of a transformational spirituality. It gives humanity a new impetus towards wholeness, or 'communal holiness' (Clark, 2010, pp. 172-82)[1]. It is a spirituality which possesses an energy epitomised by St. Patrick's breast-plate, a classic prayer from the Celtic tradition. The latter invokes a vibrant and life-giving

---

[1] See also Chapter 11.

power which pilgrims can access in their quest for a deeper vision and experience of what the Christian life is all about.

Alan Ecclestone (1975), reflecting on the lessons to be learnt from a spirituality of the kingdom which inspired earlier generations to embark on the construction of majestic cathedrals, believes that:

> Men and women today (need) to discover for themselves a life energising principle, an impulse of spirituality commensurate with the needs of the time. It (has) to be, like its forerunners, grounded deep in the earth, in the consciousness of men and women, and it (has) to soar towards the heavens in a growing unity of purpose, a consciousness of community, of mankind unified, divinised and expectant of the Christ. (pp. 96-97)

A spirituality of the kingdom community, however, can never ignore the reality of a world of pain, suffering and sinfulness. The Celts lived close to the violence and destructiveness of nature and what they often felt to be evil and mysterious powers. Many of their prayers were for protection and strength against the forces of darkness, human and satanic. The Ignatian *Exercises* show a profound awareness of a fallen world, the whole of the 'first week' being given to furthering recognition of human sinfulness and the cost of our redemption. John Wesley's understanding of holiness 'was far deeper than the absence of "wilful transgressions of a known law" (his definition of actual sin). Rather, perfection meant perfect love, including freedom not just from evil actions, but evil thoughts and "tempers" ' (*Called to Love and Praise*, 1999, 4.3.8). In 1904, John William Rowntree, a Quaker, wrote:

> No legal bargain, but a spiritual conflict, an inward change, the rejection of the living death of sin, the choice of the new birth, of the purified self, the conversion from a low and earthly to a high and spiritual standard of life and conduct – here you have the practical conditions of salvation, and in the active, free and holy love of God, ever seeking entrance, ever powerful if we but yield the gateway of our hearts, is the substance of the Gospel (*QFP*, 26.49).

The omnipresence of the gifts of the kingdom community

The Celts possessed an ever-present and intimate experience of the Trinity. They possessed 'a deep sense of the presence of God... here and now, with me, close at hand, a God present in life and in work, immediate and accessible' (de Waal, 1996, p. 65). For them 'God is companion, guest, fellow-traveller, friend, fellow-worker', writes Esther de Waal (p. 66). That experience 'flows from their real, lived-out grasp of the centrality of the incarnation... "God with us" is true!' (p. 66). At the same time, 'the Celts felt the presence of Christ almost physically woven around their lives' (Bradley, 1993, p. 33). The Holy Spirit was invoked as the ever-present source of comfort and power:

> God with me protecting,
> The Lord with me directing,
> The Spirit with me strengthening,
> For ever and for evermore,
> Ever and evermore. Amen   (Esther de Waal, 1996, p. 71)

Alongside a sense of the ever-present Trinity, Celtic spirituality constantly sought the help of Mary the Mother of Christ and of many of the saints. All 'are approachable, close at hand, woven quite naturally into life just as would be any other member of an extended family' (p. 143).

The Celts did not have any need to bring the Trinity into their daily lives 'from beyond'. God was already at work as Creator, Liberator, Lover and Teacher in every moment of the day. Thus the gifts of the kingdom community were evident in their rising and sleeping, in homemaking and farming, in hunting and fishing, in rest and in travel, in health and in sickness and in childbirth and death.

Quaker spirituality likewise embodies a deep sense of the omnipresence of God. Since the time of George Fox, Quakers have believed that 'the Light' exists within everyone. 'For a Quaker', writes Harvey Gillman, 'religion is not an external activity, concerning a special "holy" part of the self. It is an openness to the world in the here and the now with the whole of the self... In short... there is no part of ourselves and of our relationships where God is not present' (*QFP*, 20.20). In 1986, the London Yearly Meeting commented: 'The whole of our everyday experience is the stuff of our religious awareness: it is here that God is best known to us' (*QFP*, 27.38).

A classic work of spirituality not yet mentioned is *The Practice of the Presence of God* by Brother Lawrence (2008). This also bears witness to the presence of God within us and around us. Brother Lawrence, a sandal maker and kitchen servant, believed that 'God (was) always in the depth of the soul, no matter what (a man) does or what happens to him' (p. 74). Lawrence also felt God to be powerfully present in the whole of life. He spoke of his 'soul's secret experience of the actual unceasing presence of God' (p. 85). This enabled him 'to become involved in a continuous conversation with Him in a simple and unhindered manner' (p. 71) and thereby experience a mutual 'exchange of love' (p. 80).

A sacramental spirituality of the kingdom community

The spirituality of the kingdom community we have described above is regarded by many as a profoundly sacramental experience. Evelyn Underhill calls it 'the sacrament of the present moment' (1934, p. 108). The gifts of the kingdom community are also just that - gifts. As Underhill (1953) puts it: 'That which we really know about God is not what we have been clever enough to find out, but what Divine Charity has secretly revealed to us (p. 42)... (God) inspires and supports the adventure of which he is the goal' (p.107).

For the Celts 'the real presence' of God, Father, Son and Holy Spirit, was manifest and accessible within and throughout the whole of life. Ian Bradley (1993) writes that '(the Celts) had the ability to invest the ordinary and the commonplace with sacramental significance, to find glimpses of God's glory throughout creation and to paint pictures in words, signs and music that acted as icons opening windows on heaven and pathways to eternity' (p. 84). Theirs was an experience illustrated by the following prayer (de Waal, 1996):

> Each day may I remember the sources of the mercies
> Thou hast bestowed on me gently and generously:
> Each day may I be fuller in love to Thyself.
> Each thing I have received from Thee it came,
> Each thing for which I hope, from Thy love it will come,
> Each thing I enjoy, it is of Thy bounty;
> Each thing I ask, comes of Thy disposing. (p. 178)

Every moment of the working day or of the night, of the changing seasons and of the passing years, becomes a means of grace, enriched 'by a succession of rituals (which) upheld and sacramentalized (them)' (de Waal, 1996, p. 59).

In the *Spiritual Exercises* of Ignatius there is no specific reference to sacramental grace other than in the context of the mass, though the grace of God is clearly communicated to the penitent through his or her many acts of devotion.

Methodism's understanding of sacramental grace reflects its Anglican inheritance, with baptism and holy communion being to the fore, though communion services were originally more 'gospel feasts than holy mysteries' (Wakefield, 1999, p. 34). At the same time, John Wesley also identified what he called 'extraordinary' means of grace. These could be public (love feasts, watch-night and covenant services, band and class meetings), private (bible reading, prayer, devotional reading, self-denial) or 'works of mercy' (Jones, 2004, p. 160). Many of Charles Wesley's hymns likewise convey a deep sense of the sacramental or 'real presence' of God as Father, Son and Holy Spirit.

> Open, Lord my inward ear,
> And bid my heart rejoice;
> Bid my quiet spirit hear
> Thy comfortable voice;
> Never in the whirlwind found,
> Or where earthquakes rock the place,
> Still and silent is the sound.
> The whisper of thy grace. (*Hymns and Psalms*, 540)

'To (George) Fox and the early Friends the whole of life seemed sacramental, and they refused to mark off any one particular practice or observance as more sacred than others... Their whole attitude was gloriously positive, not negative. They were "alive unto God" and sensed him everywhere' (*QFP*, 27.39). Barratt Brown, a Quaker, comments (*QFP*, 27.43):

> It is a bold and colossal claim that we put forward – that the whole of life is sacramental, that there are innumerable 'means of grace' by which God is revealed and communicated – through nature and through human fellowship and through a thousand things that may become the 'outward and visible sign' of 'an inward and spiritual grace'.

4. The diaconal church - a model

Preamble

A theology and spirituality of the kingdom community can only be translated into mission through all the people of God. Thus the church must be a body which reflects a theology and spirituality of the kingdom community in every aspect of its life and work. In short, it has to become a servant of the kingdom community, or a *diaconal* church. The diaconal church is called by God to witness to the experience of community at its zenith, the kingdom community, and to work for the creation of human communities that manifest the kingdom community's gifts of life, liberation, love and learning.

The diaconal church is in many ways a mirror-image of the Christendom church, that model of church which has been dominant in the West for well over a millennium, many important features of which are still evident today. However, the diaconal church as yet remains a vision as much as a reality The mould of Christendom has to be broken if the diaconal church is to fulfil its calling as the servant of the kingdom community and a model of the latter for every institution, sacred or secular.

In this chapter we explore some important hall-marks of the diaconal church evident in the life of the historic diaconate, especially as it developed from the early nineteenth century onwards. We then go on to consider how a renewed diaconate might become a catalyst for the emergence of the diaconal church.

This chapter first appeared in *Breaking the Mould of Christendom*[1].

The Christendom model of church

The church is not the kingdom community. The church is the 'servant' (*diakonos*) of the kingdom community. The church that God is calling into being to serve the kingdom community and to meet the needs of our age is a *'diaconal* church'.

Unfortunately, the diaconal model of church is not the one that currently informs and shapes the life of the church in the West, and in

---

[1] Clark (2005: second printing, 2014) (pp. 57-69).

many places beyond. It is the model of the Christendom church that still dominates the scene. Its legacy remains so all-pervasive that unless the mould of Christendom can be broken, the diaconal church can never come into being. We shall later be looking at the differences between the Christendom and diaconal models of church. First, however, we need to describe the Christendom model of church in order to provide a template against which we can set our model of the diaconal church.

Christendom

The model of church that we in the West have inherited is that of Christendom. We define 'Christendom', in the words of Nichols (1999, p. 1) as 'a society where the historic Christian faith provides the cultural framework for social living, as well as the official religious form of the State'.

In the past, Christendom was both a religious and geo-political entity. Most historians are agreed that the Christendom era began in 313 when the Emperor Constantine declared that Christianity should have official recognition throughout the Roman Empire, though others look to Theodosius's reign (379-95) as the time when Christianity first became the empire's dominant religion.

Christendom was of profound importance. 'The experiment of a Christian political order had to be made', states Newbigin (1983, p. 34). For many centuries, Christendom shaped and sustained the life of an entire civilization, from princes and pontiffs to peasants and priests. Reflecting our earlier sociological definition of community, it offered people a strong sense of security, significance and solidarity: a sense of security founded on shared territory and a common heritage, and a sense of significance and solidarity founded on family and parish life. Christendom was also a civilization in which the 'seven ages of man' were clearly marked out, the rules well defined, sanctions formidable and boundaries firm. To this world the church offered the resources of the Christian faith to sustain and enrich communal life. The Christendom church had many assets, so much so that some people, like Aidan Nichols in his *Christendom Awake*, long for its revival.

Yet Christendom was also founded on 'coercion, control and domination' (Ustorf in Mc.Leod and Ustorf, 2003, p. 218). As the world became increasingly mobile, geographically, cognitively, socially and culturally, Christendom sought to retain its coherence by rejecting new expressions of community and resisting changes that threatened its identity and power. Far from addressing the communal dilemma – how to become open to other cultures without weakening itself as a community – it sought to extend its own culture on an ever wider scale. Hence, as a geo-political entity, it became the model for competing land-based empires that lasted into the middle of the twentieth century. However, as Howe notes (2002, p. 6), although such great historic imperial systems have collapsed during the past half-century, their legacies still shape many aspects of global life.

Throughout Christendom, the church was closely identified with secular power. Not only did it exercise spiritual domination over the lives of men and women, it frequently sought to order affairs of state as well. Even in the post-Reformation era, the church continued to carry forward its mission in Christendom mode. Indeed, Dulles argues that the Counter-Reformation led within the Roman Catholic Church to a more imperialistic form of centralization and institutionalization than ever before (p. 189). As Christendom merged into empire, 'the most powerful and widespread early-modern argument vindicating empire was a religious one' (Howe, p. 84) even if, as Porter (2004) argues, Christian missionaries were not uncritical propagandists of empire. As empire building continued apace, the attitude of all churches was that 'not only should new worlds be won for Christendom but specifically for one's own particular version of it, denying opportunities of conquest and conversion to the heretics' (Howe, p. 84).

What is still disputed is when Christendom's decline commenced. Hugh McLeod (McLeod and Ustorf, pp. 16-19) identifies three different periods that scholars claim are the decisive ones in precipitating that decline. Some see the seventeenth and eighteenth centuries, in particular the Enlightenment, as the main period of Christendom's demise. Another school of thought sees Christendom's decline as running from the French Revolution in 1879 to the end of the Second World War. However, more recently, it has been argued that it was 'the "long 1960s" from 1956 to 1973 (that) appear as a cataclysm for the place of religion in British (and European) society' (Callum Brown in Mc.Leod and Ustorf, p. 35).

Whenever Christendom's decline began there is 'no way back to the Constantinean alliance between church and state' (Newbigin,

1983, p. 34). Nevertheless, McLeod and his fellow writers believe that 'we are still living in its (Christendom's) shadow' (p. 2). Indeed the hypothesis upon which their book is based is 'that the coercion, control and domination that were part of the Christendom model of church and mission carry within themselves the seeds of the modern repudiation of Christianity in Europe' (p. 218). We accept that hypothesis.

McManners (1990, p. 665) spells out the implications of this legacy:

> Even if the dream of a culturally integrated 'common Europe home' were to be achieved, a united Europe that imagined itself to be Christendom once again could do only harm to the world-wide Christian movement... The choice between the open, diversified church and the church behind institutional and mental barricades emerges yet more clearly as the supreme issue for the next century.

Yet the fact remains that the church in the West is still moulded by the Christendom model of church. Mead (1991, p. 18) puts it as follows:

> We are surrounded by the relics of the Christendom Paradigm, a paradigm that has largely ceased to work. But the relics hold us hostage to the past, and make it difficult to create a new paradigm that can be as compelling for the next age as the Christendom Paradigm has been for the past age.

We believe that it is this continuing captivity to the legacy of Christendom that prevents the church from making its communal contribution to a world that can only survive if it becomes a global community of communities. The task before us is to liberate the church from a Christendom model of church that is exclusive and closed by discerning how the gospel can be expressed through a model of church that is inclusive and open. Newbigin describes this task as follows (1980, p. 35):

> What we have now to seek are forms of church and ministry which neither draw men and women out of the world into a private society, nor seek to dominate the world through controlling centers of power, but enable men and women to function within the secular life of the world in ways which reflect the reality of Christ's passion and thereby make the

reality of Christ's resurrection credible to victims of the world's wrongs.

At the beginning of the twenty-first century, therefore, the church is called upon to undertake yet another journey of discovery. This time, however, it is a journey that will necessitate the biggest revolution that it has faced since the emergence of Christendom. Furthermore, as that body called by God to discern and make known the gifts of the kingdom community, the church's ability to re-shape its own life and mission will have critical implications for human civilization as a whole. Grace Davie (2002) asks whether *Europe* (is) *the exceptional case* in still being held fast by the mould of Christendom. We believe that the need for the church to break that mould is as crucial for the future of every other continent as it is for Europe.

This journey is 'a divine risk' (Holloway, 1990), yet it also a divine imperative without which the resources of the kingdom community will remain untapped. It is our conviction that the church that God is calling into being to undertake this journey is the diaconal church.

Sources of the diaconal model of church

To construct a model of the diaconal church we have drawn on three main sources. The first source is the academic insights of sociology, education and theology: a source that has provided us (as we have seen in Chapter 1) with the concepts of community (sociological) and the kingdom community (theological), the latter transforming our understanding of the former.

The second source we have used is empirical. In Part III of *Breaking the Mould of Christendom* (Clark, 2005) (not included in this book) we offered a number of case-studies illustrating the hall-marks of the diaconal church.

The third source for our model is historical. The question we pose is how the model of the diaconal church (and of diaconal institutions in a secular context) might be informed by features of diaconal ministry from the early church onwards, and especially by the life and work of the diaconate from the early nineteenth century to the present day.

The history of diaconal ministry[1]

The early church and after

A wide diversity of diaconal forms of ministry permeated the life of the early church (Collins, 2002). These led to the emergence of the title of deacon well before the end of New Testament times, though the nature of the office during that period remains controversial. In the second and third centuries, deacons appear to have gained in status and power, in part because they developed a role as assistants to bishops and, in part, because they accumulated important administrative and financial responsibilities (pp. 109-110).

After Constantine offered the Christian church official recognition in 313, bishops gradually assumed the oversight of larger and larger areas. At the same time, priests took increasing responsibility for the local church which, together with a greater focus on Eucharistic worship, considerably enhanced their status. As a result, from the fourth century onwards the influence of deacons steadily declined. 'They became subordinate to the priests, their direct link with the bishop faded away, and they ended up having no specific function.' (*From the Diakonia of Christ*, p. 30). 'The functions (of deacons) which had in the past been autonomous and practical, (gradually) became stages in the career path towards priesthood'. By the tenth century, a hierarchical order of ministry, with the deacon at its base, became the norm (p. 31). This has remained the case, notably within the Roman Catholic Church, Orthodox Church and the Church of England, up to the present day.

The nineteenth century to the present day

In the early nineteenth century, there was an unexpected upsurge of interest in diaconal ministry. In 1836, Pastor Theodor Fliedner of the German Lutheran Church founded the first deaconess institute at Kaiserswerth, training women for welfare work, nursing and teaching.

---

[1] In reviewing the history of diaconal ministry, and the lessons to be learnt from it, we draw on the findings of a number of working parties that over recent years have been investigating what a so-called 'renewed diaconate' might have to offer to the life of their churches. The documents on which we draw most frequently are Anglican (*For such a time as this. A renewed diaconate in the Church of England*, 2001, and *The Distinctive Diaconate*, Diocese of Salisbury, 2003); Roman Catholic (*From the Diakonia of Christ to the Diakonia of the Apostles*, 2003); and Methodist (*What is a Deacon?* Methodist Conference, 2004).

The Church of England admitted its first deaconesses in 1862 (*The Distinctive Diaconate*, p. 19). In 1878, the Methodist Church began training Sisters of the Children, and, in 1890, the first training institute for the Wesley Deaconess Order was set up in London (Staton, 2001, p. 103). Similar developments, all relating to women, were seen in other churches across Europe, especially in Scandinavia.

The reasons for this renewed interest in diaconal ministry were largely three-fold. First, churches were possessed by a growing concern to re-engage with 'a working-class' culture. They were fast losing touch with working people as the industrial revolution gathered momentum and hundreds of thousands of people moved from the countryside to the city. Second, churches became were increasingly aware of the needs of those for whom migration brought massive deprivation. Many people not only lost touch with their communal roots but were forced to live and work in appalling conditions in the new industrial heartlands. Trying to meet their material as well as spiritual needs demanded more trained and dedicated personnel than the church then possessed.

Thirdly, women were beginning to look for ways of gaining an independent identity in a still dominantly male culture. Offering to work as deaconesses was one way of enhancing their status and self-esteem, as well as fulfilling their own sense of vocation. 'The deaconess movement in the nineteenth century' writes Staton (p. 94), 'was a pragmatic response to the needs and demands of contemporary society, not least the demands by women for recognition and fulfilment'.

The deaconess movement gathered momentum up to the middle of the twentieth century. As a result, in 1947, DIAKONIA, a worldwide federation of diaconal associations, was founded. DIAKONIA began to hold international assemblies every few years and to promote contacts, debate and reflection on the role of the diaconate across many denominations.

After the Second World War, however, the picture becomes more confusing. The deaconess orders in England declined in strength. There were a number of reasons for this. The coming of the Welfare State to some extent blunted the cutting edge of the church's involvement with those in poverty, socially deprived or unemployed. This meant that the social ministries of the urban settlements and inner-city churches and missions, on whose staff many deaconesses served, were less in demand than in decades past.

At the same time competing forms of ministry, particularly presbyteral ministry, were gradually opening up to women. The Salvation Army had begun to commission women officers as early as the mid-nineteenth century. In 1904, the Unitarians, and in 1914, the Congregational Union accepted women ministers. In 1972 that the Methodist Church opened presbyterial ministry to women, and, in 1992, the Church of England followed suit. In last two churches mentioned many deaconesses and deacons who had been 'priests in waiting', often for some time, opted to be ordained as presbyters.

These post-war developments, combined with the church's continuing ambivalence about the status of the diaconate, led the Church of England's Advisory Committee for the Church's Ministry, in 1974, to recommend the abolition of the diaconate (*For such a time*, 2001, p. 8). The recommendation was rejected. However, in Methodism, the Wesley Deaconess Order was closed to new candidates in 1978. At this point in time, therefore, it looked as if the diaconate, at least as it had developed over the preceding century, was reaching the end of the road.

However, other factors were at work paving the way for a renewal of interest in the diaconate. Vatican II had restored the 'permanent diaconate' (the term used by Roman Catholics to describe an ordained order of deacons who remain as such, and do not see their role as a stage en route to the priesthood). It was a decision that stemmed from a new theology of the church that accepted 'the diaconate as a stable order of the hierarchy' (*From the Diakonia of Christ*, p. 54). It was a decision also given impetus by the hope that a permanent diaconate might help to relieve the workload of a declining number of Catholic priests. Although the Catholic Church initially saw the restoration of a permanent diaconate as of particular importance to the African and Asian churches, it was in fact in Europe and the United States where the restoration had most impact. By 1998, there were over 25,000 permanent deacons in the Roman Catholic Church world-wide, the majority was located in the West (p. 63).

In 1986, the British Methodist Church re-opened its diaconal order, and to men as well as women. By 2004, Methodism had over a hundred active deacons. In 1988, the Church of England produced a report entitled *Deacons in the Ministry of the Church*, which encouraged the church to make provision for a permanent diaconate. A second Anglican report, *For such a time as this*, was produced in 2001. This urged that the permanent diaconate be considerably expanded, though at the discretion of each diocesan bishop. By the turn of the millennium, the Church of England had some 75 permanent deacons. In 2003, the Diocese of Salisbury, produced a lengthy report entitled *The Distinctive Diaconate*, urging that the church should encourage many more people to become permanent deacons.

A renewed diaconate as a catalyst for change

In using the history of diaconal ministry as illustrative of the hall-marks of the diaconal church, it needs to be recognized that 'there is no single normative model of the diaconate to which we can hark back' (*For such a time*, pp. 4-5). Or, as *The Distinctive Diaconate* states (p. 27), 'There is no suggestion that there is a first century model of diaconal ministry to which we can ascribe "authority" for diaconal ministry today.' Thus, although the New Testament and the early church offer us important insights into the nature of the diaconal church, it is to the history of the diaconate, especially since it renewal in the nineteenth century, and also to the quest for a renewed diaconate over more recent years, to which we must give particular attention. This is not only because 'today's theology works from today's need' (p. 119). It is because 'it seems that the diaconate has been particularly important in the church's mission at times of acute political and social change and upheaval' (*For such a time*, p. 1) typical of the present time.

It is not surprising, therefore, that in recent years, literature on 'a renewed diaconate' has proliferated world-wide. The so-called 'Lima' document of the Faith and Order Commission of the World Council of Churches, *Baptism, Eucharist and Ministry*, (1982) was widely regarded as setting the pace for a new interest in the ministry of the whole people of God, with deacons seen as exemplifying the people of God's calling to a servant ministry (*For such a time*, p. 16). This document also witnessed an important shift from an hierarchical concept of ordained ministry to a more integrated approach that grounded ministry in the nature and mission of the church. However, it was not until the early 1990s that interest in the diaconate began to move centre-stage, with John Collins' first book, *Diakonia: Re-*

interpreting the Ancient Sources, exploring the meaning of the *diakon*-words in the New Testament, a task he has continued to pursue assiduously over the next decade and more (1992, 2002).

In 1992, Christine Hall edited a symposium entitled *The Deacon's Ministry*, the back cover describing the book as filling 'an important gap' in the literature about the church's ministry, ordained and lay. In 1996, the Anglican-Lutheran Commission published the Hanover Report, *The Diaconate as Ecumenical Opportunity* and 'for the first time in the history of bilateral ecumenical dialogue, the diaconate was the sole focus of a report' (*For such a time*, p. 17). In 1997, an ecumenical and diaconal consultation was held at St. George's, Windsor. It produced *The Windsor Statement* (1997), a radical interpretation of the ministry of deacons that, amongst other roles, described the latter as 'pioneering' and 'prophetic'.

At the end of the 1990s, the Anglo-Nordic Diaconal Research Project published two volumes of papers entitled *The Ministry of the Deacon* (Borgegard et. al., 1999, 2000). These papers underlined the diverse interpretations of the ministry of the deacon in different countries and churches, and raised important ecclesiological issues concerning the future of the office. Methodism contributed to the ongoing debate with the publication in 2002 of *What is a Minister?* (Shreeve and Luscombe) which included a chapter by Sue Jackson, a Warden of the Methodist Diaconal Order, on 'What is a Deacon?'. In 2003, the Roman Catholic International Theological Commission produced a comprehensive report entitled *From the Diakonia of Christ to the Diakonia of the Apostles* in which it traced the development of the role of the deacon from biblical times to the present day and explored the office's future potential. In 2004, the British Methodist Conference approved a document entitled *What is a Deacon?* which affirmed Methodism's understanding of the diaconate as both an order of ministry and a religious order.

Why has there been this upsurge in interest in the ministry of the deacon over the past couple of decades? Why, as *For such a time as this* puts it, 'across the Christian traditions and around the world (are) the churches … rediscovering the diaconate'?

More cynical observers point to a shortage of priests. However, in the West at least, what appears to be driving the interest in a renewed diaconate is the church's consciousness of the growing gap between itself and a secular society. There is an increasing awareness that the church has to re-engage with contemporary cultures and that, as it has been shaped by Christendom, it can no longer fulfil that task. There is also a slow but growing realization of the need to enhance the role of the laity in the mission of the church, an undertaking that will require new forms of leadership for which the ordained ministry as it stands seems ill-equipped.

There are signs, however, that the upsurge of interest in the possibilities for renewal opened up by the recent interest in the role of the diaconate could wane. The response of the Church of England to its report *For such a time as this* has been luke-warm, other than in one or two dioceses such as Salisbury (*The Distinctive Diaconate*, p. 85). Within British Methodism, there are still many differences of view about the nature and potential of the diaconate. And the reinstatement of a permanent diaconate within the Roman Catholic Church has so far failed to herald any major changes in its understanding of the hierarchical nature of the ordained ministry or the role of the laity within the life of the church. All this is evidence of the church's habit of only half exploring avenues of renewal that could lead to a breakthrough in its approach to mission and ministry. Yet it is only as we are prepared to questions some of the foundational assumptions of Christendom that we will be able to look at the promise of diaconal ministry with fresh eyes and to discover its potentially radical, redemptive and re-creative contribution to the life of church and world alike.

We believe, however, that the forces leading to the current debate over the role of a renewed diaconate are here to stay and that it is a debate that has profound implications for the future. We take this position because it is believed that the concept of *diakonia* (which we interpret as 'servanthood') relates not just to a particular order of ministry, but to every aspect of the church's life and work. As *For such a time as this* puts it, 'The diaconate remains the fundamental stratum' of all ministries, ordained and lay (p. 9). Because Christ's ministry was utterly diaconal, 'so by analogy the church is a diaconal body' (*The Distinctive Diaconate*, p. 40). *From the Diakonia of Christ* makes a similar point (p. 3): 'The Kyrios, Lord, becomes the diakonos, servant, of all,' thus 'Christian existence is a sharing in the *diakonia* or service which God himself fulfilled in favour of mankind: it likewise leads to an understanding of the fulfillment of mankind'. It is this all-embracing understanding of the meaning of *diakonia* as servanthood that informs the model of the diaconal church which we set out below.

Overview of the model of the diaconal church

Diagram 3 presents some of the main hall-marks of the diaconal church. In the first column are set out key themes of relevance to both the Christendom and diaconal models of church. In the second column are laid out those features of the Christendom model of church that continue to mould the life and work of the contemporary church. Though these features apply particularly to the church in the West, their influence extends across every continent and shapes not only the mainstream denominations but also many new expressions of church. The third column summarizes the transition that needs to be made if the mould of Christendom is to be broken and the diaconal church is to come into being.

Diagram 3
From the Christendom church to the diaconal church

THEME	THE CHRISTENDOM CHURCH	THE DIACONAL CHURCH
MISSION	**Proselytism**	From church-centred to ***kingdom community-centred***
	Exclusivism	From exclusive to ***inclusive communities***
	Dogmatism	From indoctrination to ***education***
CULTURE	**Sacralism**	From a sacred to ***a secular society***
	Conservatism	From preservation to ***transformation***
STANCE	**Imperialism**	From domination to ***servanthood***
THE LAITY	**Clericalism**	From priest to ***people***

	Conformism	From dependency to *autonomy*
SOCIAL COLLECTIVES Hearing	Legalism	From venerating the status quo to *visioning*
Group	Didacticism	From instruction to *dialogue*
	Parochialism	From community of place to *communities of interest*
Network	Isolationism	From insularity to *interconnectedness*
Institution	Institutionalism	From controlling the whole to *serving the parts*
		From guarding the boundaries to *facilitating connections*
Partnership	Separatism	From competition to *co-operation*
CHURCH LEADERSHIP	Elitism	From hierarchy to *servant leaders*
	Authoritarianism	From director to *community educator*
	Paternalism	From men to *women and men*
GOVERNANCE	Centralism	From centralization to *subsidiarity*
	Unilateralism	From autocracy to *democracy*
	Statism	From establishment to *self-government*

5. *Mission, culture, stance and the laity*

Preamble

Chapter 5 explores some notable hall-marks of the diaconal church. Of particular significance is way the historic diaconate has given impetus to the shift from an authoritarian stance typified by the Christendom model of church to a stance of servanthood, a foundational feature of the diaconal church.

This chapter first appeared in *Breaking the Mould of Christendom*[1].

Mission

From church-centred to *kingdom community-centred*

The mission of the diaconal church is to be the servant of the kingdom community, the epitome of all communities. In pragmatic terms, its mission is to help create a global community of communities transformed by the gifts of the kingdom community. As Giles Fraser's puts it, the mission of the diaconal church is to be a 'vanguard of a new world order known as the kingdom. Our job is to rattle the cages of those who believe the kingdom is make-believe, and that, deep down, things can never really change' (*Church Times*, 15/4/05).

As the servant of the kingdom community, the diaconal church is a *kingdom community-centred* church. As such, it is called by God to make manifest the kingdom community's gifts of life, liberation, love and learning within its own life and work. 'Neither truth nor love can be communicated except as they are embodied in a community which reasons and loves' (Newbigin, 1989, p. 85). It is also called to build communities that, in their turn, manifest the gifts of the kingdom community.

The diaconal church serves a kingdom community whose membership is known to and determined by God alone and which

---

[1] Clark (2005: second printing, 2014) *Breaking the Mould of Christendom* (pp. 70-84). In this chapter (and Chapters 6 and 7), to help remind the reader of the main missional and ecclesiological themes set out in *Diagram 3* (Chapter 4), the hall-marks of the diaconal church are placed in italics when they first appear in the text.

requires no church-defined or church-defended boundaries. The diaconal church bears witness to a God who is both beyond us yet with us, showing us the meaning of servanthood in the life of Christ. The diaconal church is the servant of a kingdom community already omnipresent within the church and beyond, through which the grace of God is freely offered to humankind.

The mission of the diaconal church is the transformation of our world so that the kingdom community might come 'on earth as in heaven' (CIPL, Clark, B10, 1993). It is a mission concerned with the 'integrity of creation', of the preservation and sustainability of 'one inhabited earth', the stewardship of which has been entrusted to all of us. It is a mission that challenges poverty, injustice and oppression and all that destroys the image of God in men and women. It is a mission that embraces the whole of humankind, those who hold power as well as those on the margins of society. Thus it is called 'to speak of God not (only) on the boundaries but at the centre, not (only) in weakness but in strength; and therefore not (only) in death and guilt but in man's life and goodness' (Bonhoeffer in Bethge, 1979, p. 155). The mission of the diaconal church is one that calls all to account, but it is one that also offers 'an explosion of joy' (Newbigin, p. 116).

Within Christendom, by contrast, the church regarded itself as synonymous with the kingdom, or as near as human beings could get to the kingdom in this life. It was the kingdom in ecclesiastical garb. The church's rituals, symbolism and buildings offered the most visible and tangible demonstration of God's rule here on earth. The church was humankind's means of salvation, a saved and saving community. God's grace was bestowed on men and women primarily through the church and through its sacraments. The Word, when read or preached, was God-given, to be heard and obeyed.

The Christendom church sought to ensure that its members remained safe and secure within its fold, their reward being membership of a divinely ordered society and the blessings of eternal life. Such a protectionist perspective meant that the Christendom church needed to guard its boundaries, geographical, political and doctrinal, with great care. It engaged with 'alien' communities, sacred or secular, only when it felt impelled to convert them, as heathens or heretics, to the one true faith (not infrequently at the point of the sword or through threat of divine punishment). Proselytism (*Diagram*

3), the attempt to bring everyone into the fold of mother church, permeated its church-centred approach to mission.

The mission of the diaconal church is far removed from proselytism. As we have seen, its task is to be the servant of the kingdom community. In that undertaking, the diaconal church is called to enter wholeheartedly into partnership with all those furthering the purposes of the kingdom community, whether or not they are aware of that which motivates and inspires them.

From exclusive to *inclusive communities* and from indoctrination to *education*

The kingdom community-centred nature of the diaconal church impels it to challenge the church-centred exclusivism and dogmatism that are so prominent within the Christendom model of church (*Diagram 3*). The diaconal church sees as a divine imperative its task of enabling the world to move from exclusive to *inclusive communities*, and from indoctrination to *education*, so that it can build communities that manifest the kingdom community's gifts of life, liberation, love and learning (Chapter 2).

Desmond Tutu sums up the nature of such communities:

> You and I are made for goodness, for love, for transcendence, for togetherness. God has a dream that we, God's children will come to realize that we are indeed sisters and brothers, members of one family, the human family – that all belong, all white, black and yellow, rich and poor, beautiful and not so beautiful, young and old, male and female. There are no outsiders, all are insiders – gay and straight, Christians, Muslims, Jews, Arabs, Americans, Protestants, Roman Catholics, Afghans – all belong. And God says: 'I have no one to help me realize my dream except you – will you help me?'.

> (Addressing Georgetown University, Washington DC - quoted in *Look to Christ*, 2004, p.35)

Culture

From a sacred to *a secular society*

The diaconal church fully acknowledges the realities of life in today's world. It accepts that, in the West, we now live in *a secular society*; 'in the brave new world of secular secularization – that is, the permanent decline of religion' as we have known it (Brown in McLeod and Ustorf, p. 29).

By 'secular' and 'secularization' we here mean an open-ended process characterized by four main developments. First, 'differentiation': functions that the church once fulfilled are being taken over by many other institutions. Second 'disengagement' (see Glasner, 1977): responsibility for such functions is being transferred from church to state or to the latter's many associated agencies. Third, 'pluralism': there is great diversity amongst and competition between all those institutions, of which the church is only one, now seeking to 'market' themselves to a global constituency. Fourth, 'technical rationality': the increasing influence of a process whereby 'supernatural influences and moral considerations (are gradually displaced) from ever-widening areas of public life, (and are replaced) by considerations of objective performance and practical expedience' (Bruce in McLeod and Ustorf, p. 14).

The diaconal church recognizes and accepts the increasingly secular nature of society. However, it sets its face against the hegemony of secular*ism*, an ideology that denies the reality of any sacred order or, in its less extreme form, an agnosticism that treats the sacred as irrelevant to public life. At the same time, the diaconal church resists the hegemony of sacralism (*Diagram 3*, Chapter 4). Sacral*ism* is an ideology that reifies the sacred. In a sacralistic world, it is religious systems that reign supreme and deny the legitimate authority of the secular. Sacralism permeated the culture of Christendom from top to bottom. It buttressed the Christendom church's claim that it had the right to control every aspect of human life because God had placed everything under its jurisdiction.

The diaconal church's response to both secularism and sacralism is to espouse what I have elsewhere termed 'secular faith' (Clark, 1984, pp. 26-27). Secular faith rejects the closed ideologies of secularism and sacralism, but it remains open to learning from the secular milieu within which we all now live and work. Secular faith is a *Yes to God*, of which Alan Ecclestone has written with such profound insight (1975). But it is also a *Yes to Life* (Clark, 1987), the whole of life. It is a faith founded on 'reality'. As Bonhoeffer once put it, 'There can be no reality without Christ and no Christ without reality' (in Bethge, 1979, p. 156). Secular faith liberates the diaconal church to build a world transformed by the gifts of the kingdom community because it knows that our 'Yes to God' and our 'Yes to life' are always met by God's 'Yes' to us.

From preservation to *transformation*

The diaconal church is committed to radical change. Unlike the Christendom model of church, it is not founded on conservatism (*Diagram 3*, Chapter 4) or primarily concerned with preservation. The diaconal church acknowledges and affirms its Christian heritage of which Christendom has been a major part. But it knows that it can no longer be bound by 'Tradition' spelt, as by Nichols (1999), with a capital 'T'. Its concern is with the *transformation* of a world that has lost touch with the kingdom community, a transformation brought about by its making manifest and sharing of God's gifts of life, liberation, love and learning.

Stance

From domination to *servanthood*

'The church of the next (millennium) will be a servanthood church' (*Diaconal Reflections*, 1998). The concept of *servanthood* (*diakonia*) is of fundamental importance for the diaconal church because the relational qualities of servanthood are those at the very heart of the kingdom community.

Servanthood characterizes the entire life of the diaconal church. The Anglican report on a renewed diaconate, *For such a time as this* (p. 37), states that 'all Christian ministry, ordained and lay, is grounded in *diakonia* because it is all dependent on the fundamental divine commission of the church in the service of the kingdom'. *The Distinctive Diaconate* (p. 40) comments that, '*Diakonia* belongs to the whole life of the church'. *From the Diakonia of Christ*, a Roman Catholic perspective (p. 3), adds that 'Baptism confers this *diakonein*, power of service, on every Christian'. The Methodist document, *What is a Deacon?* (2004, para. 3.1.1), maintains that 'being and acting as a deacon is a particular expression of a calling to discipleship that is shared by all Methodists.'

Biblical and historical background

There are numerous biblical words that fill out the meaning of servant and servanthood. In the Old Testament, the Hebrew word *ebed* is used, whilst in the New Testament it is the Greek word *diakonia* that is most relevant to our concerns.

For the diaconal church, the meaning of what it is to be a servant derives first and foremost from the life and ministry of Christ. In turn, Christ's understanding of his own ministry drew freely on the meaning of servanthood in the Old Testament. '(The) tradition of the servant of God runs from Moses through Elijah to Jeremiah and into the portrayal of the nation of Israel as the suffering servant in the beautiful Servant Songs of Isaiah 40-55' (Croft, 1999, p. 57). These servant songs must have had a profound influence on Christ's understanding of his own ministry, and of the nature and cost of being God's mediator in the creation of redemptive relationships. Christ's public declaration of his own calling when he preached in the synagogue in Nazareth (Luke 4:18-19) also resonates with Isaiah 61:1-2.

A number of passages in the gospels exemplify the servanthood of Christ. In Mark 10:45 ('For the Son of Man came not to be served but to serve, and to give his life as a ransom for many.'), Christ indicates the fundamental stance of his life's work. John Collins' (2002, p. 28ff) insists that 'service' in this passage is intimately linked with suffering and salvation. In Luke 22:24-30, when dealing with his disciples' dispute about greatness, Christ says, 'I am among you as one who serves', dramatically reversing the expectations of those who looked to him as 'master'. In John 13:1-16, the Last Supper, Christ takes the towel and basin and washes the feet of his disciples. Here, though the word *doulos* (a meaning more akin to that of 'slave') not *diakonos* is used, Christ's actions exemplify the caring and self-effacing nature of servanthood. It is interesting to note that, by the early second century, when the office of deacon had emerged more clearly, the role was directly associated with the person of Christ (Collins, p. 13) who was at that time given the title of 'the great Deacon' (*For such a time,* p. 35).

The early church recognized the essence of Christ's ministry as fundamentally that of servanthood, a quality that should be seen to permeate the lives of his disciples and followers. As *From the Diakonia of Christ* (p. 8) puts it:

> The first fundamental fact of relevance from the New Testament is that the verb *diokenein* designates Christ's actual mission as servant (Mk 10:45 and parallels; cf. Mt 12:18; Acts

4:30; Phil 2:6-11). This word or its derivatives also designates the exercise of service or ministry by his disciples (Mk 10:43ff; Mt 20:26ff; 23:11; Lk 8:3; Rom 15:25) (as well as) ministries of different kinds in the church.

Thus the apostles are entrusted with a servant ministry (Acts 1:17; 6:4; 20:24), and Paul often refers to himself as *diakonos* (1 Cor 3:5; 2 Cor 3:6; 6:4; 11:23). Christopher Moody writes (in *The New Dictionary of Pastoral* Studies, 2002, p. 85):

In the developing order of the churches of the New Testament, *diakonia*…was shared by the whole community. It described a way of living with each other and in the world brought about by the revelation of God in the ministry of Christ as 'the one who serves'…and in the outpouring of the Spirit to equip God's people for the proclamation, service of the kingdom, and the ministry of reconciliation. The term can be applied to any individual ministry in relation to the whole church and to the whole church in relation to its service to the world (2 Cor: 3-5).

Collins (2002) argues that during the early years of the Christian church, the word *diakonos* came increasingly to be used to identify the role of deacon. In the process, its more all-embracing meaning as 'servant' became overlaid by other meanings, such as those of attendant, agent and messenger. Nevertheless, Collins also acknowledges that when the diaconate re-emerged in the nineteenth century, 'the leading edge of the new ministerial model was service…, the kind of selfless, caring and loving service that characterized Jesus in his dealings with the lame and rejected men and women who people the gospel narratives' (pp. 7-8). It is quite clear that the diaconal communities and associations which came into existence at that time saw their ministry as one primarily of service, in particular nursing, welfare work and teaching, often amongst the most marginalized and destitute members of society.

In recent years, the theme of the servant church has come increasingly to the fore. Dulles sees it as the fifth (and most recent) model of church (1976). The Roman Catholic International Commission report (*From the Diakonia of Christ,* p. 3) states that 'Christian existence is a sharing in the *diakonia* or service which God himself fulfilled in favour of mankind; it likewise leads to an understanding of the fulfillment of mankind.' The current interest in a renewed diaconate can be seen as 'a sign of the church's vocation to be the servant of Christ and of God... which could renew the church in the evangelical spirit of humility and service' (p. 57)'. 'Deacons represent to the church its calling as servant in the world', states the Lima document from the World Council of Churches (quoted in *For such a time*, p. 16).

'Servanthood' and 'service'

In the light of the life and ministry of Christ, the witness of the early church and, not least, the needs of the world today, it is the model of the church as servant, the model of the diaconal church, that must take precedence over all others.

Nevertheless, it is extremely important that we distinguish between two interrelated, but different interpretations of the nature of 'servanthood' as found in the discussions about a renewed diaconate: servanthood as 'service', and servanthood as what it means to be a 'servant'. The legacy of diaconal communities and associations founded over the last century and a half has generally been one where servanthood is equated with service, as personified in the often sacrificial endeavours of the deaconess movement. It is also this understanding of servanthood as service that permeates many of the more recent reports on the restoration of a renewed diaconate.[1]

'Service' is of course an essential aspect of servanthood. Compassion and care for others are an integral part of a servant ministry and the life of the servant church. Service embodies love for God and love for neighbour in a way that can be seen and responded to by a world that challenges the credibility of a church that does not practice what it preaches. But service does not in itself get to the heart of the biblical meaning of servanthood, and thus of the nature of the diaconal church as a servant church.

'Service' is action-focused. Being a 'servant' is person-centred. The meaning of being a servant is derived from who or what is served. The diaconal church is the servant of the kingdom

---

[1] See *For such a time* (pp. 53-55) and *The Distinctive Diaconate* (pp. 65-66), where pastoral care figures prominently; *From the Diakonia of Christ* (p. 68), which stresses 'the service of charity'; *What is a Deacon?*, 2004, para. 5. 'Core emphasis of Methodist diaconal ministry: a ministry of witness through service' - though here the concept of 'service' is given a more radical interpretation than in the other reports.

community and of the Trinitarian God who rules that kingdom. Thus the diaconal church is a servant of God, a servant of Christ (2 Cor:11-23) and a servant of the Spirit: in short of One God in three Persons. It is also a servant of humanity, of the world which God created and which he loves. As a servant of the kingdom community, the diaconal church is called to offer the gifts of life, liberation, love and learning to all in the name of Father, Son and Holy Spirit.

Features of servanthood

The diaconal church is 'a good and faithful servant' (Mt 25:21). It obeys the Triune God's call to follow him, trusts that his purposes are for the well-being of his creation, orders its life in accordance with his divine priorities and seeks to be worthy of its calling. That calling it lives out in and for the world, and throughout the whole of life.

As a servant of the kingdom community, the diaconal church is deeply concerned about the planet earth (the gift of life). However, as Archibishop Rembert puts it, our stewardship of God's creation 'is more than just a question of not polluting the earth; it becomes a whole question of what lifestyle we must live as followers of Christ, in order that the earth can be constantly regenerating itself and, as it were, renewing itself from our waste and pollution. A kind of Christian cosmology has to accompany a Christian anthropology' (quoted in Echlin, P., 1991, p. 165).

Being the servant of the kingdom community commits the diaconal church to the kingdom's work of redemption, of bringing 'human integrity and wholeness' to all of creation (Grey, 1989, p. 4) (the gift of liberation). It is a ministry of reconciliation and renewal offered to the whole of society (*What is a deacon?*, 2004, paras. 5.5, 5.7). It is a calling to address whatever causes chaos in public affairs, as well as in private life. But it is a costly calling; it involves the way of the cross (5.6). The diaconal church follows the example of Christ who became 'a suffering servant' so that through his suffering a broken world might be forgiven and healed, and God's kingdom come.

The power of the servant church is not coercive power. It is the power of redemptive love (the gift of love). As Collins (p. 39) puts it, all the sayings of Jesus on the matter of the first and the last, the great and the lowly, are teaching his followers that 'the kingdom of God establishes itself in a community of relationships' undistorted by the misuse of power. Such servanthood 'is neither menial nor servile' for 'service in Christ is true greatness and to be great is to be a servant' (*For such a time*, p. 35). The servant church also bears witness to what Stanley Hauerwas (1986) calls a 'peaceable kingdom', a community that transforms the world though quiet authenticity and authority, not by frenetic endeavour.

Servanthood involves being open to learn, to embark on a journey of spiritual discovery (the gift of learning). The diaconal church knows that it can only begin to manifest the gifts of the kingdom community when it has the humility to become a genuine learning community. Such learning is about openness to the movement of the Spirit which 'blows where it wills' (John 3:8) and about listening to 'the still small voice' however faint. The diaconal church also recognizes that is has an immense amount to learn from a secular world, a world wherein the kingdom community is omnipresent even if unrecognized.

Servanthood brings great rewards. The servant church is invited 'to enter into the joy of (its) master' (Mt 25:21) whose 'service is perfect freedom'. Servanthood brings to members of the servant church the most profound experience of life, liberation, love and learning that human beings can experience. These are gifts that the diaconal church as servant of the kingdom community cannot help but want to share with others.

As a servant church, the diaconal church presents a very different picture from that of a Christendom church that has been shaped over many centuries by belief in a kingdom founded on power and control. If the church is once again to be able to respond to its commission to proclaim the gospel and to witness to the centrality of the kingdom community in all that Christ taught and did, then such imperialism (*Diagram 3* Chapter 4) must end. There has to be a fundamental shift of stance from domination to servanthood. The preoccupation of the Christendom church with controlling and moulding, still prevalent to-day, has to give way to a spirit of affirmation, listening, learning and of 'self-giving sacrificial love'.

Comparing what he calls 'empire' and 'discipleship' (2002, pp. 36-37), John Collins writes:

> (Christ's) words 'servant' and 'slave' are introduced into (his) sayings for the purpose of identifying the extreme contrast between two social groups. The two words stand opposed to

'great' and 'first'. The imperial group pursues values which are immediately recognizable and which have been part of our historical understanding and of folklore from time immemorial. But the sayings of Jesus are insisting that discipleship does not operate by the principles that make one 'great' or 'first'. Instead discipleship operates by principles that no social organization has ever known…

If this last sentence is true, then the servant church offers a radically new vision of the future. It is a vision that will mean the most profound change in the life of the church since Christendom began. But without a vision the people perish. The church, of all bodies, does not exist to dismiss the words of Christ as naive, but to use them as pointers to the nature of the kingdom community and to seek, as far as is humanly possible, to make manifest that community for the benefit of the whole of humankind.

Joe Holland (1983, p. 85) puts this commission in a contemporary context:

The symbolic interpretation has shifted from the Davidic image of 'Christ the King', dominant since Constantinean Christianity, to a mosaic image of a 'Prophetic Servant Jesus'… We are entering not simply a new response to industrialization, but a whole new form of church – one that is altering elements that have dominated the church since the time of Constantine and perhaps since the apostle Paul and the rise of the Greek Church. The radical strategy, therefore, is not merely a short-term traditional strategy. Rather, it is a profound shift that terminates Constantinean Christianity, retrieving neglected elements of the pre-Constantinean and perhaps pre-Pauline forms.

But how can the diaconal church pursue this radical and demanding agenda? It can only do so if the church is acknowledged, in principle and practice, to be the *laos*, the whole people of God whose calling it is to be servants of the kingdom community across the world.

The laity

From priest to *people*

The diaconal church is first and foremost a body of people, 'the *laos*'. 'The *laos*' is comprised of the whole people of God and is theologically prior to any distinction between laity and clergy. In the Gospels, the servant passages were 'directed to the church as a whole' (Collins, 2002, p. 122). Throughout the New Testament church, 'the (diaconal) emphasis was on the ministry of the whole Christian community through the use of God-given gifts which included prophecy, evangelism, teaching and pastoral care (Ephesians 4:11)' (Staton, 2000, p. 18). Thus diaconal ministry becomes a way of life which reflects the servant ministry of Christ through the life and work of the whole people of God (Staton, p. 298; see also *What is a Deacon?*, para. 3.2). 'Ordination does not take anyone out of the *laos*' (*For such a time*, p. 26).

The all-embracing nature of servanthood has two important implications for the diaconal church. First, both ordained and lay are called to servanthood as the hall-mark of their Christian discipleship. Whatever role they might be fulfilling, from the leadership of worship within the church to witnessing to the nature of the kingdom community beyond it, it is as servants that both ordained and lay undertake their responsibilities. Secondly, because all are servants of Christ the Servant and his kingdom, there can be no question of those ordained claiming or being given higher status than the laity.

Christendom failed to grasp or, where it did, to acknowledge the importance of the laity in the ministry and mission of the church. Instead, clericalism gradually gained strength, setting the position and standing of priest above that of *the people* (*Diagram 3,* Chapter 4). For a variety of reasons, from a distorted sacramental theology, which took the breaking of bread to be of deeper significance than the washing of feet, to a concern to guard 'the truth', and the status and power which thereby accrued to its guardians, clericalism came to dominate the ethos of the Christendom church.

'Clericalism is the domination of the "ordinary" people by those ordained, trained and invested with privilege and power' (Stevens, 1999, p. 52). It is a 'division between clergy and laity (that) undervalues the lay lifestyle, lay talent, lay leadership, lay experience and lay spirituality' (Lakeland, 2003, p. 195).

In the diaconal church, Christendom's understanding of the relationship of clergy and laity is radically changed. We shall see later that this has important lessons to teach us about the nature of ordained leadership within the diaconal church. Here, we simply note that in the diaconal church it is the laity who move centre-stage, though the clergy remain their fellow travelers. Thus the diaconal church is one in which the focus moves from priest to people, to the whole people of God, as *Lumen Gentium*, one of the most important documents of Vatican II, made abundantly clear (Ker, 2001, pp. 9-10).

From dependency to *autonomy*

A laity that breaks clear of clericalism also breaks the mould of conformism (*Diagram 3*, Chapter 4). Gilbert (1976, p. 13) describes this as ending 'the dependency system' which dominated the social and political scene in pre-industrial England. Throughout Christendom, it was the church in alliance with the state, at all levels of society, but especially at parish level, which controlled and directed the lives of lay people. Other factors colluded to maintain this situation, such as a relatively immobile society, strong kinship ties and bonding based on a shared locality and a common heritage. The outcome was a laity so dependent on a Christendom church that their experiences, insights and skills, both religious and secular, were constantly undervalued.

The diaconal church is a church in which there has been a transition from dependency to *autonomy*. This is not a self-centred autonomy that focuses on the desires and interests of the self-sufficient individual, but what moral educators term 'altruistic autonomy', that form of autonomy which embraces both the fulfillment of self and the welfare of others.

Within the life of secular institutions the transition from lay dependency to autonomy has been ongoing for some centuries, even if it has only gained real momentum during the second half of the twentieth century, not least as a result of the coming of universal educational opportunities. Within the church, however, clericalism and conformism have retained a powerful hold. Even within much of 'Evangelical Nonconformity', the nineteenth century saw the ordained ministry gradually reasserting its authority over an initially pro-active laity (p. 58), though the ongoing contribution of lay people remained significant in the development of some denominations such as certain branches of Methodism. Yet, writes Gilbert (p. 158), 'the impetus within the professional ministry of Nonconformist organizations towards role differentiation between ministers and laymen, and the consequent marked reduction in the scope for lay initiative in pastoral and evangelistic work, was successful, in the final resort, only because the laity acquiesced with the process'.

Nor has the rise of Pentecostalism (and its near relative, the Charismatic Movement) very much altered this situation. In many cases, the professional leaders of these movements have promoted their own role and image in such a way that their followers have remained dependent on them as symbolic figures and conformist to the religious culture that they have fostered. Thus clericalism and conformism have made their mark even in churches with an ecclesiology that, at first sight, appears very different from that of the Christendom church.

Within the diaconal church, lay and ordained exercise their ministry as equal partners. The laity's experience, knowledge and skills are acknowledged and affirmed. The responsibility of all those ordained is to encourage and equip lay people to use their talents and skills to fulfil their calling as servants of the kingdom community wherever they live or work. At the same time, lay people have a responsibility to encourage and support the ministry of the ordained. In the diaconal church the relationship of lay to ordained is one of interdependence not dependence.

The laity as kingdom community builders

The ministry to which the laity are called is that of fulfilling the mission of the diaconal church. Their vocation is to be the servants of the kingdom community throughout the world. As such, they are called to be kingdom community builders by making manifest the kingdom community's gifts of life, liberation, love and learning within the church. But they are also called to be kingdom community builders within the world, empowered by and offering to others the gifts of the kingdom community.

The laity, liberated from clericalism and conformism to play their full part in the mission of the diaconal church, offer to church and world a wealth of expertise and skills. The sheer diversity of lay experience makes available to the church a vast resource of human imagination, knowledge, talents and energy hitherto latent, but for years undervalued and underused by the Christendom model of church. The liberation of the laity means that the diaconal church can be present wherever lay people live, work or play, on the margins as well as at the heart of society, to discern, to make known and to participate in making manifest the gifts of the kingdom community.

For lay people to rediscover their calling to be servants of the kingdom community, it will be necessary for the concept of Christian vocation to become as important to them as it is to those ordained (see Adair, 2000). Unless this happens, the laity will continue to see the clergy as those with the 'real' responsibility for the life and mission of the church, and themselves as the supporting cast. It is thus a top priority for the diaconal church to find ways of reinstating Christian vocation as the high calling of all lay people. It is a calling both to be about God's work of building communities that manifest the gifts of the kingdom community and also to keep moving forward on the journey of spiritual discovery by means of which those gifts can be better appreciated, understood and used.

Coming to realize that God is calling them to be servants of the kingdom community will offer many lay people new inspiration, purpose and fulfilment, over against the debilitating passivity so often forced on them by the Christendom model of church. However, we are not assuming that lay people are waiting eagerly to be liberated from the Christendom's legacy of clericalism and conformism. It will be no easy transition for *God's Frozen People* to become *God's Lively People* (Gibbs and Morton, 1964 and 1971). The changes required for this transformation to happen are as radical and demanding as those required for the diaconal church itself to come into being.

6. *Diaconal collectives*

Preamble

The diaconal church, like any other organization, must have structure and form. However, the human collectives most appropriate to the mission of the diaconal church are those most likely to further the manifestation of the gifts of the kingdom community; life, liberation, love and learning.

In order to fulfil its ministry and mission effectively, the diaconate as it re-emerged in the West in the early nineteenth century chose to adopt collective forms similar to those of the diaconal church. Notably, these were the communal group and what today would be called the network. It is collective forms such as these which need to be integrated into the life and work of a renewed diaconate.

This chapter presents the descriptions of the communal group and network contained in *Breaking the Mould of Christendom*[1].

The communal group

From community of place to *communities of interest*

Because we now live in a highly mobile world, 'membership of a permanent religious body that confronts us as a fixed objective entity cannot give us our basic social identity as religious persons', writes Charles Davis (1994, p. 148). New communal collectives are needed to facilitate the emergence of the diaconal church. Key requirements of such collectives are that they are diverse and available to all. At the same time, they must be inclusive and open if the church is to address the communal dilemma, end exclusiveness and make its essential contribution to the creation of a global community.

Not only are the structures of Christendom unable to meet this need, but their legacy locks the church into an anachronistic past. In particular, parochialism (*Diagram 3*, Chapter 4), the idea of 'church' being equated with a parish or local neighbourhood, has to be

---

[1] Clark (2005: second printing, 2014) *Breaking the Mould of Christendom* (pp. 90-95). The original chapter also contained descriptions of the hearing, the communal institution and the partnership, other typical collective forms of the diaconal church.

superseded if human collectives conducive to the growth of the diaconal church are to emerge. 'The parochial system of the Church of England (has) been one of the most durable of the nation's institutions,' writes Gilbert (1976, p. 127). The problem is, however, that the parish remains 'a fixed objective entity' too closely associated with a specific and limited geographical area. It cannot provide communities of faith adequate to support and equip a highly mobile laity who, unlike previous generations, live, work and play in many different locations.

For new communities of faith to emerge, the church must acknowledge the importance of *communities of interest*. It needs to embrace such communities, encouraging its members to come together around common interests related not only to the parish or the local neighbourhood, but to occupation, health, social and political concerns and leisure interests. At the same time, faith communities based on common interests must provide their members with a sense of life, liberation, love and learning strong enough to match the challenge of a secular, mobile and volatile society. It is here that the communal group, a mini community versatile enough to embrace a wide variety of common concerns and interests, comes to the fore.

The communal group as such has played a key role throughout Christian history. The Christian church originated from a group of twelve people. 'The church in the house' was the normative form of the early church's gatherings, in many cases the home-owners, male or female, being identified by name (Acts 12:12, Romans 16:5, 1 Cor:19, Colossians 4:15, Philemon 2). The term *ekklesia* (church) was used to refer to the communal home-based gathering and to the wider Christian community. For many years the church was composed of communal communities of faith, meeting where secrecy and safety permitted, linked by preachers and pastors mobile enough to keep them closely in touch with one another.

Subsequent centuries witnessed the communal group at the heart of the church's missionary endeavours, often providing the springboard for movements of Christian renewal. From the Desert Fathers to Benedict of Nursia and the monastic cells which gathered round him, from the Celtic missionaries keeping the faith alive on the fringes of a fragmenting Roman empire to the Franciscans and the Dominicans, from the explosion of communal Christian groups after the Reformation to the counter-Reformation spearheaded by the Society of Jesus, from the rise of 'non-conformity' typified by the small independent church, the Quaker meeting and the Methodist 'class meeting', communal groups shaped and sustained the life and mission of the church (Clark, 1984, pp. 74-75).

The nineteenth century also saw the communal group at the forefront of renewal and mission. New Roman Catholic orders appeared on the continent and new Anglican orders were founded in England. From the middle of the century, first the Salvation Army and then the Pentecostal Movement strove to create small Spirit-filled bands of Christians. As we have noted, it was during this period, too, that a new form of diaconal movement emerged, first within the German and Scandinavian churches and later within the Anglican and Methodist Churches in Britain.

In the latter half of the twentieth century, renewal movements throughout the church continued to be pioneered by small groups of Christians. Such was the case with the Christian Community Movement in the UK (Clark, 1977; 1987), the basic ecclesial communities in Latin America, the so-called 'house churches' in the UK and the more recent 'emerging churches' worldwide.

However, it must be recognized that not every group is a communal group. If we had time to examine the history of the small group in the life of the church, we would find many instances of groups that were exclusive and closed, had distorted the church's understanding of its call to be the servant of the kingdom community and negated attempts at Christian renewal.

It is the communal group which forms the collective foundation of the diaconal church. As an essential form of the diaconal church seeking to reflect the nature of the kingdom community, the communal group is a community of faith through which the kingdom community's gifts of life, liberation, love and learning are offered to all. It is a mini learning community pursuing a journey of spiritual discovery and, in that undertaking, always open to learning from and about others. It is inclusive in its relationships with other groups. Within the life of the diaconal church, every communal group becomes 'a kingdom community group'.

The communal group, as a kingdom community group, is a key resource for nurturing the life of the diaconal church not only within but also beyond the parish or local neighbourhood. One of its great assets is that it can be located anywhere. It is neither confined to a particular place, such as the parish, nor to a particular organization, such as the institutional church. Work and voluntary interests, as well as concerns about issues such as poverty, justice and peace, can bring such communities of faith into being.

Nonetheless, in a global village, the word 'globe' is as important as the word 'village'. The whole is as essential as the part. Larger diaconal collectives are as important as the communal group for building a global community of learning communities. Without devaluing the importance of the communal group, the responsibility of the diaconal church is to share in creating forms of human collective that can create a trans-world community. In this task networks and networking also have a key part to play.

The network

From insularity to *interconnectedness*

The parochialism which typified much of the Christendom era, led to community of place, especially rural place, shaping the day-to-day life of the Christian church. It was the boundaries of the parish that defined the interests and concerns of most people. But it was also a situation that led to isolationism (*Diagram 3*, Chapter 4). The spatial immobility of the population, with only the most laborious means of communication available to them, led to what we have described as cognitive and cultural, as well as social and economic immobility. The sense of being part of a universal church was still there, though largely mediated through institutional rituals and symbolic figures.

The diaconal church faces a quite different world. Especially since the middle of the twentieth century mobility in every sense has gathered momentum. Vastly increased spatial mobility, notably through air travel, and cognitive mobility, given impetus by a dramatic revolution in information technology, has presented humankind with unimagined opportunities for greater cultural and social mobility. If the church is to re-engage with this world of so-called 'flows', then the communal groups that still provide its life and energy will need to become integral parts of a much greater whole. Insularity must be replaced by *interconnectedness*. For this purpose networks assume great importance.

The word 'network' is a relatively recent term. It describes a web of interconnecting lines of communication that enable participants to exchange experiences, ideas, insights and resources, quickly, easily and on an equal footing. 'Networks' of communal Christian groups have characterized the church from its inception, even if communication between such groups was extremely slow up to the Victorian era. Such networks represent a model of the church as 'movement' rather than as 'institution'. The early church was for a number of centuries a movement, consisting of networks of Christian groups linked by itinerant missionaries like Paul and his associates. Indeed, Collins (2002, p. 113) states that 'the first written record of a church building is said to be (not until) the year 200 in the writings of Clement of Alexandria'.

With the coming of Christendom, mission gradually gave way to 'maintenance' and the church as institution gradually took precedence over the church as movement. Only when the call for the renewal of the church as institution, or the conversion of those outside it, came to the fore, did the need for the church as movement re-emerge. Thus the religious orders over many centuries, the post-Reformation 'churches' and the Methodist revival (note that Methodism still calls itself a 'Connexion'), the diaconal associations of the nineteenth and twentieth centuries, as well as the Pentecostal and charismatic movements of more recent times, have all made use of networks to link the diversity of the communal groups, that initially gave them life and momentum, into corporate and sustainable renewal movements.

The diaconal church welcomes the emergence of networks that can give identity and sustainability to the diverse and dispersed communities of faith that make it up. It recognizes, as has always been the case, that the church as movement is essential but complementary to the church as institution. Thus the diaconal church seeks to create networks that can enrich its life, work and mission. To that end, it has a special concern to create networks that facilitate communication that is open, immediate, direct, informative and interactive (Clark, 1996, p. 76).

For the diaconal church networking is also about linking the local and the global. Holland and Henriot describe such a strategy as follows (p. 85):

While (this) radical strategy is centred on the activities of communal grassroots groups that constitute the basic Christian community, there is also a significant *transnational character* to the strategy. The (diaconal) church is a genuine transnational actor, one that is present and active across national boundaries. Thus, there is a paradoxical two-way thrust to the strategy, the first towards the grassroots and the second towards the transnational arena. Thus, within the new strategy, there is a combination of decentralization and broad networking.

Though the diaconal church employs the network as pre-eminently a means of linking communities of faith, it also recognizes the network as a means of connecting Christians as individuals. This is particularly important where the mission of the laity as the church widely dispersed throughout society is concerned. The network here offers a way of enabling lay people to share their experiences, insights and skills. It makes resources available that would not otherwise be accessible. The network, too, can sometimes offer lay people a 'virtual' faith community when they might otherwise find themselves in isolated and lonely situations.

It is one of the great assets of a new millennium that the information technology needed to create networks of diverse kinds is rapidly becoming available to everyone, not least to the church. Yet, as with all types of human collective, networks can be used for good or ill. The power of information technology can promote interests (such as pornography) and activities (such as terrorism) that are deeply destructive of those values for which the kingdom community stands.

Nevertheless, the sustainability of the diverse and dispersed communal groups and individuals that make up the diaconal church and enable it to engage with the global challenges of a new era will in large part depend on the creative development and maintenance of communal networks.

7. *Servant leadership and governance*

Preamble

In this chapter we set out a vision of church leadership as servant leadership. It is a vision which emerges from a theology of the kingdom community and of the model of the diaconal church built on that foundation. We reiterate that within the diaconal church all forms of church leadership must be servant leadership.

Our particular interest here is what a renewed diaconate might contribute to the leadership of the diaconal church. Debate continues across a number of denominations about the potential of 'a renewed diaconate' as a leadership resource. Our problem is that this debate is taking place largely in the context of an understanding of ministry and mission moulded by an outdated Christendom model of church. Nowhere is a conversation taking place with the model of the diaconal church as its starting point.

The vision of servant leadership, and the roles which derive from it, which is offered below is shaped by the model of the diaconal church.

This chapter first appeared in *Breaking the Mould of Christendom*[1].

Introduction

To understand and describe the nature of church leadership within the diaconal church, it is necessary to use the insights of all academic disciplines at our disposal. We recognize that there are a significant number of people, especially amongst those who remain committed to the Christendom model of church (Nichols, 1999), who reject what they see as a 'functional' rather than a sacramental approach to church leadership. Others are put off by what they regard as 'management-speak' (Pattison, 1997). In what follows, we are not claiming that the nature of the church and its leadership can be fully understood in terms of the human sciences. The church, as a servant of the kingdom community, will always retain its mystical and sacramental character (Dulles, 1976, pp. 43 – 70). However, we are

---

[1] Clark (2005: second printing, 2014) *Breaking the Mould of Christendom* (pp. 102-129).

convinced that if the church is to have any hope of addressing the communal needs of a new millennium, it will require a form of leadership radically different from that which characterized the age of Christendom. Thus in discerning the nature of the kind of leadership needed by the diaconal church we need to draw on useful insights wherever available.

For the purposes of our analysis and of clarity, we here use the terms 'church leader' and 'church leadership' to refer to those appointed and employed (usually) on a paid basis by the church, and (usually) ordained, to oversee its life and work. This chapter focuses on the roles of church leaders within the diaconal church, and in particular on how these roles relate to the ministry and mission of the laity.

To understand what will be required of church leaders within the diaconal church, we first look at the forms of leadership that we have inherited from the Christendom church, with a brief resumé of how the leadership of the church developed from New Testament times onwards.

The historical context

As the early church grew and spread, a wide diversity of leadership roles emerged which were inevitably shaped by the missionary nature of the church's life and work. Even so, as John Collins reminds us, 'the profound obscurity surrounding the rise of forms of church order with which the Christian world is now familiar' (2002, p. 97). Nevertheless, before any clear and definitive leadership roles emerged within the early church it was commonly believed that all forms of ministry should be 'diaconal' in nature.

Collins presents a wide-ranging discussion of the diverse use of diaconal words in the New Testament. He acknowledges their highly contextual meaning, but comes to three main conclusions. First, he argues, in the face of current assumptions about the word, that 'it is no longer possible to continue claiming that social work expresses what the early church meant by the term *diakonia*' (p. 121).

Second, Collins believes that the word *diakonia* describes a broad range of ministries. These appear to be focused on three functions (*For such a time*, 2001, p. 32, and Jackson, 2002, p. 119): that of messenger – one who is entrusted with carrying good tidings; that of agent – one who is commissioned to carry out a task on behalf of someone in authority; and that of attendant – one who waits on a person on whose behalf he performs various duties. In practice, it is not easy to distinguish between these three aspects of diaconal ministry. Nevertheless, what they appear to have in common is that they embrace the concept of servanthood, that they stress the role of intermediary and that they include the task of spreading the good news of the kingdom.

Third, with respect to the last of these tasks, Collins states that *diakonia* includes a responsibility for proclaiming 'the Word' (*For such a time,* p.50) and is thus a role carrying a clear missionary connotation.

Over the first few centuries of the Christian church, three specific leadership roles identified by the titles of *diakonos, episcopos* and *presbyteros*, probably in that chronological order, gradually began to appear. As the church became more an institution and less a movement (especially after Constantine extended state recognition to Christianity in 313), the role of deacon, which had early on the life of the church gained some prominence, declined in importance. At the local level, the role of priest or presbyter gradually came to dominate the scene, and, at the level of the region, that of bishop. At the same time, the laity came increasingly to be seen more as the recipients than the instruments of ministry, and the church more as 'a community of followers' than 'a community of leaders' (Adair and Nelson, 2004, p. 190).

As the Christendom church became part of the warp and woof of society, and as its sacramental rituals move to the fore, bishops and presbyters, as its overseers and guardians, gained in power and status. The consequences were the emergence of forms of church leadership that reflected power and status, and in particular the attributes of Christendom that we have called élitism, authoritarianism and paternalism (*Diagram 3,* Chapter 4).

There were of course, even within Christendom, exceptions to this pattern of church leadership. When the renewal or mission of the church came to the fore, the roles of priest and bishop could not suffice. Such times required new movements and new forms of leadership able to nurture faith and communicate the gospel with fresh vision, zeal and energy. The monastic movement was one such movement. Other movements were associated with the Reformation and the Counter-Reformation. Likewise, Nonconformity was a movement before it developed into different denominations. So were the Methodist revival and subsequent 'evangelical' revivals, as well as the early international missionary movements associated with the age of empire.

Mission movements of this kind have continued up to the present day. Those leading them have pursued ministries that have far more in common with the New Testament understanding of *diakonos*, in particular the role of the messenger who proclaims 'the Word', than with that of *presbyteros* or *episkopos*. Despite this fact, such movements have done little to break the mould of Christendom, of the élitism, authoritarianism and paternalism of its leadership and of the lowly position often occupied by the laity.

Church leadership within the diaconal church

From hierarchy to *servant leaders*

Leadership within the Christendom church was élitist (*Diagram 3*, Chapter 4) in the sense that there was a clear and unassailable order of 'merit', with lay people at the bottom, the priest in the middle and the bishop at the top of that order. The church was a hierarchical institution where those who were 'above' ruled, and those who were 'below' obeyed.

The failure of the Christendom church to acknowledge that the church is 'a community of leaders', and that different 'orders' of ordained ministry are of equal value and status, is one of the most tenacious of all problems facing the emergence of the diaconal church. The assumption, within society as well as church, that there is a hierarchy of ministries that reads 'bishop, priest, deacon and laity', in that order of precedence, remains deeply entrenched. The diaconal church radically questions this legacy of Christendom. It regards all (ordained and lay) as servants of the kingdom community, and all ministries (ordained and lay) as having equal standing even though they entail different responsibilities. The only 'privileged' position enjoyed by the ordained leadership of the diaconal church is that of being *'servant leaders'* of the laity (Philip Mawer, in Adair and Nelson, 2004, p. 92).

Reports from working parties on the nature of a renewed diaconate argue that the deacon has a special responsibility to model a servanthood ministry (see Chapter 4). A 'diaconal, servanthood ministry means being a healing, accepting, encouraging presence to others, enabling them to experience God's unending, unconditional love and forgiveness' (*Diaconal Reflections*, 1998). However, though servanthood is 'the key to understanding the call to diaconal ministry' (*Diaconal Reflections*), it is not an attribute of the ministry of the deacon alone. Servanthood is likewise a hall-mark of the ministries of presbyter and bishop. Thus for the diaconal church to single out the deacon as having a particular calling to exemplify the meaning of servanthood would not only be invidious but also deny the fact that presbyter and bishop, as well as deacon, are servant leaders.

One would have hoped that the literature on a renewed diaconate would have produced a radically new vision of church leadership. One would also have hoped that these reports would have recognized the laity as the leaders in mission and those ordained as supporting them, with lay and ordained alike being seen as having equal value and status. However, the conclusions, in particular of the Anglican and Roman Catholic working parties on a renewed diaconate, are ambivalent if not contradictory on these issues. Their reports assert with some conviction that all ordained ministries are diaconal (servant ministries) in nature, but then go on to argue for the retention of a hierarchical order of church leadership.

On the one hand, the Church of England working party set up by the House of Bishops states that the diaconate is 'the *sine qua non* of all ordained ministry, the base line, the template on which it is fashioned' (*For such a time as this*, p. 37), a sentiment echoed by the Diocese of Salisbury report on *The Distinctive Diaconate* (2003, p. 5). The Roman Catholic Church's International Theological Commission believes that the 'representation of Christ as Servant ...should be considered a characteristic common to every ordained minister' (*From the Diakonia of Christ*, 2003, p. 80).

On the other hand, the hierarchical three-fold order of bishop, priest and deacon remains firmly entrenched. The Anglican Church, in *For such a time as this*, states that (permanent) deacons operate 'under the oversight of the parish priest and both deacon and priest are subject to the oversight of the bishop' (p. 56). The Diocese of Salisbury report at least acknowledges that 'there may appear to be a tension between our desire for an integrated approach to ministry and the seemingly hierarchical context of the Anglican church (as well as the Roman Catholic and Orthodox churches) whereby from the *laos* some are called as deacons, of whom some are called as priests, of whom some are called as bishops' (p. 39). But the report's attempt to resolve this dilemma by talking of 'cumulative responsibility for the edification of the church', still leaves the diaconate as such at the bottom of the ladder, a fact brought home by its recommendation that the deacon's stipend is to be 'as other *assistant* clergy' (p. 83, our italics).

The Roman Catholic Commission similarly notes that Vatican II, despite reinstating the permanent diaconate, still upheld 'different "degrees" of Holy Orders' wherein 'deacons represent the "lowest" degree in the hierarchical scale, in relation to bishops and priests' (*From the Diakonia of* Christ, p. 83). In short, the relegation of the deacon to a transitory grade of ministry 'placed after the bishop and the priests' (p. 20), remains the norm.

From director to *community educator*

Authoritarianism (*Diagram 3,* Chapter 4), in the literal sense of taking authority to oneself, typified the leadership of the Christendom church. Its leaders were certainly not into the business of equipping the church to be the servant of the kingdom community. Their task was to instruct and train, not to educate. As guardians of the church, they were there to direct its affairs and protect the souls of the faithful.

In contrast, church leaders of the diaconal church are *community educators* not directors. In this context, presbyter, deacon and bishop have two major responsibilities. The first is that of enabling the church to become a *community* that makes manifest the gifts of the kingdom community. All its church leaders are working to nurture and sustain a body of people who are open to receiving God's gifts of life, liberation, love, and learning and who are passionate that others should have the opportunity to receive these gifts. Presbyter, deacon and bishop are there to help the laity to interpret the Christian faith not as a closed book, but as an ongoing journey of spiritual discovery in search of the meaning of the kingdom community.

Within the diaconal church, the second major responsibility of church leaders, presbyters, deacons and bishops, is that of equipping lay people to be kingdom community builders. This means helping them to discern and to make known the gifts of the kingdom community already omnipresent in the world. It means helping lay people to be kingdom community builders empowered by the gifts of the kingdom community in whatever situations they find themselves.

Presbyter, deacon and bishop fulfil their role as community educators in at least four ways.[1] They are *catalysts* rousing a Christendom church from its slumbers and challenging the laity to break clear of their dependence on the clergy. They encourage lay people to engage in visioning what a world manifesting the gifts of the kingdom community would be like. They work to raise the awareness of the laity to their vocation to be the servants of the kingdom community in the world.

As community educators, church leaders within the diaconal church are *enablers*. They build up the confidence of lay people by affirming the knowledge, experience and skills that they already possess. They encourage them to reflect on how these attributes can enrich their life as a faith community and enhance their ministry in the world. They help lay people to learn how faith can inform work, and how work can inform faith, and to discover how both processes can inform their calling as kingdom community builders. They work with lay people to enable them to become 'reflective practitioners' (Schön, 1991).

As community educators, presbyter, deacon and bishop are also *intermediaries*. Their responsibility is to link lay person with lay person so that beliefs, experiences and ideas can be shared, learning advanced and the sense of being a team be strengthened. They work to create local team ministries that bring together presbyter, deacon and laity. They seek to foster links with other churches committed to an ecumenical vision of mission. They are also on the look out for creative connections that can be made between the church and a secular society, especially connections that can create networks and partnerships to further community building.

---

[1] In Appendix 1, written a decade later than this chapter, we suggest that the role of servant leader, in a secular as well as ecclesiological context, is somewhat broader than that of community *educator*. We describe it as embracing six subsidiary roles - visionary, strategist, animator (similar to the role of catalyst), enabler, intermediary and educator. The role of *resource person* mentioned below informs all six roles.

Through all these facets of their role as community educators, presbyter, deacon and bishop operate as *resource persons*. They offer the resources of the church, through worship, education and pastoral care, to enable lay people to gain a deeper understanding of Christian faith, to learn what it means to be a learning community and to prepare for their calling to represent the church in the world.

At the present time, when we still await the liberation of the diaconal church from the legacy of Christendom, it is our belief that the deacon has a particular responsibility to fulfil the roles of catalyst and enabler (see Chapter 9). Complementary to these diaconal roles, the presbyter might be seen as having a special responsibility to undertake the role of resource person, and the bishop to fulfil that of intermediary. Nevertheless, in suggesting such a 'division of labour', we would not in any way want to undermine the all-important fact that deacon, presbyter and bishop all remain community educators, those equipping the laity to be kingdom community builders, and, at one time of another, will be called upon to play out every facet of that role.

Gender issues

From men to *women and men*

All positions of leadership within the diaconal church are open to *women and men*. This is a far cry from the Christendom model of church in which patriarchy and paternalism (*Diagram 3,* Chapter 4) were the norm.

In the early church, women appear to have worked as equals alongside men in exercising informal leadership, despite the gender discrimination evident in certain of the Pauline letters and the reservations about the role of women as leaders in the pastoral epistles. Even though the status of Phoebe, designated a *diakonos* (Romans 16:1), and that of the women 'deacons' mentioned in I Timothy 3: 11, is disputed (see Collins, p. 99, as against *The Diakonia of Christ,* p. 21), there is little doubt that women leaders figured prominently during this period. However, as the leadership of the church became more formalized, women were increasingly excluded from positions of authority.

Even when designated 'deaconesses', women were only in evidence in the Eastern Church and then exercised a ministry largely confined to the needs of other women. Indeed 'in the west there is no trace of any deaconesses for the first five centuries' (*The Diakonia of Christ*, p. 26). From then on deaconesses continued to fulfil a lowly 'ecclesiastical function' in both East and West (p. 27), though their ministry developed unevenly in different regions.

With the emergence of female monastic communities, a number of women came to exercise a notable ministry as their leaders. However, in relation to the order and governance of the institutional church they continued to be treated as subordinate to men.

It was not until the nineteenth century, as we have seen (Chapter 4), that deaconesses, as members of a re-invigourated diaconate undertaking a ministry of nursing, social welfare and teaching, again came to the fore. However, they were usually seen as exercising a 'lay' ministry. Few were given any voice in matters of church governance. In fact, the deaconess associations of this era did not press for such a voice, did not take a great interest in church politics and were not much involved in 'feminist causes' as a whole (Staton, 2001, p. 68).

During the twentieth century, deaconess associations began to lobby for their role as church leaders to be recognized by their being accepted into the presbyteral ministry of the church. Women were ordained as presbyters within the Congregational Union in 1914. In Methodism, the Wesley Deaconess Order began debating the ordination of women as early as 1920 (p. 159). In 1947, the Methodist Diaconal Convocation again pressed for deaconesses to be given the opportunity to be ordained as presbyters, a request declined by the Methodist Conference (p. 210) even though many deaconesses were then working in presbyteral appointments because of a shortage of male ministers during the war. Not until 1972, was the Methodist ministry opened to women. Staton goes so far as to describe the treatment of the Wesley Deaconesses in the Methodist Church during the period from 1932 (the union of Methodism in the United Kingdom) to 1972 as 'a paradigm of subordination and the exploitation of feminine good nature!' (p. 250).

In the second half of the twentieth century there were similar moves to ordain women as priests within the Church of England. Increasing numbers of women opted for the diaconate but mainly in the hope of eventually being able to become priests (700 women were ordained deacon, as the first step towards priesthood, in 1987!). In

1992, the General Synod at last voted to open the priesthood (though not the episcopate) to women. The first ordinations of women to the priesthood of the Church of England were held in 1994 (*For such a time*, p. 8).

It is worth noting here that the coming of greater gender equality within the life of the church also raised the issue of equal opportunities for men. Thus many diaconal associations and communities, once entirely female, are now open to men, though women continue to be a large majority.

However, within the Roman Catholic and Orthodox Churches the reinstatement and revival of the permanent diaconate still relates only to men. Nor in those churches has there been any official movement towards the ordination of women to either the diaconate or the priesthood. At the same time, a similar male dominated form of church leadership characterizes many Pentecostal and charismatic churches.

The ordination of women to presbyteral ministry has certainly challenged Christendom's legacy of paternalism. Thus it could be a major step towards the emergence of the diaconal church in which positions of church leadership are open equally to women and men. However, there is some danger that the opening of presbyteral ministry to women could inadvertently continue to perpetuate the Christendom model of élitism and clericalism. For if the opportunity for women to be ordained only leads to an increase in the number of priests and presbyters, it could perpetuate rather than challenge hierarchical orders of ministry. Of major consequence also, the diaconate could continue to be seen as a subordinate office, and the ministry of both deacon and lay people continue to be devalued as a result.

Presbyter, deacon and bishop

The local church and the dispersed church

Before we examine the roles of presbyter, deacon and bishop within the diaconal church, we need to identify two forms of church that are vital to its life and work: *the local church* and *the dispersed church*. By the local church, we mean the people of God as servants of the kingdom community gathered to worship, learn, care for one another and enjoy each other's company. By the dispersed church, we mean the people of God dispersed throughout society to serve the kingdom community by building communities that manifest its gifts of life, liberation, love and learning.

One of the most crippling weaknesses of the Christendom model of church is that no church leader is specifically designated explicitly to serve the laity as the people of God *in the world*. This is a huge omission. It is one that we believe lies at the heart of the church's marginalization in our day and age. Thus it is imperative that the diaconal church creates a form of church leadership explicitly concerned to equip and support the laity as kingdom community builders dispersed throughout society. We argue below that in future this responsibility should become that of a renewed diaconate. This would mean the deacon's role differing radically from how it is seen to-day, even in literature on a renewed diaconate.

A threefold form of church leadership

We distinguish three main spheres of church leadership within the diaconal church. That of *'presbyter'* is seen as relating to *the local church*; that of 'deacon' to *the dispersed church*; and that of *'bishop'* as concerned with linking and integrating the life and work of both *the local* and the *dispersed church*. In what follows, the title of 'presbyter' is taken to be synonymous with the titles of 'priest' or 'minister'.

We keep the titles of presbyter, deacon and bishop simply because they are the ones in common usage today, as well as their linking us with the early church and our Christian heritage. However, we need to make clear that we see the titles as such as relatively unimportant. It is the leadership *roles* that relate to these titles that are of real significance. Indeed, in future years these titles may well be superceded by new ones that have greater affinity with the everyday language of a secular society, as well as with the ethos of the diaconal church.

Diagram 4 outlines the main features of the role of presbyter and deacon within the diaconal church. Each role is described as what, in sociological terms, is called an 'ideal type'. Each ideal type brings together the key features of a particular leadership role, though all the features will rarely be evident in the ministry of any one individual. We do not include the role of bishop in the diagram because, as we explain later, we see his or her role as linking and integrating the roles of presbyter and deacon.

In the discussion that follows, the headings in the left-hand column of the diagram will appear in italics in the text.

Diagram 4
The roles of presbyter and deacon in the diaconal church

	Presbyter	Deacon
COMMON FEATURES	*Servant leaders of the laity* *Community educators* *Women and men*	
FORM OF CHURCH	Local (gathered)	Dispersed
PEOPLE SERVED	The laity in the church	The laity in the world
PRIMARY TASK	Church as medium of the kingdom community The church as 'the Body of Christ'	Church as messenger of the kingdom community The church as 'the people of God'
FOCUS OF MINISTRY	Community of place The church as workplace	Communities of concern, occupation and interest The church as home base
BOUNDARIES OF MINISTRY	Working within the boundaries of the church	Moving across the boundaries of church and world
WORSHIP	'The Word' for the church Baptism as a sign of belonging Holy communion as 'the breaking of bread' Christian rites of passage	'The Word' for the world Baptism as a sign of discipleship Holy communion as 'the washing of feet' Secular 'rites of passage'

LEARNING	Learning about the faith	Learning about Christian vocation
	Doctrine	Ethics
	Spirituality of growth in the Christian life	Spirituality of work
	Learning about the church	Learning about the church in the world
	Reflection on faith Discussion	Reflection on practice Dialogue
PASTORAL CARE	The laity in the church	The laity in the world
	Those in need associated with the church	Those in need beyond the church
MANAGEMENT RESPONSIBILITIES	The local church Team ministry co-ordinator	The dispersed church
AS SYMBOLIC FIGURE	Represents the church as an institution	Represents the church as a movement
'ECUMENICAL' MINISTRY	Working with other churches	Linking Christian and non-Christian collectives
PIONEERING MINISTRY	'Planting', supporting and developing 'emerging churches'	Exemplifying, advocating and working for the furtherance of kingdom community values in the world

The presbyter

Within the diaconal church, the presbyter is both a servant of the kingdom community and a servant leader of the laity. He[1] is also a community educator, enabling the laity to become kingdom community builders, and his style of leadership will reflect this.

The *form of church* with which the presbyter is mainly concerned is the local church, and the *people served* who are his particular responsibility are those who are members of that local congregation. His *primary task* is that of building church members into a community that makes manifest the gifts of the kingdom community; life, liberation, love and learning. The corporate image most clearly associated with this expression of church is 'the Body of Christ'.

The *focus of ministry* for the presbyter is the church as a community of place, usually meaning a particular building within a particular locality (such as a parish), even though the members of his congregation may come from further afield. The local church building serves as the presbyter's main place of work, in the sense that his office may be there, that he meets people there during the week and that worship takes place there. The *boundaries of ministry* for the presbyter are defined largely by the church as a community focused on the local neighbourhood, and as an institution.

In the context of *worship*, the presbyter is seen as a minister of 'Word and Sacrament'. He celebrates the sacrament of baptism as a sign of belonging, and holy communion as 'the breaking of bread', as well as other Christian rites of passage. For the presbyter, *learning* has faith and doctrine as its main focus, as well as the history and traditions of the particular denomination he represents. As with any community educator, the presbyter encourages reflection and discussion. He also seeks to nurture the laity in a spirituality that helps them grow in the Christian life. For the presbyter, *pastoral care* is focused on the members of the local church, especially on their personal and family concerns, and on the needs of others closely associated with the church or living in the immediate neighbourhood.

The presbyter's *management responsibilities* encompass organizational, administrative and financial matters related to the life of the local church. The presbyter has the important task of co-

---

[1] We use the word 'he' throughout this chapter as interchangeable with 'she'.

ordinating any team ministry associated with the work of the local church. Such teams will be made up of ordained (including deacons in their new role) and lay members. Their style of operating will be collaborative and consensual.

As a *symbolic figure*, it is with the church as a public institution that the presbyter is most clearly identified.

The presbyter's wider ministry has two main foci. *Ecumenically*, his main concern is working in partnership with (local) churches of other denominations. Where he undertakes a more *pioneering* role, his work will often be focused on church growth or how 'emerging' forms of local congregation, the latter usually linked to his own church, can be created and nurtured.

The deacon

Within the diaconal church, the deacon, like the presbyter, is a servant of the kingdom community and a servant leader of the laity. He, too, is a community educator.

However, it is of importance to recognize that the *form of church* for which the deacon takes the main responsibility is the dispersed church, the people of God called to be the servants of the kingdom community in society and world. Thus the *people served* by the deacon are the laity as that church dispersed is the world.

The *primary task* of the deacon is to challenge and equip lay people to fulfil their calling as messengers of the kingdom community. This means that he will be equipping them to be kingdom community builders empowered by and offering to others the gifts of life, liberation, love and learning.

The deacon's task is 'to enable (lay people) to see that mission is not an optional extra, but central to what it means to be the church...called not merely to maintain itself but to proclaim God's kingdom' (Atkinson). He helps 'the church to have confidence in God by recognizing his constant presence' (Atkinson) throughout the whole of society. The deacon's responsibility is to maintain 'a permanent focus on the servant ministry of Christ by attempting to embody that role and encouraging and enabling the church to do so too' (Atkinson, 2005).[1] The corporate image most clearly associated with this expression of church is 'the people of God'.

Although, like the presbyter, 'the central community of the diaconal minister's life and ministry is the congregation' (Lambert, 1999, p. 16), the *focus of ministry* for the deacon is the communities of interest, occupation or concern in which lay people are involved on a daily basis. The deacon is thus involved not only with community education within the local church as such but, following up the ministry of the laity, with community education well beyond. The local church is not so much the deacon's place of work as a home base and launching pad for his ministry within wider society.

The *boundaries of* the deacon's *ministry* do not limit him to working within the institutional church. He criss-crosses the boundaries of church and society in order to discover ways in which he can better enable the laity to fulfil their vocation as the dispersed church. He also moves across these boundaries to enhance his own knowledge, experience and resources.[2] The deacon's boundary role gives depth

---

[1] The role of the deacon as one facilitating the ministry of the laity in the world receives attention from a number of commentaries on a renewed diaconate. For example, *For such a time as this* (quoting the Anglican-Lutheran Hanover Report of 1996) describes the deacon's role as 'enabling and resourcing the ministry of the laity' (p. 18). *For such a time as this* argues that a renewed diaconate should 'model, encourage and coordinate the diaconal ministry of the people of God' (p. 36). It adds that 'a renewed, distinctive diaconate, operating as a catalyst for Christian discipleship, in the mission space between worship and world, can help the church to become more incarnational' (p. 30). *The Distinctive Diaconate* report for the Diocese of Salisbury states that 'the deacon does not do the work of others but encourages and enables the ministry of others' (p. 106). For the Methodist Church, *What is a Deacon?* states that 'the primary purpose' of diaconal ministry 'is to help all Christians discover, develop and express their own servant ministry' (2004, para. 5.4), adding that the deacon 'encourages and enables others to undertake their ministry with greater effectiveness in their daily lives' (para. 3.3 (b)).

[2] In this connection, some commentaries on a renewed diaconate misinterpret what it means for a deacon to be 'a boundary worker'. They speak as if it is the deacon himself who is the 'go-between', the 'bridge' or the 'envoy' (*For such a time as this*, p. 22), or the 'ambassador' or 'agent' working on behalf of the church (*The Distinctive Diaconate*, p. 42). Within the diaconal church, however, it is the people of God in the world, not the deacon, who are the 'go-betweens', 'the envoys' and 'agents' linking church and world. The responsibility of the deacon is to inspire, enable and resource the laity to fulfil that ministry. If the deacon's

and breadth to his understanding of the communal needs of society. It is a role that 'may also involve social and cultural analysis' (Lambert, p. 11). It offers him a unique vantage point from which to discern the presence of the kingdom community in wider society. It is a position that enables him to keep the servant ministry of the dispersed church constantly under review, and from which he can identify the most appropriate resources for educating and equipping the laity for that ministry.

The laity, as the dispersed church, also need to gather together in order to renew themselves for mission. When this happens, it is the deacon's primary responsibility, through worship, education and pastoral care, to help the laity reflect on and renew their calling as the church in the world and to equip them for that ministry.

In relation to *worship*[1], 'liturgical involvement holds great potential for expressing a diaconal minister's identity as a *public* (our italics) minister of the Word' (Lambert, p. 12). The deacon ensures that 'the Word', through preaching or prayers of intercession, is applied not just to the life of the church but also to the mission of the diaconal church within the world.

His presence points to baptism to be a sign of discipleship. It also points to 'holy communion' as a sacrament of servanthood, in this case symbolized by 'the washing of feet'. Endowing this sacrament

---

boundary role were interpreted in this way, then some fears that a renewed diaconate could devalue the ministry of the laity, and a new form of clericalism thereby re-assert itself, would be allayed (see *For such a time*, p. 46; *The Distinctive Diaconate*, pp. 46 and 73; *From the Diakonia of Christ*, pp. 65-66).

[1] Commentaries on the renewed diaconate affirm a number of the features of the liturgical role of the deacon mentioned above. For example, in the Anglican reports, the deacon's responsibility is seen as reading the gospel, offering prayers of intercession and dismissing the people with an appropriate blessing (*For such a time*, p. 55 and *The Distinctive Diaconate*, p. 63). In the Diocese of Salisbury's report, it is argued that the deacon should also preach. (p. 72). At the Roman Catholic mass, the deacon reads the bible and occasionally preaches (*From the Diakonia of Christ*, pp. 61-62). However, these Anglican and Catholic commentaries fail to make a clear connection between the deacon's liturgical role within the local congregation and his ministry to the laity as the church dispersed in the world. Their approach is dominated by the deacon's liturgical responsibilities as an assistant to the presbyter (priest), especially in relation to the celebration of the Eucharist or Mass.

with much greater significance than has been the case in the liturgy of the Christendom church is one of the deacon's most important contributions to the worship of the diaconal church. Thereby the deacon offers a potent symbol not only of the grace bestowed by the kingdom community's gifts of life, liberation, love and learning but of the way in which the diaconal or servant church should seek to make them manifest in the world.

The deacon should have responsibility for sending the congregation out with a prayer of dismissal emphasizes their calling as the people of God in the world. The deacon should also help the church to acknowledge and celebrate secular 'rites of passage'; those important transitional experiences which mark significant stages in everyday life: from home to school, from school to work, from job to job, from work to retirement, and from place to place.

The deacon has an important role in relation to *learning*. One focus of the deacon's ministry in this context is to strengthen the laity's sense of vocation as the people of God in the world. In this his task is to challenge, inspire and equip them to become kingdom community builders. Facilitating theological reflection on daily life and work, and developing the idea of dialogue as mission are other tasks central to the deacon's role as community educator. Christian ethics will figure prominently in the deacon's repertoire. All these responsibilities will involve the deacon exercising his educational skills through the use of hearings and groups. He will also enable lay people to develop a spirituality of work related to their working situation and their personal needs.[1]

The deacon, along with the presbyter, exercises *pastoral care*. However, the deacon's caring ministry is primarily concerned with nurturing, encouraging and supporting the laity as they seek to live out their calling in daily life. His job is to understand and address the inevitable strains and stresses experienced by those seeking to serve the kingdom community in a secular and sometimes hostile society.

---

[1] These aspects of the deacon's role as applied to learning are far removed from the catechetical role of the deacon portrayed in commentaries on the renewed diaconate. In these reports, the 'educational' role of the deacon is generally interpreted in the narrow sense of teaching church members about the faith and preparing people for Christian rites of passage. In few commentaries is the deacon's role explicitly associated with strengthening and developing the vocation of lay people as the church dispersed in the world.

At the same time, the deacon is always ready to care for those outside the church, as the situation demands and his time and energy allow.[1]

The deacon's *management responsibilities* require him to oversee the work of all those supporting the ministry and mission of the dispersed church. Ideally, he will gather groups of people with relevant skills, especially educational skills, to assist him on a paid or voluntary basis. At the same time, 'diaconal ministry is not a "lone ranger" activity' (Lambert, 1999, p. 17). Thus the deacon will be an active member of any team ministry that seeks to integrate the work of the local and dispersed expressions of the diaconal church.

As *a symbolic figure*, the deacon is most closely identified with the church as a movement. He represents the diaconal church in its more mobile form, dispersed throughout society and able to respond to the call to serve the kingdom community anywhere and anytime. However, for the public at large, it is almost invariably the presbyter who still represents the church, and a church moulded by Christendom at that. This makes it all the more difficult for the diaconal church to present the deacon to society as an equally symbolic figure.

The deacon fulfils an *'ecumenical' ministry*. His role here is primarily that of an intermediary. Whereas the presbyter focuses his attention on connecting local church with local church, the deacon looks to build creative connections between the church and the diversity of Christian collectives active in society (voluntary organizations, church schools, religious orders and so on). The deacon also fosters links between the church and secular collectives which share the former's concerns for community building.

On occasions, the deacon's intermediary role will take him into broader fields of engagement. He may find himself operating as a person seeking to connect secular collective with secular collective in

---

[1] Commentaries on the renewed diaconate again miss the point. They interpret the deacon's pastoral role as relating primarily to the needs of the local church and its neighbourhood and not to those representing the dispersed church as such. For example, in some Anglican commentaries the deacon is regarded as the person who 'spearheads pastoral care in the parish' (*The Distinctive Diaconate*, p. 64). This is seen as his 'pivotal' responsibility (*The Distinctive Diaconate*, p. 65). The Roman Catholic International Commission also goes a good way to reinforcing this parochial approach with its emphasis on the deacon's ministry as being 'the service of charity' within the parish (*The Diakonia of Christ*, p. 68).

an attempt to build a more communal society. He may also interpret his 'ecumenical' role as relating to 'the whole inhabited earth' (the literal meaning of the word 'ecumenical') and become involved in ecological issues of preservation and conservation. Here, however, we are touching on the role of deacon as pioneer.

Like the presbyter, the deacon may sometimes be called upon to undertake a *'pioneering* and prophetic' *ministry* (*Windsor* Statement, 1997).[1] The role of deacon as pioneer may be expressed in three main ways. He identifies with the marginalized (see *Voices from the margins*, Methodist Diaconal Order, 2005). As *Diaconal Reflections* puts it (1998, p. 2): 'In identifying with Christ, (the deacon is) identifying with the suffering of the world, with the oppressed, the poor, the disenfranchised, the abused'. Second, the deacon as pioneer is an agent of change: 'The prophetic role of diaconal ministry is to see God's intention for the creation, to critique what is going on in church and world, to protest against evil and injustice, and to call the church and world – all people – to respond in ways that will transform the world' (p. 2). Third, the deacon as pioneer is pro-active in striving for a more just world, in working for peace and in serving the vulnerable and marginalized, especially where their needs are acute. It is a role that entails 'prophetic, political, social and environmental action directed towards peace, justice and reconciliation...' (*What is a Deacon?* para. 5.4).

Nevertheless, in focusing on the role of deacon as pioneer it is important to remind ourselves of the hall-marks of the diaconal

---

[1] Though most of the commentaries on the renewed diaconate major on the deacon's liturgical, catechetical and pastoral responsibilities in relation to the local church, some do touch on his role as pioneer. *For such a time as this*, for example, claims to be offering 'a vision of the renewed diaconate at the cutting edge of the church's mission' (p. viii). *The Distinctive Diaconate* believes that 'the deacon is the church's representative person in a liminal ministry among those who would never cross the threshold of the church on their own' (p. 106). *The Diakonia of Christ*, for the Roman Catholic Church, notes that 'in various places particular efforts have been made to make the diaconate a "threshold" ministry, which aims to look after "the frontier church"' (p. 69). The Methodist Church is particularly strong on this aspect of the deacon's role, stressing the deacon's pioneering role as 'crossing boundaries, making connections between alienated and fragmented groups, including those beyond the margins, overturning unjust structures, standing in solidarity with the vulnerable and helping them discover their own voice' (*What is a Deacon?* para. 5.7).

church and of the deacon's role within it. Within the diaconal church, the deacon only assumes the role of pioneer where it is one which cannot be fulfilled by lay people. Within the diaconal church, the deacon's primary responsibility is to educate and equip the laity for ministry and mission, pioneering or otherwise. His task is not, as is suggested in *From the Diakonia of Christ* (p. 56), 'to penetrate secular society in the same way as lay people' unless lay people are unavailable to meet the need or address the issue concerned. Any deacon, indeed any church leader, however dynamic, courageous, or sacrificial his ministry, who takes over what could be the ministry of the people of God in the world, devalues the church's greatest resource and perpetuates clericalism.

If the lack of any Christian presence means that it is necessary for a deacon to take up a pioneering role in wider society, he will seek to move aside as soon as possible so that the skills, energy and resources of others can come to the fore. Such 'stepping aside' is of the essence of the deacon's ministry as a servant leader.

One final but important point needs to made here. Even within the diaconal church there may be times when a presbyter is required to play the role of deacon, or a deacon to play the role of presbyter. In these circumstances the presbyter must be given full authority to undertake diaconal responsibilities. At the same time, the deacon must be given full authority to undertake presbyteral responsibilities, including if necessary presiding at the Eucharist. However, it remains essential to maintain a division of labour between the role of the presbyter, primarily focused on the local church, and the role of the deacon, primarily focused on the dispersed church, if the communal life of the local church is to be enriched and its mission as the servant of the kingdom community in the world effectively fulfilled.

The bishop

As with the role of presbyter and deacon, there is only 'fragmentary New Testament evidence about the office of *episcopos*' (bishop) (Croft, p. 146). In the early church the broad picture is that of an *episcopoi* initially exercising oversight of local congregations alongside presbyters, but gradually assuming a wider remit as the church expanded numerically and geographically. In time, the bishop came to oversee both presbyters, who were beginning to take greater responsibility for the work and worship of the local church, and deacons, who were assuming a more itinerant and administrative brief, the latter often acting as the eyes and ears of the bishop who authorized their ministry. With the emergence of Christendom this threefold order of ministry became normative, with power and influence accruing to the bishop at regional level and to the presbyter at local level. Meanwhile the office of deacon lost its earlier responsibilities and status and was eventually relegated to a first brief stage en route to the priesthood.

In this section we use the title 'bishop' to encompasses not only the office of bishop as present in the Anglican and Roman Catholic Churches, but any office (such as that of chair of district or moderator) with which the title can be equated in other denominations. The Christendom church has left us with the problem that the title, in the eyes of both church and society, describes those regarded as at the 'top' of the ecclesiastical pyramid. However, within the diaconal church, the role of bishop would differ markedly from that with which it is currently associated.

Within the diaconal church, the bishop, like the presbyter and deacon, is a servant of the kingdom community and a servant leader of the laity. Like the presbyter and deacon, he is also a community educator, taking responsibility for ways in which the laity are equipped to be kingdom community builders. A subsidiary role of the bishop as community educator is that of *intermediary* (as against the common interpretation of *episcope* as an 'overseer' or director). To repeat Wenger's words on the leadership of organizations, the role of the bishop is not to 'sit on top but to move in between, not to unify by transcending but to connect and disconnect, not to reign but to travel and to be shaped and appropriated in the context of specific practices' (1998, p. 247). The bishop is 'a go-between leader' serving a 'go-between God' (Taylor, 1979). From his 'go-between' position he is able to learn, to monitor (Rudge, 1968, pp. 55-57), to connect and, if necessary, to initiate.

The bishop is the servant of the *laos*. His task is to integrate the local and dispersed forms of church, across a wide area, into a dynamic whole. It is a task he fulfils largely by affirming and supporting the ministries of presbyter and deacon. His responsibility is to enable them to share their visions, experiences, knowledge and skills so that the church can make manifest the gifts of the kingdom community and, through its lay people, offer those gifts to all.

The bishop helps deacon and presbyter to recognize that their ministries are complementary. He enables them to hold together baptism as a sign of belonging and baptism as a sign of discipleship; worship as 'the Word' for the church and worship as 'the Word' for the world; holy communion as 'the breaking of bread' and holy communion as 'the washing of feet'; learning about the faith and learning about Christian vocation; pastoral care to nurture the laity 'at home' and pastoral care to support the laity 'at work'. The bishop also has the task of maintaining strong links between the church as an institution and the church as a movement.

The bishop is a servant leader, always seeking to discern and understand more clearly the workings of the kingdom community in church and world. The exercise of *episcope*, of being an intermediary, is crucial in enabling the whole church to see and acknowledge the ministries of presbyter and deacon as complementary and collaborative. It is also crucial in enabling the laity to recognize that their ministry as the dispersed church is as important as their work within the local church, and that, unless these two expressions of Christian ministry are given equal validation, the mission of the church will remain unfulfilled.

The bishop, like the presbyter and deacon, is a symbolic figure within church and world. However, his authority as such derives not from any kind of traditionally ascribed status, but from the fact that he represents the holistic nature of the church, local and dispersed as a servant community.

Though the bishop's primary role within the diaconal church is to support and integrate the ministries of presbyter and deacon and, through them, to affirm the ministries of the people of God, he also has important ecumenical responsibilities. His task is to help link the servant ministry of the churches for which he has overall responsibility with that of churches within other denominations. Likewise, he seeks to link the churches for which he has responsibility with secular organizations also committed to the communal transformation of society.

From time to time the bishop may exercise a pioneering role. As a pioneer, the bishop may be engaged with urgent issues or critical needs which the dispersed church is not able to address effectively, or which require the involvement a person representative of a wider

Christian constituency. However, the bishop's role should not become that of the focal person on which the ultimate success of such interventions comes to depend. Thus he will assume a pioneering role only where the ministries of presbyter or deacon, and above all the ministry of the laity, are not operative or adequate. He will also seek to delegate responsibility for such interventions as soon as possible.

Governance

In our exploration of the main features of the diaconal church, we have made only passing reference to issues of governance. How is the diaconal church to govern itself, make decisions, look after its finances, maintain its buildings, and, especially, handle organizational conflict over matters both spiritual and temporal?

We recognize that these are critical concerns, and that the diaconal church could all too easily be undermined by the day-to-day challenges of being an institution within which convictions will inevitably diverge and passions run high. We recognize too, that breaking the mould of Christendom would be little more than iconoclastic if no appropriate form of church governance were put in its place.

Our conviction is, however, that it is more important to set out a number of principles on which the governance of our model of the diaconal church is based rather than to make any attempt to present a detailed blue-print for governance. Thus we offer three principles of diaconal governance: *subsidiarity*, *democracy* and *self-government*. We believe that they have the potential to break the mould of Christendom because they are the antithesis of the principles on which the governance of that model of church is based: centralism, unilateralism and statism.

From centralization to *subsidiarity*

Over against centralism (*Diagram 3*, Chapter 4) the diaconal church is committed to the principle of *subsidiarity*. It encourages the dispersal of leadership and the devolution of power. Interestingly enough, for a church that is perhaps still the one most influenced by the legacy of Christendom, it was the Roman Catholic Church that in a papal encyclical of the late nineteenth century first enunciated the principle of subsidiarity. Stamp quotes Hans Kung (CIPL, G3, 1992): the principle of subsidiarity states that 'the behaviour of the community in regard to the individual, and that of the superior community in regard to the subordinate community, is subsidiary'. Kung continues:

> The principle of subsidiarity 'allows as much liberty as possible and as much association as necessary. But this implies, too, that the community has no right to shut itself off like a sect. Its autonomy is not absolute, but in many ways relative, inasmuch as subsidiarity carries with it an obligation to solidarity...with other communities, with the regional church and universal church.'

From autocracy to *democracy*

Unlike governance within Christendom church, decision-making within the diaconal church is never unilateral (*Diagram 3,* Chapter 4). It is *democratic* not autocratic. We define democracy here, with the Oxford Dictionary, as 'government by all the people, direct or representative', as well as 'a form of society...tolerating minority views'. This form of church governance is derived, on the one hand, from the principle of subsidiarity, and, on the other, from the assumption that the leaders of the diaconal church are servant leaders of the laity.

Some people reject the idea of the church being a democracy, not only on theological grounds, but because of the dangers of 'heresy', conflict and fragmentation to which such a form of governance could lead. Some evidence for this is offered by Werner Ustorf who informs us that 'Christianity today is split into approximately 34,000 separate denominations' and is 'a massive Babel of diversity' (McLeod and Ustorf, 2003, p. 220). However, the fundamental issue here is how much longer the church can continue to reject democratic forms of governance in an era in which the autocracy that characterized Christendom is no longer tenable?

We remind ourselves that human civilization is facing a high-risk future and that we must learn how to create a global community of communities or chaos will ensue. All of us need to be involved in that enterprise and all of us are responsible for its outcome. The governance of the global community we seek cannot be based on anything other than democratic principles, whatever particular form such democracy may take. If the church if to be true to its calling to be the servant of the kingdom community, the latter offering a vision of community desperately needed by a world in crisis, then the church too must ultimately find ways of taking democracy into its system. The risks it faces in so doing are no greater than those faced by the world of which it is an integral part (Holloway, 1990). Unless the church is prepared to take such risks, it will have little to offer to a world in which inequality and injustice is still endemic in all societies.

From establishment to *self-government*

The diaconal church is a *self-governing* church. The principles of subsidiarity and democracy reinforce this requirement. Thus statism (*Diagram 3,* Chapter 4), the Christendom model where the church is supported by the state and civil law in respect of its doctrines, worship and discipline (often described as 'establishment'), is no longer an option.

All established churches, and especially those in a relationship with the state exemplified by the position of the Church of England, benefit in one way or another from the privilege, patronage and power bestowed on them by the legacy of Christendom (Hobson, 2003). In England, for example, the Church of England's senior bishops sit in the House of Lords, its cathedrals are nationally symbolic places and its leading clergy are treated as nationally symbolic persons. Its parish system encompasses the entire country and its incumbents are accorded a status higher than those of any other denomination.

In contrast, the diaconal church cannot accept privileges and patronage bestowed on it by the state because these call in question the church's freedom to fulfil its mission as the servant of the kingdom community, a mission that may at times involve strong opposition to or denunciation of the state itself (for example, as should have happened more publicly in Germany under the Third Reich). Any privilege and patronage bestowed on it by the state also undermines the diaconal church's stance of servanthood and its calling to serve the kingdom community not from a position of strength but from one of vulnerability.

Another problem has confronted established churches in recent years. They can give the impression that the church is an organization offering its services to the general public as a beneficent parent. Thus the relationship of the general public to an established church can mutate into an experience of what Grace Davie terms 'vicarious religion' (2002, p. 19). This term refers to the fact that 'for particular historical reasons... significant numbers of Europeans are content to let both (established) churches and churchgoers enact a memory on their behalf. In this situation, people come to take the church for granted. They do not see themselves as having any responsibility for the maintenance of an institution which to survive must in the long-term require their tangible support.

If, in this situation, the state withdraws privileges and patronage from an established church and its clergy (as is gradually happening in much of Europe today), what is then left is a church without 'emperor's clothes'. Its laity will be poorly equipped to take responsibility for a church previously protected by the state from the consequences of declining support. And the general public, which has depended for so long on a vicarious religious experience, will no longer have the services of a church supported by the state on which to draw. Nor will other churches, which over the years have been weakened by the domination of an established church, have anything like the same public credibility or resources to be able to step into the breach.

The diaconal church needs to be independent of the state in order that its laity can acknowledge that they are responsible, as partners with the clergy, for its maintenance and mission. Those who are drawn to explore the meaning of Christian faith will then find, not the hollow shell of an established church abandoned by a secular state and left to fend for itself by a wider populace, but a living and sustainable Christian community.

This does not mean that the diaconal church should ignore the state. It means that the diaconal church should seek to enter into a genuine partnership with the state, just as it would with any other institution, and whenever possible work closely with government in order to build a society which manifests the gifts of the kingdom community.

Appendices[1]

Preamble

In Appendix 1 we argue that the model of the diaconal church, including the servant leadership roles which typify it, need to become normative for every institution if the gifts of the kingdom community are to be made manifest within society and world. In defining the meaning of servant leadership, we suggest a number of complementary roles[2] which are vital for the task of helping to make manifest the gifts of the kingdom community. Appendix 2 summarizes the hall-marks of the diaconal church identified in earlier chapters. Appendix 3 summarizes the hall-marks of all diaconal institutions, sacred or secular.

Appendix 1

The diaconal church and its leadership – a model for all institutions

God calls not only his church but also his world to manifest the gifts of the kingdom community. Because the diaconal church acknowledges that it is the servant of the kingdom community, it has the potential and the responsibility to become a model for every institution, sacred or secular. Becoming such a model is the diaconal church's great privilege, as well as daunting responsibility (Clark 2005, pp. 128-129; 2008a, pp. 199-211).

Consequently, the stance, collective forms, mode of communication, membership and leadership of all institutions needed to create a world that manifests the gifts of the kingdom community will reflect the stance, collective forms, mode of communication, membership and leadership of the diaconal model of church set out above. Only when this transformation happens will we be able to say that we are living in a diaconal world; a global community of

---

[1] These Appendices are taken from Clark (2014) *The Kingdom at Work Project* (pp. 112-120).

[2] These offer a broader perspective than that of community educator, though we still regard the latter as a key aspect of servant leadership described earlier in this chapter.

communities whose understanding of community is informed and transformed by the images of the Trinity and the kingdom which reveal God's inclusive and universal gifts of life, liberation, love and learning.

In a diaconal world, all institutions, sacred and secular, would embrace the stance of servants of humankind, if not consciously and explicitly of servants of the kingdom community. The diaconal institution would create and sustain communal groups, networks, and partnerships. Its normative mode of communication would be dialogical. Membership (employees) of the institution, at all levels, would be regarded as the latter's primary asset, their experience, insights and skills seen as an indispensable human resource. All would be expected to become community builders within the life and work of their organizations, institutions and wider society.

Within the diaconal institution, leadership roles would be akin to the leadership roles within the diaconal church. That of servant leader would be pre-eminent.

Servant leadership

The implications of a theology of the kingdom community are that all institutions should be servants of that community and thus diaconal in nature. The leaders of such institutions should likewise be servants of the kingdom community and of humankind. Such servant leadership in either church or world focuses on six subsidiary and complementary roles each embodying one or more of the gifts of the kingdom community. These roles are depicted in *Diagram 5*.

Diagram 5
The servant leader

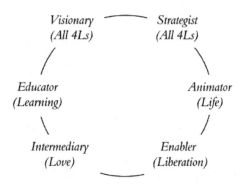

Visionary (All 4Ls)

The servant leader is a visionary who seeks to offer insights into the nature and form of a church and world transformed by the kingdom community's gifts of *life, liberation, love and learning* (the 4Ls). He or she has the ability to communicate that vision to and inspire others, by example and word. At the same time, the servant leader as visionary seeks to foster others' visions of a church and world transformed, encourages them to share these visions and to reflect on their practical significance.

Strategist (All 4Ls)

The servant leader is a strategist who has the competence to turn visions of a church and world transformed by any or all of *the 4Ls* into reality. The role of strategist has much in common with that of 'the designer', a role identified by Peter Senge as essential for the creation of learning organizations (1990, pp. 341-345). The strategist can be described as an 'organizational architect' (p. 343), a person who has the ability to enable visions, values and purposes to inform and shape every aspect of the life and work of the institution concerned, not least in how it can engage effectively with the wider world. Strategists have the ability to discern when the time is right to intervene. They have a clear overview of how human collectives operate and of how change might be brought about. They know where resources, human and otherwise, are to be found and how these might be best employed. The strategist does not raise false hopes or lead people up blind alleys.

Animator (Life)

The servant leader is an animator who seeks to create a church and world that manifest the kingdom community's *gift of life*. The role of animator is, literally, one which animates - it brings the church and secular institutions to life. It is a role which encourages innovation, creativity and risk-taking. The leader as animator inspires people to bring energy and commitment to their task. The animator generates a culture of enthusiasm and enjoyment. He or she fosters respect for the natural environment and concern for the preservation of the planet.

Enabler (Liberation)

The servant leader is an enabler who endeavours to bring into being a church and world that manifest the kingdom community's *gift of liberation*. The enabler is an attentive listener. He or she looks for the best in their colleagues, as fellow workers and as people. Enablers are concerned with helping people free themselves *from* over dependence on others, not least those who are enablers. They seek to bring release to those held captive by fear, failure and guilt. They strive to free people *for* communal transformation by helping them to employ their insights, skills, and abilities for the redemption and renewal of every human collective. The servant leader as enabler has the ability to stand aside once the person or collective with which they are engaged is able 'to go it alone'.

Intermediary (Love)

The servant leader is an intermediary whose task is to create a church and world that manifest the kingdom community's *gift of love*. The intermediary builds new and creative connections between person and person, collective and collective. He or she is actively concerned with how experiences, insights and resources can be enhanced and enriched through formal and informal exchanges and sharing. The intermediary plays an active part in resolving conflicts and disagreements, where necessary exercising the skills of reconciler, mediator or negotiator. The leader as intermediary has the ability to draw people together into creative and supportive communities of practice (Wenger, 1998 and 2002).

Educator (Learning)

The servant leader is an educator who strives to create a church and world that manifest the kingdom community's *gift of learning* (Senge, 1990, pp. 353-357). 'Any monastery that fails to become a learning organization will soon fade away', state Kit Dollard and others, the authors of *Doing Business with Benedict* (Dollard, 2002, p. 63). So it is with diaconal institutions. The educator encourages the questioning of evidence, the challenging of values and the testing out of received wisdom. It is a role which fosters new ideas, experimentation and the development of fresh paradigms. Servant leaders as educators sometimes operate as coaches (Fox, 2011) or mentors. They help others to see and embrace learning as a journey of discovery.

Complementarity and collectivity

Though each of the above roles has an affinity with a particular gift of the kingdom community, all draw inspiration and insights from one or more of the other gifts. It is only when all roles and the gifts on which they draw are recognised as complementary that servant leadership as a whole reveals its deepest meaning.

No one person has the ability, skills and resilience to fulfil all the roles which go to make up servant leadership. Thus servant leadership within church *and* world is invariably a collective phenomenon. This means that the concept of the leadership *team* needs to be very much to the fore though, as the Benedictines acknowledge, 'the challenge is (always) to change the team into a community' (Dollard, 2002, p. 114).

Appendix 2

Eighteen theses for the diaconal church

1. In the millennium ahead, our world faces a *choice between chaos and community*.

2. If it is to survive, human civilization has *to choose to become a global community of character*, ranging from micro communities (the family) to macro communities (major institutions and nation states).

3. *The Christian vision of 'the kingdom community'* is the supreme exemplification of all such communities, and thus a model for world and church.

4. *The gifts of the kingdom community are life, liberation, love and learning.* They are gifts manifest within the nature of the Trinity and in Christ's teaching about the kingdom of God. They are *universal gifts* offered to all.

5. The *mission* of the church is to model and to build communities of character that are transformed by and manifest the gifts of the kingdom community. *The credibility* and *viability* of the church depends on how faithfully it fulfils this mission.

6. Such a mission can only be fulfilled if the church becomes *a 'diaconal' (servant) church*. The diaconal church is *the servant of the kingdom community* and *of humankind*.

7. The diaconal church *respects the autonomy of a secular culture* but *rejects the domination of sacralism* or *secularism*.

8. *The human collectives that make up the diaconal church* – hearings, groups, networks, the institution as an entity and partnerships – are all *communal* collectives.

9. *Dialogue* is fundamental to the means by which the diaconal church communicates its message.

10. The diaconal church *liberates its laity* to build learning communities that are transformed by the gifts of the kingdom community.

11. The diaconal church has *two main forms*:

     - as the Christian community *local* for worship, learning and caring;

     - as the Christian community *dispersed* to fulfil its mission in the world.

12. To equip the laity to be the servants of the kingdom community *new forms of church leadership* are needed. These are embodied in the roles of *'servant leader'*. The latter necessitates leaders being trained to equip lay people to become kingdom community builders within church and world.

13. *Leaders* of the diaconal church are *women and men*.

14. The leadership of the diaconal church is exercised through three particular roles:

     - that of *'presbyter'* - whose task is to equip the local church to model the kingdom community in its life and work;

     - that of *'deacon'* - whose task is to equip the dispersed church to build learning communities that manifest the gifts of the kingdom community in the world;

     - that of *'bishop'* - whose task is to be an intermediary who supports and resources presbyters and deacons and, through them, the laity.

15. The diaconal church embraces *a collective form of church leadership*.

16. Within the diaconal church all work *collaboratively*.

17. The diaconal church is a *democratic* and *self-governing* church, based on the principle of *subsidiarity*.

18. For the diaconal church to fulfil its mission, *the mould of Christendom must be broken*.

Appendix 3

Eighteen theses for the Christian or secular diaconal institution

1. In the millennium ahead, our world faces a *choice between chaos and community*.

2. If it is to survive, human civilization has *to choose to become a global community of character*, ranging from micro communities (the family) to macro communities (major institutions and nation states).

3. *The Christian vision of 'the kingdom community'* is the supreme exemplification of all such communities, and thus a model for world and church.

4. *The gifts of the kingdom community are life, liberation, love and learning.* They are gifts manifest within the nature of the Trinity and in Christ's teaching about the kingdom of God. They are *universal gifts* offered to all.

5. Alongside the primary task for which it was established, the *mission* of each institution is to model and build communities that are transformed by and manifest the gifts of the kingdom community. *The viability* of each institution depends on how faithfully it fulfils its primary task *and* communal mission.

6. Its communal mission can only be fulfilled if the institution becomes *a 'diaconal' (servant) institution*. A diaconal institution is *the servant of the kingdom community* and *of humankind*.

7. The diaconal institution *respects the autonomy of a secular culture* but *rejects a culture dominated by sacralism* or *secularism*.

8. *The human collectives that make up a diaconal institution* – hearings, groups, networks, the institution as an entity and partnerships – are all *communal* collectives.

9. *Dialogue* is fundamental to the means by which a diaconal institution communicates.

10. A diaconal institution *liberates its members* to build communities that are transformed by the gifts of the kingdom community.

11. A diaconal institution has *two main forms* –

     - as a *local* community, fulfilling its primary task and communal mission through its own life and work;

     - as a *dispersed* community, fulfilling its primary task and communal mission in the world.

12. To equip the members of a diaconal institution to be the servants of the kingdom community *new forms of institutional leadership are needed.* These are embodied in the roles of *'servant leader'.* The latter necessitates leaders being trained to equip the members of their institution to become community builders within that institution and within the world.

13. *Leaders* of a diaconal institution are *women and men.*

14. The leadership of a diaconal institution is exercised through three particular tasks:

     - that of *equipping the local institution* to model the kingdom community as it engages in the primary task for which the institution was established;

     - that of *equipping the dispersed institution* to build communities that manifest the gifts of the kingdom community as it engages in the primary task for which the institution was established;

     - that of acting as an *intermediary* who supports and resources the two roles described above and, through them, the members of the institution.

15. The diaconal institution embraces *a collective form of leadership.*

16. Within the diaconal institution all work *collaboratively.*

17. A diaconal institution is a *democratic* and *self-governing* institution, based on the principle of *subsidiarity.*

18. For diaconal institutions to fulfil their communal mission, *the mould of sacred and secular Christendoms must be broken.*

8. *Mission as discernment and intervention*

Preamble

Even if a diaconal church, its mission and its leadership are in place, how do its members go about engaging with society and world? In particular, how do Christians dispersed in society and world become active participants in a mission of communal transformation?

In what follows we identify the heart of the missionary methodology of the diaconal church as being the art of discernment, and the skills of intervention in response to what has been discerned. Discernment is the art of becoming aware of the gifts of the kingdom community - life, liberation, love, and learning - already present in daily life. We look at some aids to discernment. Intervention is the task of helping to make those gifts more fully manifest and their Giver more clearly recognized. We briefly review some ways in which Christians might intervene to further the communal transformation of society.

The material in this chapter was originally written as an introduction as to how the process of discernment and intervention might apply to the world of work, one vital but often neglected field of mission.[1] Although most references to the world of work have been retained, many of the points made are applicable to every field of mission.

Introduction

The ever-present and intimate experience of the Trinity and its gifts which typify the communal spirituality described in Chapter 3 is highly relevant to mission within the world of work. It is an experience which shows us that the kingdom community's inclusive and universal gifts of life, liberation, love and learning are ever present and on offer within the workplace. From the production line to the office, from the school to the hospital ward, from the bank to the town hall, the gifts of the kingdom community are on offer and ours for the taking. Whether we are based in the same location each day or constantly on the move, whether at our desk or doing business on our

---

[1] Drawn from Clark (2014) *The Kingdom at Work Project* (pp. 76-83).

i-phones or i-pads, the gifts of the kingdom community are intimately present. Thus at any moment of day or night, the world of work can become a means of grace, a way of enabling work and the workplace to be transformed by and manifest those gifts.

The purpose of mission as we have defined it is to create a world transformed by the gifts of the kingdom community: life, liberation, love and learning. Therefore our first responsibility as Christians is to discern where the gifts of the kingdom community are in evidence, or where they are being neglected or negated. Our second responsibility is to use the signs of the kingdom community discerned to inform and shape the kind of intervention in which we engage so that society and world might manifest the gifts of the kingdom community more fully.

The art of discernment

'Seeing is no simple matter. Even to claim to see things of God is a dangerous business, yet, says the Christ, men must be on the watch, prepared to see, looking for the coming of their Lord, awaiting the onset of His Kingdom' writes Alan Ecclestone (1975, pp. 42-43). Charles Elliott (1985) states:

> People do not look for the Kingdom to break in around them, because they do not expect to find anything if they do. And yet when they do look, they are astonished and delighted at what they discover. This is not to say that if you go to Wigan or Wichita, your will find the Beatitudes fulfilled in the High Street. The process is more subtle, more ambiguous, more provisional: it needs discernment and the eye of faith to see where God is working' (p. 128).

Here, as Jonathan Sacks (2011) puts it, we share in the experience of Elijah listening to the 'still small voice', of Paul looking 'through a glass darkly' and of Wordsworth's 'sense of something far more deeply infused' (p. 285).

Discernment of the kingdom community's gifts of life, liberation, love and learning requires what the Celts call 'rinsed eyes' (de Waal, 1996, p. 88) and Benedict calls 'the ear of your heart' (Parry, 1990, p. xviii). Brother Lawrence describes such awareness as 'the practice of the presence of God'. For Brother Lawrence such 'practice' was a matter of 'train(ing) yourself to dwell in His presence all day long'

(2008, p. 90). However, states Ecclestone (1975), 'It is not the job of spirituality today to turn men and women into second and third rate mystics' (p. 41). Its job is to enable us, with all our sinfulness and limitations, to become as aware as possible of the presence of the gifts of the kingdom community so that, by accessing what they offer, we can make our modest contribution to the transformation of workplace and the world beyond.

The journey in and the journey out

The art of discernment can be enhanced in a number of ways. Prominent amongst these are prayer and worship. However, here attention is focused more explicitly on the *practice* of discernment. The practice of discernment can operate at a number of levels of human experience. One is that of the self-awareness. This can be called 'the journey in'. Another is that of human relationships. A third is our experience of the natural world. The last two can be called 'the journey out' (Clark, 1997, pp. 78-81).

The journey in

Eckhart Tolle describes the journey in as shaped by 'the shift from thinking to awareness' (2005, p. 117). It is the art, recognized within many forms of spiritual direction, of freeing our minds from their constant preoccupation with past or future, and allowing ourselves to become fully aware of the present. Tolle puts it succinctly: 'Life is now' (2002, p. 23). All four forms of spirituality discussed earlier (Chapter 3) offer ways in which this journey in can be nurtured and enriched. They suggest means of discernment through which we can be empowered by the presence of the Trinity and transformed by its communal gifts.

The journey out

Unless we are committed to the journey in we will be unable to discern the kingdom community's gifts of life, liberation, love and learning, in our relationships with others or with the natural world. However, the journey in needs to be complemented by the journey out if we are to access and employ the gifts of the kingdom community for that purpose for which they were intended.

Like the journey in, the journey out is about the practice of discernment, that is becoming more aware of the presence of the gifts of the kingdom community in what is commonplace. 'The most effective way Brother Lawrence had for communicating with God was simply to do his ordinary work' (2008, p. 72). In his case, this meant working for many years in the monastery kitchen and, in later life, repairing sandals. Much of Celtic and Quaker spirituality likewise indicates that the journey out entails our learning to become aware of the presence of God in the daily encounters and events of life and work. Nevertheless, the journey out should spur us on to look for the gifts of the kingdom community even in the midst of poverty and deprivation, conflict and violence.

The journey out can also involve us in a deeper relationship with the natural world. This means that we seek to align ourselves with what Matthew Fox (1994) calls 'the "Great Work" of creation itself – the work of creation unfolding, the work of evolution or creativity in the universe' (p. 61), of which God is the instigator and sustainer. That journey may also take us onto 'the high ground' of the theological and philosophical quest for meaning and truth.

Implications for mission in the world of work

If we are to be involved in the task of transforming the world of work we first need to practice the art of discerning the hall-marks of the kingdom community already present within the workplace. What ways are there of equipping ourselves for this undertaking?

Aiding the art of discernment

There are a number of aids available to assist the Christian in the art of discernment. We mention four of these below.

Celtic and Quaker approaches

The kind of spirituality represented by the Celtic and Quaker traditions, as well as that espoused by Bother Lawrence, is one way of helping us to engage more fully in 'the practice of the presence of God'. At first sight, this form of discernment may seem unstructured and informal. However, we know that 'the Celtic way of prayer was learnt from the monasteries; (and that) it was from its religious communities that the people learnt to pray. As a result they learnt that there was no separation of praying and living; praying and working flow into one another' (de Waal, 1996, p. 3). This also meant that the prayer life of the people followed the rhythm of the monastic day. It was likewise for Brother Lawrence. Although his letters and conversations imply a spontaneous approach to practising the presence of God, his membership of the Carmelite Brotherhood offered him an important training ground and the daily practice of corporate prayer. Reflecting this need for discipline, a minister in secular employment speaks of following 'a personal rule, using my cellphone's reminder feature to set times for prayer during the day' (*Spiritual Direction*, 2011, p. 17).

For Quakers, their meeting for worship, which Thomas Kelly describes as grounded in and founded on 'the Real Presence of God' (*QFP*, 2.40), is their school for discernment. Their *Advices and Queries* state that their meeting for worship 'is our response to an awareness of God... When we join with others in expectant waiting we may discover a deeper sense of God's presence... and the power of God's love drawing us together and leading us' (*QFP*, 1.08). Thus behind the apparent informality of Quaker practice, there lies a form of communal discernment which equips them well for their ministry within the working world.

The Examen - an Ignatian approach

Ignatian spirituality provides a more overtly structured approach to discernment and developing an awareness of the gifts of the kingdom community in daily life. One method it offers is known as 'the examination of conscience' or 'Examen' (*Spiritual Exercises*, 2004, paras. 24-44, pp. 12-18). As a rule, 'the General Examen' takes place at the end of each day and 'the Particular Examen', which focuses on a particular fault to be addressed over days or weeks, in the middle of the day. The forms for the Particular and General Examen, as set out in the *Spiritual Exercises*, have in many cases been adapted to working life. The *Exercises*, and in some cases the Examen, are often facilitated by a mentor.

The General Examen suggests five matters for recollection and prayer which can be summarized as follows:

- recalling one is in the presence of God
- looking back over the day with gratitude
- reviewing how one has lived the day
- asking for forgiveness
- resolutions for the future and a prayer of commitment.

The General Examen offers a structured approach for discerning the gifts of kingdom community in daily life. However, it focuses more on the individual than Celtic or Quaker spirituality and on the way in which he or she is living out their faith in daily life.

Theological auditing

In the 1990s, the South London Industrial Mission was involved in facilitating an approach to discernment in the workplace called 'theological auditing'. Peter Challen, who developed this method, describes its three main stages (in Clark 1997, pp. 115-116) as:

> - an exploration by 'the client' (the lay person at work) of comprehensive themes of faith relevant to daily life: such as creation (ecological issues), jubilee (justice implications) and covenant (in contrast to contract), etc;
>
> - examining where these themes are experienced in the workplace and how they might suggest a new approach to mission;
>
> - examining where these themes are being blocked or negated and how the client might prevent this situation continuing.

The theological audit is facilitated by an 'auditor'. Challen stresses that the value of the audit depends on the building of trust between client and auditor. Such theological auditing has also been undertaken with groups and not only as a one-to-one exercise.

The power of discernment

'Awareness is the power that is concealed within the present moment' (Tolle, 2005, p. 78). A communal spirituality which discerns the presence of and is able to accesses the gifts at the heart of the kingdom community is an immensely powerful resource. 'For the kingdom, the power and the glory are yours' - the doxology to the Lord's Prayer reminds us that 'the kingdom' and 'the power' go hand in hand. However, such power is never coercive or destructive, as one particular paraphrase of the Lord's Prayer seeks to emphasize (Clark, 2008):

> Your kingdom is always with us.
> We are humbled and thankful to be members of it.
> *Yours is the power that never crushes and the glory that never dazzles.*
> You love and care for us – beyond life and death, time and space.
> For all you are to us, we praise you and thank you.

Their communal spirituality enabled the Celts to tap into the power of the Trinity's gifts from rising up to going to bed, and throughout every season. They regarded this power as given for their protection, as epitomized by St. Patrick's breastplate, or lorica:

> For my shield this day
>> A mighty power:
>> The Holy Trinity!
>> Affirming threeness,
>> Confessing oneness,
>> In the making of all
>> Through love… (de Waal. 1996, pp. 22-23)

However, the power of a spirituality which embodies the kingdom community's gifts of life, liberation, love and learning is not only concerned with providence and protection. It is a power far beyond human power offered as a means of transformation, as reflected in the Methodist spirituality of Charles Wesley:

> Give me the faith which can remove
> And sink the mountain to a plain;
> Give the childlike praying love,
> Which longs to build they house again;
> They love, let is my heart o'erpower,
> And all my simple soul devour.

Only the power offered by a communal spirituality can break the mould of those customs and structures which would negate or ignore the gifts of the kingdom community. Celtic and Ignatian spirituality, in particular, saw accessing this power as the way to overcome what they regarded as 'the enemy' (*Exercises*, paras. 324-326, pp. 97-98) - those tenacious forces of evil which annihilate love and compassion and perpetuate injustice and violence.

Implications for the world of work

Discernment of the presence of the gifts of the kingdom community, and the power which these gifts offer, brings with it the promise of, as well as our responsibility for the communal transformation of the world of work. It is a commission at the heart of which is a quest for communal wholeness[1]. As Esther de Waal puts it in her reflections on

---

[1] This concept and how it relates to that of the kingdom community is explored more fully in Chapter 11.

Celtic spirituality, it is a call to move away from 'the highly individualistic, competitive, inward-looking approach common in today's society' towards 'the promise... of (the) healing of the many fractures that maim and corrupt each of us and the world in which we live' (1996, p. 6).

It must be stressed that a communal spirituality for the world of work is not about pouring oil on troubled waters. It is a spirituality which has no truck with a global culture that exalts utility but devalues creativity, promotes the accumulation of wealth and possessions but neglects what it means to be human, furthers vested interests yet turns a blind eye to injustice and exploitation, seeks to indoctrinate not educate, and squanders the resources of the planet at the expense of generations to come. The purpose of a communal spirituality is to raise searching questions about how, when and where the kingdom community's gifts of life, liberation, love and learning are being denied as well as affirmed at every level of economic endeavour, from a particular workplace to the global economy.

Because a communal spirituality for the working world is about the task of transformation, it is a political spirituality. Elliott writes: 'There can be no spirituality without... politics' (1985, p. 146). That sentiment is echoed by Graham Ward in his thesis on the nature of discipleship when he states: 'Praying is... the most political act any Christian can engage in' (2009, p. 281). Discernment and intervention are about transforming workplaces into kingdom communities which can blaze a trail for the transformation of every sphere of life.

Intervention

In *The Kingdom at Work Project* (Clark, 2014), a major section is concerned with various forms of intervention which mission might take.[1] Although these are there applied to mission at work, they are just as relevant to every field of mission.

Intervention builds on the Christian first discerning how, when and where the gifts of the kingdom community are present within daily life. What form of intervention is then undertaken depends on a host of variables which can only be decided within the particular mission context. However, some broad forms of the intervention

---

[1] This section offers a very brief summary of a comprehensive discussion of forms of intervention covered in *The Kingdom at Work Project*.

process which could apply to any situation can be identified. The importance of Christians coming together in small groups to discuss their own situations and to help them decide how they might intervene is of vital importance.

The choice of methods of intervention touches on issues such as whether or not the mission task is of an individual or collective nature (pp. 238-264). Individual intervention is often spontaneous, informal and of short-term duration. Thus it effectiveness in making the gifts of life, liberation, love or learning manifest is dependent on how fully the individual Christian has developed an awareness of those gifts well before intervention. Collective intervention involves others, Christian or not, in the intervention process. As such it usually needs to be better prepared for and planned. This gives more time for the Christian at work, wherever possible with colleagues, to reflect on how the gifts of the kingdom community might inform, guide and give impetus to the intervention process and shape the outcome.

Another issue is whether the Christian at work leaves the Christian motivation for their intervention implicit or explicit. It is not easy to decide if and when Christian symbols, messages (pp. 293-295) and language should be introduced into what is regarded as a secular culture. Intervention which taps into the transforming power of the gifts of the kingdom community carries its own authenticity and it can be a sign of our lack of faith in the efficacy of those gifts if we feel that we must always strive to make the implicit explicit. This applies especially to dialogue (pp. 265-292) where the open or closed nature of the conversation in itself bears witness to whether the gifts of the kingdom community are present or blocked out. Nevertheless, there will be certain occasions when, given openness and trust, it is clear that it is appropriate to introduce Christian concepts and images into a conversation.

One other form of intervention which is considered in *The Kingdom at Work Project* is prayer and worship (pp. 296-323). The huge variety and form of prayers, personal and collective, which can be used, on or off church premises, is an exciting discovery for many. And worship too can come alive when it is open to reflection on and preparation for the time and place for intervention.

Part 2
A renewed diaconate
as an order of mission

9. *A renewed diaconate*

Preamble

Part 2 of this book focuses on the essential part that a renewed diaconate has to play in breaking the mould of Christendom and enabling the diaconal church to engage in building communities transformed by the kingdom community's gifts of life, liberation, love and learning.

Chapter 9 undertakes a review of the changing role of the deacon since the diaconate's re-emergence in early nineteenth century. It argues that deacons, as members of a renewed diaconate and servant leaders of the diaconal church, should now assume the role of community educator[1] in order to liberate the laity to fulfil their calling as kingdom community builders in society and world.

This chapter originally formed part of the conclusion to *Breaking the Mould of Christendom*[2].

The deacon as change agent

It is our belief that the role of the diaconal church as the servant of the kingdom community must begin with the liberation of the laity, the primary resource that the church has for the fulfilment of its mission in the world. It is also our conviction that the liberation of the laity will only be achieved if, within the leadership of the church, there are those given the explicit responsibility of enabling lay people to fulfil their servant ministry in the world. A renewed diaconate would be in pole position to assume that role.

It seems highly unlikely that any attempt to transform the Christendom model of church will be initiated from 'the top down'. In all churches, hierarchical forms of church leadership continue to dominate the scene, with the laity located at the base of the pyramid. It would be a totally unexpected development if those at 'the top' of

---

[1] In Chapter 7, and in Chapter 10, we have added to the role of community educator a number of other leadership roles which deacons might need to fulfil if they find themselves operating in situations where the dispersed church is weak or non-existent.

[2] Clark (2005: second printing, 2014) (pp. 273-284, 292-295).

the church's hierarchy agreed to turn that pyramid on its head. Nor are presbyters likely to bring about radical change of this kind. Their time and energy are increasingly consumed in striving to ensure that the local church survives and largely in Christendom mode. Even chaplains and ministers in secular employment who are attempting to help the church re-engage with a secular world find it very difficult to break clear of their traditional presbyteral role.

Nor does it seem likely that the liberation of the laity can be brought about by the laity themselves, from 'the bottom up'. The legacy of Christendom has for centuries conditioned the laity to acknowledge their lowly place in the ecclesiastical order of things and accept their dependency on clerical leadership, even within the post-Reformation churches. Where lay people, not least women, are questioning that legacy, lack of time, energy and resources and, increasingly, the decline of personal commitment, militate against their ability to alter the status quo. Where, then can the change agents needed to give impetus to the liberation of the laity be found?

We believe that a renewed diaconate constitutes the order of ministry best placed to undertake this task. In Chapter 7 (*Diagram 4*), we set out an overview of the role of the deacon as one of the three main forms of leadership within the diaconal church. In what follows, we argue that if a renewed diaconate of the kind we have already described (and expand on more fully below) came into being, a way would open for the liberation of the laity to represent the church in the world far more effectively. This could happen as follows:

> A renewed diaconate would make its prime task that of equipping the laity to become kingdom community builders and to reclaim their vocation to serve the kingdom community as *the church dispersed* in the world.

> As a consequence, presbyters, through their ministry to *the local church*, would be able to give greater attention to their own responsibility for nurturing lay people in the faith. As Crain and Seymour put it (2001, p. 35), a renewed diaconate 'has the potential to redefine the ministry of the laity and reinvigorate and refocus the ministry of the elder (presbyter)'.

> These shifts in the responsibilities of deacon and presbyter would, in turn, enable bishops, or their namesakes, to re-claim their role, notably as intermediaries, of linking and co-

ordinating, and thus energizing, the re-focused ministries of deacon and presbyter across *the whole church.*

Why the diaconate?

Current literature on a renewed diaconate

The importance of the office of the deacon as a servant of the kingdom community is prominent in a number of reports. *For such a time as this* (2001), the Church of England's report on the future of the diaconate, states unequivocally that, 'The deacon is an instrument of God's purpose, of the Kingdom of God' (pp. 35-36). The Methodist Church states that 'the Good News of God's Kingdom... is the foundation of, and template for, diaconal ministry' (*What is a Deacon?*, 2004, para 4.4).

However, we have argued that it is only by equipping the laity to be kingdom community builders and thus servants of the kingdom community in the world that a renewed diaconate would meet a long neglected need. A number of reports reflect this view

In 1996, in a report to commemorate fifty years since DIAKONIA, the World Federation of Diaconal Associations and Communities was founded (*DIAKONIA – Challenge and Response*, 1996, p. 59), Reinhard Neubauer writes: 'The diaconate... is the group of people in the church committed to support and co-ordinate the diakonia of all Christians. If only that were clear!'. The Hanover Report of the Anglican-Lutheran Commission (1996) states that the diaconate should ' "have a multiplying effect, leading others to their own specific tasks of service", showing the way, enabling and resourcing the ministry of the laity' (quoted in *For such a time as this*, p. 18).

The Church of England's own report, *For such a time as this*, argues that 'deacons are to be found playing a vital role in enabling the people of God to exercise their personal and corporate discipleship' (p. vii). It goes on to state that 'the touchstone of a renewed diaconate is whether it builds up the diverse gifts and callings of the members of the Body of Christ' (p. 46). The Roman Catholic Church, though more cautious, acknowledges that the permanent diaconate could 'be a sign of the Church's vocation to be the servant of Christ and of God' and that 'the presence of the deacon, consequently, could renew the Church in the evangelical spirit of humility and service' (*From the Diakonia of Christ*, 2003, p. 57). The Methodist Church is as forthright as any church stating that: 'The primary purpose in focusing diaconal ministry is to help all Christians discover, develop and express their own servant ministry. Deacons therefore engage in educational and nurturing activities to enable people to see God's activity in daily life and world, and to encourage them in expressing their faith in relevant ways' (*What is a Deacon?* para. 5.4).

Assets of the diaconate as change agents

The diaconate has a number of other assets which makes deacons well placed to become agents of change in the transformation of a Christendom model of church. All churches recognize the diaconate as an authentic form of ministry that goes back to the days of the early church. In this sense, the role of deacon is already well 'embedded in the system' so to speak, and cannot be dismissed as a transient form of church leadership. The fact that, after centuries of neglect, the importance of a renewed diaconate is being considered across all denominations bears witness to this 'embeddedness'. Furthermore, because of the fact that the diaconal office has been in the shadows for many centuries, the diaconate has not been seen as tainted by the élitism and authoritarianism so often associated with the offices of priest and bishop.

For many deacons their life as a community is also a great asset in enhancing and enriching their ministry. Being part of a community 'is a way of belonging where differences are accepted, where broken relationships can be restored, where skills are developed and where companionship can be found. It is a place of reconciliation and forgiveness where individuals are respected.... This sense of community exists even when members are separated by great distances' (*Diaconal Reflections*, 1998, p. 3). Here we simply note that the communal nature of the diaconate is particularly important in energizing and informing its task of enabling lay people to bear witness to the gifts of the kingdom community in daily life. We will return later to significance of the diaconate being strongly communal when considering the work of the Methodist Diaconal Order[1].

---

[1] As we shall argue in Part 3, the Methodist Diaconal Order offers a seminal model of the diaconate as both an order of ministry *and* 'a religious order' (*What is a Deacon?* paras. 6.1 to 6.5). With particular reference to the latter, *What is a Deacon?* states that 'Methodist deacons make a public, lifelong commitment to following (a) Rule of Life and living as members of a religious community.'

Changing diaconal roles

Stages of development

Though the diaconate might be in principle the form of church leadership that is best suited to renew and re-energize the laity for their ministry in daily life, is the diaconate to-day in a position to undertake such a demanding task?

In Chapter 4 we offered an overview of how and why the interest in diaconal ministry began to surface in the mid-nineteenth century and has continued to the present day. During that time the role of deacon has moved through three main stages. We believe that only the most recent of these, a stage that has barely begun, fully recognizes the potential of the diaconate to liberate the laity to fulfil their kingdom community building ministry within the world.

Stage One The deacon as carer - 'works of mercy'

The first stage in the re-emergence of the diaconate ran from the middle of the nineteenth century to the 1960s or even 1970s. It was the era of largely female associations, institutes and mother houses, pre-eminently within the Lutheran tradition, and of deaconess orders in the case of churches such as Methodism. The dominant role of the deaconess in both cases was undertaking what were known as 'works of mercy' – nursing, social work, pastoral care and some teaching – often in impoverished areas of towns and cities.

(para.6.2). This rule of life speaks of deacons as 'careful stewards of God's gifts, faithful in all relationships and willing servants' (p. 27). It covers a commitment to worship, personal devotions and reflection, as well as to praying daily for members of the Order, participating in area groups and attending an annual Convocation' (p. 28). 'Following the Rule of Life is one key way in which deacons commit themselves to nurturing a sense of identity, belonging and responsibility' (para. 6.4).

'Being a religious order, however, has much greater significance than simply supporting fellow deacons,' states *What is a Deacon?* (para. 6.7). It also contributes to 'encouraging and enabling other Methodists – through representing and modelling a way of discipleship, (and through)... reminding the whole Methodist Church of its calling to be an open and welcoming learning community that reaches out beyond itself: a learning community where disciples share what they have and are, and lovingly watch over, build up and encourage one another in order to serve God in the world' (paras. 6.7.1 and 6.7.2).

This stage saw a diaconate that was formally structured and regulated. It was restricted to single women (though a few male deacons were in evidence). Where the diaconate was closely aligned with the work of the institutional church many sisters had a role subservient to the presbyter or priest.

The later years of this stage of development witnessed a growing ambiguity within the institutional church about the significance of the office of deacon. On the one hand, as a result of Vatican II, the permanent diaconate was reinstated within the Roman Catholic Church, though only for men. On the other hand, in 1974, the Advisory Committee for Church of England's Ministry recommended abolishing the diaconate altogether (though its General Synod declined this), whilst British Methodism closed its Wesley Deaconess Order in 1978.

Stage Two The deacon as activist - a diversity of works

Stage Two, running from the 1980s to the present time, has seen major changes in how the diaconate was viewed in principle and its ministry expressed in practice. A new appreciation of the importance of the diaconate that had been surfacing for some time did not make universal headway until this period. Debate about the nature of 'a renewed diaconate' was triggered by the publication, in 1982, of the Lima Document of the Faith and Order Commission of the World Council of Churches, *Baptism, Eucharist and Ministry*. That document stresses that the diaconate is as an integral and essential part of the threefold order of ministry of (many) churches, but heralded 'a move away from a dominantly structural and hierarchical approach to ordained ministry towards a more integrated ecclesiological approach, grounding ordained ministry in the nature and mission of the church' (*For such a time as* this, p. 16). The Lima Document set the stage for a proliferation of articles, books and reports, especially from the early 1990s onwards, on the theme of a renewed diaconate.

The outpouring of publications on a renewed diaconate during Stage Two has gone hand in hand with major changes in the way in which the role of the deacon has developed in practice. The view of the diaconate as a body of women offering sacrificial and sometimes menial service to church and world was seen as a relic of the past. Most churches have come to regard the diaconate as making a distinctive contribution to the leadership of the church but also having an active role to play in the life of society.

'Works of mercy' have remained an important part of diaconal ministry. The diaconate has continued to make a vital contribution to meeting the acute material, physical and social needs of desperately disadvantaged countries, especially in Africa and parts of Asia and Latin America. In the Western world, too, pastoral care is still an important aspect of the deacon's role, not least pastoral care associated with the local church.

Nevertheless, worldwide, deacons have been taking on an ever greater diversity of ministries. They are engaged, often with professional qualifications to match, not only in fields such as counselling and social work, but in youth work, community work, the health service, the probation service, the prison service, teaching, the media and so on. An increasing number of deacons are also occupying chaplaincy roles relating to a wide variety of fields such as education, health, the prison service, industry, commerce and the retail trade.

Accompanying this move into an increasing diversity of ministries, many deacons have begun to take a more active role in the pursuit of issues such as justice, peace, the environment and human rights, including women's rights. This proactive stance has been reflected in a number of commentaries on the role of the deacon. For example, in 1997, the *Windsor Statement*, produced by an ecumenical consultation of all the diaconal bodies in the United Kingdom, included the following statement:

> We increasingly perceive our role to be pioneering and prophetic... *proactive* (our italics) in opportunity through commitment to mission and pastoral care within and beyond the church. Opening doors of opportunity, encouraging others to take risks, the contemporary diaconate acting in its capacity as 'agent of change', engages imaginatively and collaboratively with issues of justice, poverty, social and environmental concerns.

A number of other diaconal associations have also adopted a pro-active approach to their ministries, such as deacons in the Uniting Church of Australia where issues of race and immigration have been to the fore. This group of deacons describe themselves as ministers 'ordained to work primarily in the non-church community, dealing with issues of social justice, empowering the marginalized to regain a measure of power in the community'[1].

One further notable feature of Stage Two has been the opening of many diaconal associations and communities to women *and* men. In 1986, British Methodism re-opened its diaconal order, this time to men as well as to women. However, many exceptions remain, with the Roman Catholic Church continuing to restrict the permanent diaconate to men and a number of other bodies, such as the Lutheran Deaconess Association of the Evangelical Lutheran Church in America, still only admitting women.

This description of Stages One and Two has been painted with a broad brush. In practice, the development of the diaconate in relation to these two stages has been different within different churches. For example, in the case of the Roman Catholic Church, the (all male) role of the permanent deacon remains largely liturgical and pastoral. He is still seen as belonging 'to the lowest degree of hierarchy' (*From the Diakonia of Christ*, p. 60). In the Church of England, the roles stressed are still pastoral, liturgical and catechetical, in that order (*For such a time as this* pp. 53-57), even though other expressions of diaconal ministry are not ruled out. In that church, too, deacons are still largely viewed as a 'lower order' of ministry than that of priest or bishop. In these and other respects, the attitude of many of the ordained ministry towards the diaconate within the Roman Catholic and Anglican Churches still seems more closely aligned with the practice and ethos of Stage One than with that of Stage Two.

A diaconate diverted and the dispersed church neglected

Deacons as carers (Stage One) and activists (Stage Two) have made and will assuredly continue to make a major contribution to the life of church and society. However, if deacons are to be agents in harnessing the resources of lay people to further the mission of the church dispersed in the world, it is essential that their role develops beyond that described in Stage Two.

Relative to other forms of church leadership, the diaconate is not strong in numbers. Nor will deacons have the time and energy left to equipping the laity for mission in daily life if they continue their

[1] DIAKONIA (2004) - www.diakonia-world.org

personal engagement with the wide diversity of pro-active ministries described above. Deacons being employed to fill presbyteral 'vacancies' or to take up chaplaincies of a traditional kind only exacerbates the loss of their potential to serve the dispersed church. However creative and dynamic the endeavors of such deacons may be, the fragmentation and diversion of their energies leaves them with no opportunity to fulfil their servant leadership role of equipping the laity to be the church in the world. It is, therefore, imperative that there is as swift a transition as possible to Stage Three.

Stage Three The deacon as community educator – liberating the laity

Stage Three would be one that brings into being a renewed diaconate. In this stage the deacon would assume the role of community educator. This means that, following the Lima Document, their ministry would be 'grounded in the... mission of the church'. That mission is one undertaken primarily by the laity, called to build communities that are transformed by the gifts of the kingdom community. The task of a renewed diaconate would be, first and foremost, to equip the laity to build such communities.

This would involve the diaconate in rousing lay people from their dependency on the clergy, raising their awareness to their calling to be servants of the kingdom community in the world, preparing and equipping them for this task and working alongside them in responding to the needs of a constantly changing society. To liberate the laity from the legacy of Christendom, a renewed diaconate would need to apply two important facets of the role of community educator, that of catalyst (or animator) and that of enabler.

Deacons would need to become catalysts (or animators) because the laity still remains *God's Frozen People* (Gibbs and Morton, 1964) half a century on from when that book was written. The task of liberation would require a paradigm shift in attitudes and practices, from the passive acceptance of the Christendom model of church to a wholehearted commitment to the diaconal model of church. Nevertheless, we believe that, offered a vision and given a lead by a renewed diaconate, the laity can and would respond to this challenge. The Christendom church is often seen as irrelevant because its leaders have taken such a low view of lay people's readiness to re-visit the issue of their vocation and, as a result, have denied them the tools for the job. The diaconal church is founded on the conviction that all lay people have the capacity to fulfil their kingdom community building ministries in a deeply committed, informed and credible way.

As liberators of the laity, deacons would also be enablers. Much more is required than simply bringing lay people to an awareness of their calling as kingdom community builders. Vocation is also about discipleship and discipleship is a life-long learning process. Thus a renewed diaconate would equip lay people to fulfil their high calling. This would entail offering them the means of acquiring the knowledge, skills and resources for their ministry as kingdom community builders, and, in accord with the nature of any learning community, providing them with the opportunities of sharing their experience and insights with one another.

The move into Stage Three would not be an easy transition for deacons to make. In many ways, to be carers, to be pastors, to be active within a range of 'secular' occupations, and to be proactive in the pursuit of justice and peace, are more clear-cut forms of diaconal ministry. These forms of ministry often bring the rewards of face-to-face encounter or the excitement of occupying a hands-on pioneering role. But if the laity are to be liberated to serve the kingdom community in the world, and the diaconal church set free from the legacy of Christendom, it is now imperative that a renewed diaconate of the sort that we have described comes into being.

To fulfil the roles of catalyst (or animator) and enabler, deacons would need to be up-to-date in their understanding of the communal needs of the world and how these might be addressed. This means that their experience and training would need to embrace knowledge and skills relevant to an era in which building kingdom communities is an all-important task.

To fulfil their ministry in Stage Three, a renewed diaconate would need to progress further towards becoming an international and ecumenical 'religious order', though always shaped by the indigenous cultures within which diaconal ministry is exercised. Such an international religious order would be inclusive and open, and marked out by the minimum number of rules needed to give it a coherent and sustainable communal identity. It would be both a means of support and of mutual accountability. Because deacons are as yet relatively few in number and because they come from many different denominations and countries, belonging to such an order would offer the diaconate a new communal synergy. It would also give the diaconate a deeper understanding of what it means to be a worldwide kingdom community, an experience that would be of immense benefit not only to the diaconal order itself but to the church and the world.

This stage would see a diaconate fully open to women and men working together as partners to fulfil their common calling.

In Stage Three, deacons may well be called upon to undertake works of mercy, as well as to be activists or pioneers, especially in places where poverty, disease, or oppression dominate the scene. However, these roles would increasingly be expressed in a way that could catalyze and enable the laity to fill the roles that such deacons were occupying. Such forms of diaconal ministry should not be allowed to divert energy and resources from a renewed diaconate's primary task of equipping the laity to be kingdom community builders in the world.

The way ahead

The emergence of a renewed diaconate

The responsibilities we are placing on the shoulders of a renewed diaconate are formidable. We are arguing that deacons become change agents and community educators to liberate the laity from captivity to the Christendom model of church. Where would the human resources come from for this undertaking? We suggest that they would come from two main quarters, from the worldwide diaconate and, not least, from 'deacons' currently beyond the diaconate.

The worldwide diaconate

As we have already noted, the diaconate worldwide is relatively small in numbers. It is estimated (2005) that some 23,000 diaconal workers, deacons and deaconesses are associated with DIAKONIA, the World Federation, though this number excludes Roman Catholics and most Orthodox deacons. Nevertheless, it is with a renewed diaconate that we believe the task of liberating the laity must begin. It is the quality not the quantity of the diaconal models of community that emerge that will help people to catch the vision of what such a movement of liberation is all about, and encourage them to make that vision a reality in their own situation.

Though the diaconate worldwide is small, it has the synergy of a group of people who share a deep commitment to the God of the kingdom community, to one another and to the wider church. If that synergy, produced by the whole becoming greater than the sum of the parts, can lead to the creation of a renewed diaconate who dedicate themselves to the task of the liberation of the laity, then 'the God of Surprises' (Hughes, 1985) will have a lot of surprises in store for us.

In the creation of this synergy, DIAKONIA has an important part to play. It currently (2005) consists of some 80 member associations and communities from across the globe. It is playing an increasingly active role in enabling deacons and deaconesses across every continent and many denominations to connect, to share visions, to tell stories, to worship together and to shape the diaconate to come. In 1979, DIAKONIA's thirteenth international assembly gathered for the first time in the Third World (Manila). In 2005, its nineteenth assembly met in Durham, England, and some 500 delegates from 50 to 60 different countries attended. Assemblies have continued to meet since then.

DIAKONIA is thus in a unique position to stimulate and encourage deacons, on both an ecumenical and international basis, to develop their ministry as servant leaders of the laity and to liberate the diaconal church to help build a global community of learning communities that manifest the gifts of the kingdom community.

'Deacons' beyond the current diaconate

Nevertheless, a renewed diaconate faced with the demanding responsibility of equipping the laity to be kingdom community builders needs more human resources than a worldwide diaconate can offer. Where will these additional human resources come from?

The answer is that the church is filled with 'deacons'[1]. There is a multitude of priests and presbyters, in particular those working as sector ministers, chaplains or as leaders of centres and organizations concerned with furthering lay ministry, who are, in reality, engaged in what we see as a new diaconal rather than presbyteral ministry. The vision, the skills and the passion of these 'deacons in waiting' are urgently needed to lead a revolution in the life of the Christendom church.

---

[1] See Chapter 13 where this point is discussed in relation to Methodism.

The emergence of this hidden 'diaconate' beyond the diaconate will depend on those concerned, ordained or lay, becoming aware that their ministries are in reality diaconal, and committing themselves to develop their work even further in this direction. However, the importance of their contribution to the birth of the diaconal church will depend even more on such leaders recognizing themselves as leaders of the church as the servant of the kingdom community, and being ready to connect with those in a similar position across all churches to share insights, experiences, expertise and resources. This cohort of 'deacons' beyond the diaconate will also need to connect with the existing diaconate in ways that will produce even more synergy than the existing diaconate on its own can produce.

There is one other group of people who might be described as 'deacons' beyond the diaconate. This group is made up of the many lay people occupying leadership roles in the life of the church, on a paid or voluntary basis, who are currently exercising a diaconal ministry. This group of lay people often operates in the back rooms of a Christendom church in which clericalism is still rampant. Nevertheless, they too could make an invaluable contribution towards liberating the laity to build kingdom communities in daily life. Such lay people may not be in a position to offer the amount of time that the ordained leadership of the diaconal church could offer, but they would be another vital source of experience and expertise.

Where next?

We see two immediate steps that could be taken to begin the task of liberating the laity for their kingdom community building mission and facilitating the emergence of the diaconal church. One would be to seek out actual examples of how lay people are already acting as kingdom community builders, to affirm and support these initiatives and to disseminate their stories. DIAKONIA, amongst other diaconal associations, could play an important role in this process. New beginnings are often small and vulnerable, undertaken against the odds and frequently neglected because they do not 'fit' the established patterns of a Christendom model of church. But small is not only 'beautiful', it can also be 'powerful'. Such micro examples of the diaconal church in action would be of great value, far beyond their size or immediate achievements, in enabling the diaconal church to discover how the task of kingdom building community might be undertaken in to-day's world.

A second step would be a radical change in the way in which women and men are trained for the diaconate.[1] The common practice of training deacons alongside presbyters, and then hoping that 'the diaconal bit' can be bolted on as time and circumstances permit, needs to cease. Church and world require the ministry of a renewed diaconate as never before. However, the task required of deacons requires a range of targeted competences. It is thus beholden on those with responsibility for the training of church leaders within every denomination to equip deacons properly for their role as community educators.

The growth of the diaconal church will inevitably be slow and, in many situations, unobserved and unacknowledged. It will not be a sledge-hammer that breaks the mould of Christendom. It will be a host of tiny shoots revealing the nature of the diaconal church for those with eyes to see and ears to hear. The new grand narrative, 'the story that God would tell if God could tell a story' (Cox, in McLeod and Ustorf, 2003, p. 206), that must now replace the tired narrative of Christendom, and the increasingly hedonistic narrative of secularization, is about a kingdom community quietly at work through 'a thousand tiny empowerments' (Sandercock, 1998, p. 6).

All that has been written here is in the conviction that God is willing a new kind of church, the diaconal church, given leadership and impetus by the creation of a renewed diaconate, to come into being to fulfil his purposes for humankind. When this happens we shall be witnessing the most fundamental change in the life of the church since Christendom. What matters now is our commitment to liberate the diaconal church to become the servant of the kingdom community and to engage in building a global community of communities that manifests God's gifts of life, liberation, love and learning.

---

[1] See Chapter 10 and Part 3 for further discussion of the training of deacons.

10. The diaconate as an order of mission

Preamble

In Chapter 9 we set out the case for a renewed diaconate. In contrast to the somewhat limited vision of a number of recent reports on the same theme, we believe that the primary responsibility of a renewed diaconate must be the liberation of the laity for the building of communities transformed by the gifts of the kingdom community - life, liberation, love and learning. We contended that to facilitate that mission a renewed diaconate would need to undertake the role of community educator.

Our vision of a renewed diaconate set out in Chapter 9 was written over a decade ago. In Chapter 10 we revisit the nature of a renewed diaconate within the diaconal church.[1] The chapter builds on what was written earlier. However, our conclusion and conviction is that a renewed diaconate should become *an order of mission*. It should be an order whose purpose is distinct from but complementary to that of presbyters. We believe that the latter should become *an order of continuity* which is committed to the ongoing transformation of the local church as the servant of the kingdom community.

We believe that the imperative of a renewed diaconate becoming an order of mission (and presbyters an order of continuity) has been implicit in the material contained in previous chapters. It is a development which has come to the fore because offering the gifts of the kingdom community to a world ever more urgently engaged in the quest from community is now at the top of the global agenda.

The hall-marks of a renewed diaconate as an order of mission cannot be discovered by referring to the old Christendom paradigm. Nor can they be found simply by reviewing current diaconal practice which often remains determined by the same paradigm.[2] They can only be identified with reference to the mission of the diaconal church, a church founded on a theology of community, a spirituality of community and an ecclesiology of the servant church.

---

[1] This chapter has not appeared in print before.
[2] This is the fundamental weakness of Orton and Stockdale's (2014) otherwise commendable research into the current practice of Methodist deacons.

Chapter 10 offers a profile of a renewed diaconate as an order of mission. However, because the roles of deacon and presbyter are complementary it does so alongside a profile of presbyteral ministry as an order of continuity. The creation of an order of mission and an order of continuity are an imperative development if the diaconal church is to be able to engage effectively with today's world, whilst addressing the ongoing transformation of its own life in the process.

Diagram 6 sets out the key features of a diaconal order of mission alongside those of a presbyteral order of continuity. It draws a number of these features from *Diagram 3* (Chapter 4) which depicted the roles of presbyter and deacon as we identified them in 2005.[1] In *Diagram 6* the profiles of diaconal and presbyteral ministry are seen as complementary *orders* of ministry and new features added

As in the case of *Diagram 3*, in *Diagram 6* the roles of deacon and presbyter are described as 'ideal types'. Each ideal type brings together the key features of the leadership role concerned, though all the features will rarely be evident in the ministry of any one individual and in practice there will always be some overlap.

In this chapter our concern is with church leadership as expressed through the ministries of deacon and presbyter (priest). We have already outlined the role of the bishop within the diaconal church in Chapter 7 and do not expand on that discussion further.

Diagram 6 and the associated text offer few practical examples of the work of the diaconate as an order of mission. Examples of what the responsibilities of such an order might mean in practice are offered in Appendix 2 at the end of Chapter 13.

---

[1] Clark (2005: second printing, 2014) *Breaking the Mould of Christendom* (pp. 112-113).

Diagram 6

Orders of ministry within the diaconal church

Presbyters - an order of continuity
Deacons - an order of mission

MISSION	*The transformation of the world by the gifts of the kingdom community - life, liberation, love and learning*	
STANCE OF CHURCH	**Servant of the kingdom community**	
FORMS OF CHURCH	**Local** The church as a community of place	**Dispersed** The church as individuals situated within communities of kin, occupation, concern or interest
	Institution	**Movement**
FORM OF LEADERSHIP	**Servant leader**	
	Working with the local church	**Working alongside the dispersed church**
MINISTRY	**Presbyters - an order of continuity**	**Deacons - an order of mission**
CALLING	Building a church transformed by the gifts of the kingdom community - life, liberation, love, learning	Building a world transformed by the gifts of the kingdom community - life, liberation, love, learning
BOUNDARIES OF MINISTRY	Working within the boundaries of the church	Working across the boundaries of church and world

		Engaging the local church with the life and work of its area
HUMAN RESOURCES	The laity within the church	The laity within the world
LEARNING	Educating the laity to be kingdom community builders Educating the laity in faith and practice	**Primary task** Educating the laity to be kingdom community builders - through the deacon working within the local church - through the deacon working in the world Equipping the laity with the skills of discernment and intervention
WORSHIP	**Primary task** Proclaiming 'the word' for the church Celebrating the sacrament of the breaking of bread Blessing	Proclaiming 'the word' for the world Celebrating the sacrament of the washing of feet Commissioning
PASTORAL CARE	Of those associated with the local church	Of those associated with the dispersed church
MANAGEMENT	Team ministry leader	Team ministry member
	Working beyond the local church	**Working beyond the dispersed church**
CALLING	Pioneering - planting 'sister' churches transformed by the	Pioneering - initiating ways of building a world

	gifts of the kingdom community	transformed by the gifts of the kingdom community - alongside Christian agencies and institutions - alongside secular agencies and institutions
AS A SYMBOLIC FIGURE	Representing the church as an institution for continuity	Representing the church as a movement for transformation
ECUMENICAL TASK	Building one church	Building one world
Communal models and support		
COMMUNAL MODEL	The local church as a model of how the gifts of the kingdom community can be made manifest through institutions	The diaconate (as a religious order and an order of mission) as a model of how the gifts of the kingdom community can be made manifest through movements
COMMUNAL SUPPORT	**For presbyters - the local church** Local teams and regional gatherings Pastoral care Economic security	**For deacons - the religious order** Rule of life Regional and national gatherings Regular circulation of news of the order Mutual pastoral care Economic security

The diaconal church

MISSION	*The transformation of the world by the gifts of the kingdom community - life, liberation, love and learning*

The mission of the diaconal church has already been described at some length in Chapter 4. Here we simply reiterate that the diaconal church's primary purpose is to be the servant of the kingdom community and to seek to make the latter's gifts manifest within church and world. A new diaconal order of mission and a new presbyteral order of continuity would both be committed to the mission of the diaconal church.

FORMS OF CHURCH	**Local**	**Dispersed**
	The church as a community of place	The church as individuals situated within communities of kin, occupation, concern or interest
	Institution	**Movement**

The diaconal church takes two forms. One is the church which regularly gathers in a specific place. We call this the local church (sometimes referred to as the gathered church). It is primarily a community of place because its members usually live near to one another (though these days some will travel a good deal further to meet than when most lived within the same parish). Its pre-eminent hall-mark is Sunday worship. Organizationally the local church takes the form of an institution.

The other form of diaconal church is that of the dispersed church. This refers to the church made up of individual Christians when dispersed to live, work or play. Members of the dispersed church belong to what are sometimes designated as communities of kin, occupation, concern (about current issues) or interest (for example, leisure pastimes). As the dispersed church, it represents the Christian community engaged in mission. Organizationally the dispersed church takes the form of a movement.

The church as institution and the church as movement are complementary. Both are essential aspects of the life and work of the church as a whole. As an institution the church draws on the resources of the past and ensures continuity from one generation to another. As a movement the church engages with and seeks to make its message meaningful to a constantly changing world. However, any church which becomes captive to its form as an institution risks becoming inflexible and moribund. Any church which relies too heavily on its life as a movement risks becoming captive to transient cultural and social trends.

Church leadership - the local and dispersed church

FORM OF LEADERSHIP	Servant leader	
	Working within the local church	**Working alongside the dispersed church**
MINISTRY	**Presbyters - an order of continuity**	**Deacons - an order of mission**

Ecclesiologically, most churches accept in principle that servanthood (*diakonia*) underpins every form of ministry, including that of the laity. However, in practice in many denominations a hierarchical and thus contradictory approach to servant leadership continues to hold sway. In these situations the office of deacon is either regarded as transient and simply forming the first rung on the hierarchical ladder, or as permanent but assistant to the presbyter (priest) liturgically and pastorally.

Within the diaconal church all leaders are equally servants of the kingdom community. They express that leadership on an equal footing through responsibilities that reflect the nature of servanthood, presbyters as an order of continuity and deacons as an order of mission. Deacons are regarded within and beyond the church as having the same leadership status as presbyters. Such equality is reinforced by stipendiary and economic equality with presbyters. A threefold order of ministry may in principle remain but there is no formal hierarchy.

In the remainder of this chapter, the middle column refers to the ministry of presbyters as an order of continuity, the right-hand column to the ministry of deacons as an order of mission.

CALLING	Building a church transformed by the gifts of the kingdom community - life, liberation, love, learning	Building a world transformed by the gifts of the kingdom community - life, liberation, love, learning

Within the diaconal church, the primary calling of presbyter and deacon is equipping the laity to be kingdom community builders within church and world. This means the creation of sacred and secular collectives transformed by the kingdom community's gifts of life, liberation, love and learning.

For the presbyter this calling is focused first and foremost on sustaining a local church transformed by these gifts. The primary calling of the deacon is building a world transformed by the same gifts. If the local church does not exemplify the gifts of the kingdom community, the ministries of presbyter and deacon will be severely compromised. If the dispersed church fails to engage in kingdom community building, the ministries of deacon and presbyter become pointless.

The inclusive and universal nature of the kingdom community means that both presbyter and deacon make addressing the needs of the excluded, the marginalized, the poor and the vulnerable a priority.

BOUNDARIES OF MINISTRY	Working within the boundaries of the church	Working across the boundaries of church and world Engaging the local church with the life and work of its area

In the diaconal church, presbyters are based within and focus their endeavours on the local church. Consequently most of their time and energy is spent within the boundaries, geographical or organizational, of that form of church. If presbyters have oversight of more than one local church they operate within the boundaries of each of those churches and of any ecclesiastical unit (parish, deanery, circuit, area, etc.) which embraces them.

Deacons also have a home base within the local church. However, as an order of mission the diaconate operates across the boundaries of church and world. In doing so deacons are able to gain first-hand experience of the situations and issues faced by lay people in their daily lives, can ascertain what is needed to equip the latter for mission and assist the local church in providing the support and resources required for such a mission.

Deacons also seek to engage the local church with the life and work of its area. The word 'work' should here be taken literally to indicate all the places of work within the locality. This means raising awareness of the needs of the groups and organizations situated in the same area as the local church and facilitating community building connections between these collectives, and between the latter and the local church.

HUMAN RESOURCES	The laity within the church	The laity within the world

The antidote to clericalism is the acknowledgement of the laity as the church's primary human resource for ministry and mission. Presbyters are committed to the liberation of the laity to help ensure the·continuity of the local church. Deacons are committed to the liberation of the laity to engage in mission in the world.

LEARNING		**Primary task**
	Educating the laity to be kingdom community builders	Educating the laity to be kingdom community builders - through the deacon working within the

149

		local church - through the deacon working in the wider world
	Educating the laity in faith and practice	Equipping the laity with the skills of discernment and intervention

Presbyters as an order of continuity and deacons as an order of mission place access to the kingdom community's gift of learning high on their agendas. However, in the case of deacons operating within the local church, educating the laity to be kingdom community builders in the world is their primary task.

There are a number of notable features of the deacon's role as a community educator (Chapter 9). One is the deacon's responsibility for enabling lay people to understand and identify with the role of kingdom community builder where they live, work or play. Another is the deacon's task of helping the laity to develop the art of discerning the gifts of the kingdom community. A third feature is the role of equipping the laity with the skills and resources for forms of intervention which can bring about fuller expression of those gifts in the situations in which they are set. The deacon's educational role can be undertaken on a one-to-one basis or, often more usefully, in small groups. The latter will usually meet within the catchment area of the local church.

Sometimes deacons, for example as chaplains, will find themselves able to fulfil an educational role alongside the dispersed church, as individuals or in groups, beyond the local church and often across denominational boundaries. In such situations, the deacon's particular task is to help those concerned to share their experiences, insights and resources so that their mission as kingdom community builders can be undertaken more effectively.

One of the presbyter's educational tasks is to work for the continuity of the local church as a model of a kingdom community. This means equipping members of the congregation to discern whether the local church manifests the kingdom community's gifts of life, liberation, love and learning and to intervene to make these gifts more evident. An important part of the presbyter's task will involve deepening lay people's knowledge and experience of Christian faith and practice.

WORSHIP	**Primary task**	
	Celebrating the sacrament of the breaking of bread	Celebrating the sacrament of the washing of feet
	Proclaiming 'the word' for the church	Proclaiming 'the word' for the world
	Blessing	Commissioning

As a member of an order of continuity, the primary task of the presbyter is responsibility for the conduct of worship. The presbyter's responsibilities in worship are focused on the ministry of word and sacrament. The former ministry is here called proclaiming 'the word' for the church because it is with the church as the enduring embodiment of the gifts of the kingdom community that the presbyter is concerned. The latter's ministry is focussed on the celebration of holy communion (or Eucharist) at which and the presbyter will normally preside.

Within the worship of the diaconal church the deacon also plays a clearly identifiable role. The reports on the nature of a renewed diaconate referred to in previous chapters recommend that the deacon should read the gospel, offer intercessions, preach when appropriate and dismiss the people at the end of the service. However, as a member of an order of mission, the participation of the deacon in worship should always be undertaken with the calling of the people of God to be the church dispersed to build kingdom communities in the world as pre-eminent. In that context, the sacrament of the washing of feet should come much more to the fore and the deacon should normally preside over this. When spoken by the deacon, the prayer of dismissal should be a prayer of commissioning for mission in daily life.

It has already been noted that if the ministries of presbyter and deacon are to be seen as of equal importance then the meaning of ordination, and not least its current hierarchical mode, needs reviewing. It is our contention that both deacons and presbyters should be ordained to a ministry of word *and* sacrament and that each should undertake responsibility for those ministries in worship along the lines indicated above.

However some occasions may occur when the presbyter will preside over what are usually diaconal aspects of worship and the deacon over what are normally presbyteral responsibilities. These situations underline the fact that that within the diaconal church the contribution of presbyter and deacon, not only to worship but to the whole life and work of the church, are complementary and not exclusive.

PASTORAL CARE	Of those associated with the local church	Of those associated with the dispersed church

The pastoral care of those associated with the local church is an important responsibility of the presbyter even when this is sometimes delegated to lay leaders. As a member of an order of mission, the deacon's pastoral responsibilities are concerned with the support and encouragement of the laity forming the church dispersed in the world.

MANAGEMENT	Team ministry leader	Team ministry member

Because the roles needing to be played out within servant leadership are so many and varied, it is a form of leadership synonymous with team ministry. However, team ministry needs to be managed and co-ordinated. Because the local church provides the base camp for the whole congregation, it is the presbyter who is usually in the best position to lead the team. However, in order that continuity and mission can inform and complement one another, the deacon needs to be an active member of that team.

Church leadership - beyond the local and dispersed church

	Working beyond the local church	Working beyond the dispersed church
CALLING	Pioneering - planting 'sister' churches transformed by the gifts of the kingdom community	Pioneering - initiating ways of building a world transformed by the gifts of the kingdom community - alongside Christian agencies and institutions - alongside secular agencies and institutions

There are many places within society where no lay presence is in evidence. In such situations the gifts of the kingdom remain present even if hidden. However, this means that their fuller expression and potential for individual and collective transformation may well be neglected. It is here that the presbyter or deacon as pioneer (embracing the servant leadership roles of visionary, animator or intermediary) can have an important role to play.

Where no local church exists, presbyters may play a pioneering role by seeking to encourage the 'planting' of 'sister' congregations. In that role, the presbyter will endeavour to work in partnership with those holding Christian convictions, or otherwise, who regard the 'planting' of a new church as of communal value for the neighbourhood concerned. Skills for the 'planting' of congregations should be one facet of the training of all presbyters. It is a role which should not be delegated to a special category of presbyters called 'pioneer ministers' who can all too often become lone rangers.

Beyond the local church, deacons may also face the need to operate as pioneers (visionaries, animators or intermediaries). However, they will still need to address how the gifts of the kingdom community may become more transformative within secular communities of kin, occupation, concern or interest. Their special concern will be communities which have become introverted or exclusive and thus exacerbate the communal dilemma[1] (Chapter 2).

When the deacon is working beyond the dispersed church it is likely that the role of intermediary will often come to the fore. The Methodist report on *What is a Deacon?* (para. 5.7) identifies this role very clearly when its states that the deacon should be involved in 'crossing boundaries, (and) making connections between alienated and fragmented groups, including those beyond the margins'. The report adds that the deacon as pioneer should also give special attention to 'overturning unjust structures, standing in solidarity with the vulnerable and helping them discover their own voice'.

The most important outcome of diaconal intervention is the building and development of kingdom communities, whether or not they are overtly recognized as such. Deacons as pioneers *and* enablers will seek to pass over the leadership of what they have pioneered to others motivated by a similar communal vision as soon as feasible.

AS A SYMBOLIC FIGURE	Representing the church as an institution for continuity	Representing the church as a movement for transformation

In the public eye, presbyters as an order of continuity become the representatives of the church as an institution. It is a role which differs little from that which currently exists.

Deacons as an order of mission become the representatives of the church as a movement. This is role very different from that, if any, which the church and the public currently associate with the role of deacon. Deacons being identified as representatives of the church as a movement will only come about when the distinctiveness yet equal standing of the roles of presbyter and deacon are recognized.

---

[1] 'The problem human collectives face when needing to become increasingly open to one another without undermining or weakening their own sense of community or that of others.'

One of the problematic factors in being a symbolic figure comes when a presbyter takes up the role of chaplain and, sometimes, of a minister in secular employment. Both are situations in which the presbyter, if reflecting the norms of the Christendom church, majors on the role of pastor and, when requested to do so, of worship leader.

This can raise a major difficulty for the mission of the diaconal church. Because the presbyter as chaplain or minister in secular employment is regarded as *the* symbolic figure representing the church in the world, the public often comes to equate the role of pastor and worship leader, that is the church in its institutional form, with the total picture of what the church is about.[1] The church as a movement for the communal transformation of society, within the diaconal church represented by the laity and deacons serving them, becomes invisible. Thus in the eye of the public it is the Christendom model of church which remains the norm whilst the model of the diaconal church remains totally foreign. Furthermore, as the public finds the Christendom model of church to be less and less attractive, church membership continues to decline and the vital contribution of the diaconal church to the communal transformation of society and world remains unrecognized and untapped.

ECUMENICAL TASK	Building one church	Building one world

The ecumenical movement is struggling to retain its impetus. This is largely because no mainstream church has accepted the *sine que non* of breaking the mould of Christendom. The old order still rules and even emerging churches world-wide soon succumb to this outmoded model of church. As a consequence 'ecumenicity' has become a word for forms of partnership which, though usually undertaken in a spirit of goodwill and offering occasional signs of hope, bring little lasting change. Even declining numbers and lack or financial resources have so far failed to concentrate denominational minds sufficiently to herald a new beginning. The disastrous consequence is that the message 'one in Christ' (Gal 3:28) is not reflected even by the church. Consequently the world is denied any model of how the inclusive and

---

[1] See Clark (2014) *The Kingdom at Work* Project (pp. 359-381).

universal nature of the gifts of the kingdom community can be manifest in practice.

As the servant of the kingdom community, the diaconal church offers a model of church as an inclusive and universal community. Within that church the presbyter's particular concern is building one church and the deacon's is the creation of one world. This does not mean the negation of denominational, cultural and social identities. It does mean presbyter and deacon ensuring that sacred and secular identities do not become a divisive barrier but are seen as a rich resource to be acknowledged, appreciated and shared by all. Both presbyters and deacons are called to make the original meaning of 'ecumenical', the integrity of the whole inhabited world, a reality.

Communal models and support

COMMUNAL MODELS	The local church as a model of how the gifts of the kingdom community can be made manifest through institutions	The diaconate (as a religious order and an order of mission) as a model of how the gifts of the kingdom community can be made manifest through movements

The local church seeks to be a model of how the gifts of the kingdom can be passed on from one generation another. In particular it exemplifies the nature of communal continuity for institutions, sacred and secular. In this context, educating the family, the traditional Christian model of continuity, to be able to express the gifts of life, liberation, love and learning, is of special concern for the presbyter

Within the diaconal church, a renewed diaconate as a religious order offers a model to church and world of how movements, often more vulnerable to a changing culture than institutions, can more effectively sustain their life and fulfil their calling.

COMMUNAL SUPPORT	**For presbyters - the local church** Local teams and regional gathering	**For deacons - the religious order** Rule of life Regional and national gatherings Regular circulation of news of the order
	Pastoral care	Mutual pastoral care
	Economic security	Economic security

Amongst those communities which offer presbyters communal support, the local church is often the most prominent. Herein they are able to access colleagueship (ordained and lay), pastoral care and economic security. However, the local church can offer only short-term support as presbyters are likely to move from one to another numerous times during their careers. Beyond the local church, some presbyters find the wider church communally important to them. However, the infrequency of meeting colleagues from further afield and the need to travel a considerable distance to access such colleagueship inevitably weaken this resource.

Their links with the dispersed church cannot offer deacons the degree of communal support available to presbyters. However, deacons as members of a religious order are able to make up for this deficit (see Part 3). The religious order, in particular through its rule of life and mutual pastoral care, can offer deacons, throughout their life and wherever they may be located, a powerful and personal communal resource for undertaking their calling as an order of mission.

Part 3

Methodism and the Methodist Diaconal Order – a movement for communal holiness

Preamble to Part 3

Part 1 of this book described the nature of the kingdom community and the hall-marks of the diaconal church as the servant of that community. In Part 2 we set out the main features of a renewed diaconate as an order of mission.

In **Part 3** we select a British church and diaconal order to explore how the latter might become an order of mission and, in the process, give impetus to a church seeking to develop as a movement for the building of kingdom communities. To this end, we have chosen the Methodist Church, because it already embodies many characteristics of the diaconal church, and the Methodist Diaconal Order, because it has certain attributes which could help it to develop as an order of mission. We explore a number of changes which will need to take place within Methodism if the developments noted are to occur.

11. *Methodism as a diaconal church*

Preamble

In this chapter we present evidence showing that Methodism possesses many hall-marks of the diaconal church. We undertake this exploration because we believe that only a diaconal church is in a position to give birth to a renewed diaconate. Because the theological foundations on which the diaconal church is based (Chapter 2) are of fundamental importance, we major on the similarity between a theology of the kingdom community and what we describe as Methodism's theology of communal holiness.[1] We then identify other characteristics of the Methodist Church which resemble features of the diaconal church described in Part 1.

---

[1] The section on communal holiness draws from Clark (2010), *Reshaping the mission of Methodism* (pp. 172- 183).

The mission of Methodism - to witness to the gospel of communal holiness

'The Wesleyan movement was a commitment to a holiness project' (McMaster, 2002). In interpreting the nature of that project, Wesley knew that holiness, though a profoundly significant hallmark of the Christian life, must 'never (be) understood as an individualistic affair'. He declared that 'the gospel of Christ knows no religion but social: no holiness but social holiness' (*Called to Love and Praise*, 4.3.9). It should be remembered that Wesley was here setting the word 'social' over against the term 'solitary', and referring to how Christians should help one another to grow in the faith, not least as members of a group (or a class meeting as it was called in early Methodism). He was not here specifically concerned with the pursuit of social justice. Nevertheless, as McMaster argues, 'Today social holiness needs to be extended beyond ecclesial *koinonia*'.

Our conviction is that if the concept of social holiness is taken into and 'extended' to become that of 'communal holiness', it takes on a radically new dimension and has the potential to become the gospel for our time. Below we explore the meaning of communal holiness and its implications for the future of Methodism and wider society.

There are a number of reasons why Methodism should (re)embrace the concept of communal holiness. First, the Methodist Church needs to reclaim its holiness heritage and deflect Hempton's criticism that Methodism lost its way when, by default, it relinquished this calling to 'its Holiness offspring ... Pentecostalism' (2005, pp. 208–209). Secondly, by 'extending social holiness beyond ecclesial *koinonia*', and enabling it to take on the mantle of communal holiness, we ground Methodism's holiness project in both the sociology and theology of *community*.[1] This development would enable Methodism to make a uniquely important contribution to a world facing the critical choice between chaos and community. Its mission could then be seen as a call to build a global community transformed by the gift of communal holiness.

This approach to the mission of Methodism raises two important questions. First, what do the concept of the kingdom community,

---

[1] In what follows the reader needs to refer to the theology of the kingdom community described in Chapter 2.

which lies at the heart of the mission of the diaconal church, and the concept of communal holiness, have *in common*? Secondly, is there a *distinctive* contribution that the concept of communal holiness makes to our understanding of the diaconal church as the servant of the kingdom community? We look at these two questions in turn.

The kingdom community and communal holiness – common ground

The concepts of communal holiness and the kingdom community share some key features. Both include 'community' as a foundational word. Thus anything learnt from religious or 'secular' disciplines about the nature of community will help to inform and enrich our understanding of the concepts of kingdom community and communal holiness.

Kingdom community and communal holiness are both means of grace. The gifts they bestow are neither a reward for effort nor good conduct. They are offered to humankind simply because God loves the world which he has created. They can be either refused, or accepted and used in the service of humankind.

The kingdom community and communal holiness both derive their transforming power from that of the Trinity. It should be remembered that the Trinity was one of 'the essential doctrines on which (Wesley) insisted' (Williams, 1960, p. 17). It is also of note that, since the 1980s, references to the doctrine of the Trinity have come increasingly to the fore in reports commissioned by the Methodist Conference (Shier-Jones in Marsh, et al., 2004, p. 86).

Called to Love and Praise (an extremely insightful Methodist Conference report on the distinctive character of Methodism) sees the communal nature of Trinity and kingdom as closely related. It comments: 'The synoptic gospels' understanding of the kingdom of God, and the Trinitarian understanding of God, implicit in the New Testament and developed in subsequent tradition, show how the church is a community both of worship and mission' (1.4.1). Complementing the communal attributes connecting kingdom and Trinity, Snyder (2007) believes that the communal characteristics of holiness and Trinity are, likewise, closely linked. He writes: 'Mind-blowing as it sounds, holiness means sharing the very character of God – communion with the Trinity … (Thus) Christians are to be specialists in building community to the glory of God' (pp. 74 and 78).

The gifts of the kingdom community (life, liberation, love and learning) and the gift of communal holiness are gifts of the Trinity and reflect the latter's essentially communal nature (Clark, 2005, pp. 21–27, 37–40). However, it can be argued that the gift of communal holiness embodies and deepens our understanding of the four core gifts of the kingdom community, as we indicate below:

o The kingdom community's gift of *life* reflects the nature of God as Creator. It is a gift whose meaning is encapsulated in the phrase 'the glory of God is human beings fully alive' (Irenaeus).

For Wesley, this gift was that which enables men and women to become part of 'a new creation' (Wilkinson, 2004, p. 150–1). That creation is holy, or, as we shall contend later, a creation made whole. It brings into being a holy people eager to celebrate life in all its fullness. It calls them to worship, to thanksgiving, to service and to stewardship of the planet of which they are an integral part. Wesley preached and wrote much about individual responsibility in this connection. However, as Jones (2004) puts it, 'Holiness is the fruit of responsible grace in both the private and public spheres' (p. 161).

o The second gift of the kingdom community is *liberation*, both personal and collective. It is a gift manifest in the work of Christ as Liberator. Through this gift, we are freed *from* self, fear and a sense of failure. We are thus privileged, as individuals and human collectives, together with the whole of creation, *to* experience the glorious liberty of the children of God (Romans 8: 21).

Liberation is also a core feature of communal holiness. Carter (2002) writes: Methodism's 'experience of salvation (holiness) is at one and the same time intensely personal and totally corporate' (p. 4). Personal liberation is the process of being made whole, forgiven and restored to our true selves through the grace of the liberating Christ. However, this experience of liberation, or 'healing holiness' as Craske calls it (1999a, p. 178), is offered to each and all. It is also about the redemption of the entire creation and encompasses the cosmic nature of communal holiness.

o The third gift of the kingdom community is divine **love**, or *agape*. It is a gift which enables us to share the unity, or fellowship, of the Holy Spirit. It is a gift that has a profound affinity with communal holiness.

It is through 'love divine, all loves excelling' that we receive the promise of becoming 'pure and spotless' and of being 'changed from glory into glory' (Charles Wesley). It is the 'Wesleyan emphasis on holiness as perfect love (that gives) Methodist spirituality its own distinctive character' and expresses 'the heart of Methodist ecclesiology' (*Called to Love and Praise*, 4.3.9; 4.3.10), a view echoed by Forster in his endorsement of Methodism as a world faith (2009, p. 146). As Snyder (2007) puts it, 'Holiness ... is not first of all a doctrine but ... a love relationship with God in Jesus Christ and the Holy Spirit' (p. 82).

o The fourth gift of the kingdom community is **learning**. It reflects the nature of the Trinity as a learning community (Clark, 2005, pp. 37–38). This gift is a vital aspect of our search for communal holiness and answer to the communal dilemma, and summons us to an ongoing journey of spiritual discovery and growth.

Dawes (2003) writes, 'It is a journey from new birth to spiritual maturity, from sinfulness to perfection, from "original sin" through "justification by faith" to "entire sanctification".' Or as Wesley might have put it, learning is the journey towards perfect love. It is a gift which requires the people called Methodists to become 'a community of seekers' (Deeks, Team Focus, p. 5) rather than those who never move beyond what they have received from their forebears. It also requires that they are open to engage with those whom Curran calls 'questers' (2009a, p. 109), seekers in the wider world.

The four gifts of the kingdom community and the gift of communal holiness, which also embraces them, are universal and inclusive. They are yet to come in all their fullness, but are already among us, not only within the church but throughout our world. The mission of the diaconal church is to discern, make known and enable the gifts of the kingdom community, embodied in the gift of communal holiness, to bear fruit wherever they are found.

The universality of these gifts is reflected in Wesley's Arminianism, or 'the vision of "allness"', as Richard Andrew calls it

(1999, p. 22). Methodism's 'special vocation within the universal church,' Andrew states, is to push 'the logic of "catholicity" in the direction of its widest possible focus, the unity (and, we would add, the communal holiness) of *all* humanity' (p. 22). Such a world is an 'ecumenical' world, in the fullest and richest sense of an often misunderstood and narrowly defined concept.

The gift of communal holiness embodies and enriches our understanding of the four gifts of the kingdom community. However, the concept of communal holiness also offers a *distinctive* contribution to our understanding of those gifts and, in particular, their relationship to one another.

Communal holiness as wholeness

Informing the distinctiveness of the gift of communal holiness is a theology of integrity. This sees 'holiness' as 'wholeness', in the fullest and deepest sense of wholeness. As Craske comments, holiness, coming from the same Germanic root as wholeness, links to a range of concepts 'about healing, being complete, having integrity' (1999a, p. 178). Thus we can offer the following definition.

> **Communal holiness** is a divine gift which, embodying the kingdom community's gifts of life, liberation, love and learning, transforms humankind into whole persons, whole families, whole institutions, whole cities, whole societies and one world, and reveals the integrity of creation.

Holiness as wholeness is about 'the call to personhood' (McFadyen, 1990). It is about individuals, families, social collectives, cities, societies and humankind becoming, by divine grace, what God intended them to be (Clutterbuck, 2004, p. 68). Holiness as wholeness is also about the entire cosmos made whole, 'the integrity of creation' as the World Council of Churches describes it (WCC, Seoul, 1990). In short, communal holiness as communal wholeness is about our human and divine destiny.

Because communal holiness is a unifying concept, it integrates the kingdom community's gifts of life, liberation, love and learning. It enables us to see that the gift of life which energises us, the gift of liberation which redeems us, the gift of love which bonds us and the gift of learning which enables us to grow and develop are complementary gifts which, by God's grace and human endeavour, empower humankind to become whole.

Holiness as wholeness does not mean homogeneity. As a gift rooted in the nature of the Trinity, it affirms distinctiveness, though as an integral aspect of a profound unity. Holiness treasures the riches of diversity, though it is a diversity that affirms interdependence. It embraces difference, sometimes disagreement and even conflict, but as human exchanges. These can open up new horizons and give impetus to humankind's quest for community and the building of a society and world which are communally whole.

The gift of communal holiness knows no divide between the 'sacred' and 'secular'. Consequently the mission of the diaconal church involves building partnerships with those embracing other faiths and other convictions who are also striving to build communities that manifest the gift of communal holiness, whether or not that gift is recognised or acknowledged as such.

The gift of communal holiness is offered to a world that is unholy, is far from whole. It is offered to a world that is divided, fragmented, broken and at war with itself, because of humankind's inhumanity, greed, arrogance and selfishness. It is a gift given to address the profound challenge of the communal dilemma. The failure of individuals and collectives to accept the gift of communal holiness, and the gifts of life, liberation, love and learning which it embodies, exposes the destructive power of all that is unholy. The result is that, though communal holiness reveals the immensity of God's grace, it is a gift that comes at a price to both Liberator and receiver. To offer that gift meant a self-emptying and cross for the Liberator - to receive that gift means, for us, taking up our cross and following him. As the title of an important consultation on the future of Methodism held in 2009 reminds us, 'holiness and risk' are inseparable.

Called to Love and Praise regards 'the essential nature of the church as *koinonia*' (3.1.6–3.1.10; 5.5). In this respect, the legacy of communal holiness bequeathed to the people called Methodists is an immense asset. One aspect of this legacy is 'an emphasis on "relatedness" as essential to the concept of "church"; another is on the importance of "fellowship"' (*Called to Love and Praise*, 4.7.1). Thus, in reshaping its approach to mission, it must never downplay its commitment to *koinonia*, but affirm and nourish the genuine richness of its common life.

Methodism needs to be proud of and upfront about its long quest for communal holiness. It is a legacy enriched by passion for the coming of the kingdom, by a commitment to an adventurous journey of spiritual discovery and growth, and by generous and costly service to those marginalised by society. Above all, its historic mission is to find new ways of discerning, accessing and witnessing to the gifts of life, liberation, love and learning as a movement of communal holiness.

Other hall-marks of the diaconal church evident within Methodism

Methodism and the spirituality of the kingdom community

In Chapter 3, we explored the contribution of different denominations to a spirituality of the kingdom community, in particular how they focused on and enriched the gifts of life, liberation, love and learning. We stated that Methodism had made a significant contribution to the experience of the gift of love, noting that *Called to Love and Praise* (1999), with its perceptive title, had been one of the most insightful reports recently published on the life and work of Methodism. We also noted that it is through its hymnology and 'singing the faith', that Methodism has throughout its history given passionate expression to the gift of love.

Of course Methodist spirituality also adds its own contribution to the gifts of life, liberation and learning (see also Chapter 3). But that Methodists are not only a people in tune with the kingdom community's gift of love but have expressed it so wholeheartedly within the fellowship of their groups and societies, as well as in their concern for the poor and vulnerable, closely aligns them with the nature and mission of the diaconal church.

The 'priesthood of all believers' - the laity as the people of God in the world

Methodism reflects a number of other hall-marks of the diaconal. Crucial here is the pre-eminence it gives to the laity as the church's primary resource for the ministry and mission in the world. Its Deed of Union also rules out a hierarchical view of the ordained ministry. We quote from *Reshaping the mission of Methodism* (pp. 184-186):

> From its beginnings, Methodism has possessed 'a profoundly missionary ecclesiology' (Atkins, 2009). It has always prided

itself on being a body 'structured for mission, able to respond pragmatically and flexibly when new needs or opportunities arise' (*Called to Love and Praise*, 4.7.1). For Methodism to be able to share its 'vision of (communal) holiness' (Craske, 1999, p. 78), and help church and world become 'specialists in building community to the glory of God' (Snyder, 2007, p. 78), it is to the ministry of its lay people in the world that it must turn.

There is no chance of the mission of Methodism being fulfilled if it is seen as predominantly the responsibility of its ordained ministry. Simply as a matter of fact, there are too few ministers available to shoulder such a major undertaking. Furthermore, many ministers have lost personal contact with the world of work beyond the church even if, as a first career, they were once actively engaged in it. Far more important, however, is the fact that the mission of the diaconal church not only cannot be, but *should* not be the responsibility of the ordained ministry. It is lay people who are the church's primary missionary resource for Methodism, as they are for the diaconal church.

The Methodist *Deed of Union* declares that 'the Methodist Church holds the doctrine of the priesthood of all believers and consequently believes that no priesthood exists which belongs exclusively to a particular order or class'. Methodism was, and continues to be 'a movement of lay witness' (*Team Focus* 2007, pp. 17–18). The Methodist Conference's report on *The Ministry of the People of God in the World* (1990) confirms Methodism's conviction that 'the ministry of the people of God in the world is both the primary and normative ministry of the church, for the church is as much itself "in the world" as it is "in church" ' (pp. 539- 540). Atkins underlines this conviction when he writes (2007):

> In terms of the missionary nature of the church ... it is clear that only the releasing of the gifts, energies and skills of the whole people of God will enable large swathes of our culture and society to encounter Christianity in any authentic and meaningful way. Anything less will be insufficient (pp. 191–192).

Option for the poor

Reflecting the priorities of the diaconal church, Methodism has throughout its history made a significant contribution to the church's engagement with the challenges posed by the needs of the poor and marginalized. Of particular note here was the so-called 'Forward Movement' at the end of the nineteenth century, 'the last great attempt to reach those alienated from all the churches', as John Munsey Turner describes it (2005, p. 57). At this time, Methodism, exemplified by the leadership of Hugh Price Hughes in the West London Mission, poured massive resources into many inner cities.

A commitment to transforming the life of those on the margins continued for well over half a century from that time until radical changes in welfare provision weakened the witness, and often viability, of many Methodist city centre missions. However, from 1983 to 1996, Methodism was again actively engaged in a programme entitled 'Mission alongside the poor' (Holden, 1989).

Connexionalism

As a diaconal church Methodism recognizes that if the medium is to be the message its circuits and districts need to manifest what it means to be kingdom communities. In particular communal holiness requires that Methodism becomes 'a Connexion'. *The Nature of Oversight* (2005) expresses this point in an exceptionally perceptive way.

> Connexionalism is the Methodist way of being church ... (Methodists) cherish connexionalism as part of the tradition and gift which they have inherited ... (It) describes a way of relating in which individual people and individual groups (e.g. interest groups; working groups; fellowship groups; local churches; circuits; districts; denominational institutions, offices and agencies) do not exist by and for themselves but with and for others ... They are inter-dependent and discover their true identity and develop their full potential only in and through mutual relationships ... Connexionalism therefore characterises an experience of belonging that is shaped both by inter-dependence and also by sharing in holiness and witness, worship and mission (2.1; 2.3).

In connexionalism, Methodism has long experience of, and possesses a model for what it means for every institution, civic as well as ecclesial, to be a communal whole. As Richard Andrew (1999) puts it:

> (The identity of Methodism) is linked to enabling the whole church to fulfill its 'catholic' vocation in relation to the rest of humanity … (That) 'catholic vision' is constituted not only by the unity of faith and the outreach of divine love; it also looks to the ultimate unity of humanity as the object of our common hope (pp. 19 and 22).

We believe that if Methodism can retain the power of connexionalism as a manifestation of 'a sharing in all that God intends for human wholeness' (Clutterbuck, 2004, p. 68), it will be offering the gospel of communal holiness and a model of what it means to be a kingdom community of vital importance for the future of church and world.

Methodism as institution and movement

In its early days Methodism became a dynamic movement for communal holiness. Nevertheless, it turned to the Church of England to provide it, through the latter's network of parish churches, with the continuity that only an institution can give. When this partnership failed to materialize, Methodism was obliged to assume an increasingly institutionalized form.

In recent years, as its decline in the West has gained momentum, Methodism has been compelled to try and find new ways of expressing its mission. Some have wisely urged it to reclaim its identity as a movement. For example, Martyn Percy in his comments on the contributions to *Unmasking Methodist theology* (Marsh, 2004, p. 210) offers some highly significant reflections:

> It is my belief that Methodism should focus and reflect on its core strength - those gifts and charisms that gave it a strong movement identity in the first place… Methodism… as an intelligible and vibrant movement, is more like the leaven in the lump than it may ever have realized. I suspect that the future of Methodism - at least in Britain - may lie in the church saving itself from becoming too 'churchy'… So instead of trying to operate like a modernist meta-organization, Methodism may need to revisit some of its primary and generative spiritual roots. To return to being a movement, and in so doing, to renew not only itself, but also those other denominations around it that

need to learn from the fusion of its dynamic evangelistic heritage and capacious social witness. To be sure, this could be a costly decision. To journey from being a movement to a church, and then back to being a movement, is not a development that many in the Conference or Marylebone Road would welcome. But I wonder what the Wesley brothers would have had to say about it?

The problem is that the progression from movement to institution has been the destiny of every Christian revival movement, including Methodism, throughout history. Only through the more durable structures and resources of an institution can a movement, inevitably a creature of its own age and culture, retain its viability. It is no surprise, therefore, that Methodism's transition from a movement to institution has in some ways, for example in its increasing clericalism and parochialism, led to it being gradually moulded to the still dominant model of the Christendom church.

However, there is a way in which Methodism can reclaim its heritage as a dynamic movement for the salvation of society and world. It is a way forward which depends on Methodism's readiness to prioritize and resource the transformation of its diaconal order into an order of mission to proclaim and earth the gospel of communal holiness. We explore how this vision of a transformed Methodism might be made a reality in the remaining two chapters.

12. *The Methodist Diaconal Order as a religious order*

Preamble

In this chapter we focus on the attributes of the Methodist Diaconal Order as a religious order which manifests the kingdom community's gifts of life, liberation, love and learning. We do so because we believe that being a religious order with these attributes enables the Methodist Diaconal Order to be a model and inspiration for the whole Methodist Church. We also believe that being a religious order with these attributes means that the gifts of the kingdom community become a huge resource for the Methodist Diaconal Order in its development as an order of mission.

In order for the reader to understand better where the Methodist Diaconal Order stands at this moment in time, a brief description of its origins and history is given at the outset.

Origins and history of the Methodist Diaconal Order

Beginnings

The life and work of the Methodist Diaconal Order had its origins in the emergence of a number of Methodist deaconess associations in the late nineteenth century. As with many other deaconess organizations of this era, the Methodist associations came into being to meet the acute social needs of rapidly growing cities with their squalid living conditions and totally inadequate medical care, welfare provision and education for the poor.

In 1869, the Rev Thomas Bowman Stephenson founded the Children's Home (later called the National Children's Home and Orphanage and, more recently, Action for Children). He was greatly influenced by the work of Pastor Theodore Fliedner, the founder of a Lutheran deaconess community in 1836 in Kaiserswerth, Germany. In 1878, Bowman recruited women to work for the Children's Home as Sisters of the Children. This initiative triggered the idea of an order of women employed in three main fields: moral and spiritual education; ministry to the sick poor and evangelism.

In 1890, Stephenson built on these foundations to set up the Wesley Deaconess Order, a body distinct from the sisters working for the Children's Home. The work developed rapidly. In 1894 the first deaconess was sent to work in South Africa, the beginning of a long tradition of overseas service by the Order. In 1901 deaconesses were officially 'recognized' as a lay form of ministry by the Wesleyan Methodist Conference. In 1902, a Wesley Deaconess Institute College was founded in Ilkley to provide accommodation and training facilities for 27 students. By 1907, there were 98 fully trained deaconesses, 56 probationers and 19 accepted for training (Lloyd, 2010, p. 249). Bowman set down three principles which in time became a classic frame of reference for the Order (Graham, 2002, p. 241):

> There should be vocation but no vow…
> There should be discipline but not servility…
> There should be association but it should not exclude freedom…

Meanwhile other Methodist deaconess associations were coming into being. In 1887, Katherine Price Hughes, actively supported by her husband the Rev Hugh Price Hughes, set up the Sisters of the People based at the Wesleyan West London Mission. The association was neither subject to nor officially recognized by the Wesleyan Conference thus, unlike most sisterhoods, was relatively free from male control. This helped it to embrace an active stance towards women's rights (Lloyd, p. 251).

These initiatives encouraged the Rev Thomas John Cope of the United Methodist Free Churches based in Pimlico, London, in 1890 to set up a sisterhood on similar lines. A year later he founded a deaconess institute for these sisters. In 1907, this branch of Methodism amalgamated with the United Methodist Church and the sisters took the title of the United Methodist Deaconess Order (Graham, pp. 337-363).

In 1891, the Rev James Flannigan, a Primitive Methodist minister based in Southwark, inspired by the example of the West London Mission, began to recruit women for another association of deaconesses also known as Sisters of the People.

These deaconess orders grew and flourished over subsequent decades. They all adopted a collective discipline and regarded themselves as religious communities. Their training was taken very seriously, at Ilkley deaconesses undergoing 'at least two years' of study and practical placements (Graham, p. 352). They worked long hours. Almost all were paid though they existed on a very small 'allowance'. Most deaconesses were between twenty-two and thirty five years of age (Lloyd, p. 252) and had to remain unmarried if they wished to remain in their associations. Overall control of the different associations remained very largely in male hands.

The unification of Methodism and after

1932 saw the unification of Wesleyan Methodism, the United Methodist Church and Primitive Methodism. Within two years the deaconess associations of all these branches of Methodism came together under the title of the Wesley Deaconess Order. Overall this then had a membership of some 370 deaconesses (Graham, p 353). In 1936, the Methodist Book of Offices included a service of ordination for deaconesses who before than had been 'consecrated'. However, ordination was to a lay order and took place at Convocation not the Methodist Conference. The years following unification were not easy for the Order due to circuit re-organization and the economic depression. However, World War II saw deaconesses actively engaged in a very wide diversity of roles.

The post-war period brought a revolution in both state welfare provision and the role of women in society. These and other changes had a major impact on the Wesley Deaconess Order. From 1963 onwards deaconesses who married were permitted to remain in the Order In the late 1960s the membership of the Order dropped to some 70 active deaconesses. This decline in strength led, in 1968, to Ilkley House being closed. Training was moved to Handsworth College in Birmingham and combined with that of presbyters. Three years later a new headquarters was opened near the college.

Another major change in the life of the Order occurred when Methodist presbyteral ministry was opened to women in 1973. Between 1973 and 1982, some 65 deaconesses were ordained as presbyters. It was suggested that a Methodist Order of Deacons be formed for those wishing to remain in the Order and that the latter be open to men. However, events overtook these proposals and, as a result of many deaconesses opting to become presbyters and a decline in numbers, the Methodist Conference decided that recruitment to the Order should cease from 1978.

Re-opening of the Order

The years following the cessation of recruitment led to much heart-searching not least because of the valued legacy of the Wesley Deaconess Order and an ongoing conviction that its life and work were in transition rather than facing termination. As a result, in 1986, the Methodist Conference agreed to re-open the Order to men as well as women. From that time onwards, the Order which had in the past had a good deal of financial, administrative and educational independence came more fully under the direction of the Methodist Conference. In 1988 the Order's name was changed to the Methodist Diaconal Order and in 1990 the first ordinations to the new Order took place.

Reports in 1992, 1993 and 1995 led to the Methodist Conference accepting the Methodist Diaconal Order as an order of ministry (thus bringing the designation of deacons as lay people to an end) and agreeing that admission into the Order should be by ordination at the Methodist Conference not Convocation. In 1998 the Conference for the first time received all members of the Methodist Diaconal Order into what in Methodism is known as 'full Connexion', thus formally instituting the Methodist Diaconal Order as an order of ministry. The stipend of and accommodation for a deacon became the same as that required for a presbyter.

Since its re-opening, the Methodist Diaconal Order had been developing its life as a religious order. Elements of this way of life, though differing from some of the hall-marks of the traditional religious orders, reach well back into the days of the Wesley Deaconess Order. However, in the early 1990s, a rule of life was drawn up by members of the Order and in 1995 the Methodist Diaconal Order was affirmed as a religious order by the Methodist Conference.

The twenty-first century

In 2004, a report called *What is a Deacon?*, which set out a profile of the Order as an order of ministry and a religious order, was accepted by the Methodist Conference. Over the first decade of the twenty-first century the membership of the Methodist Diaconal Order steadily grew. In 2015 there were 145 active deacons (including 26 probationers), 20 student deacons and 121 retired (or supernumerary) deacons. However, the contraction of the membership of the Methodist Church led to increasing financial constraints and, in 2014, the diaconal house in Edgbaston, Birmingham, was sold and a decision taken to move the Order's headquarters to Methodist Church House in London, the implementation of which is, in late 2015, still a work in progress. Meanwhile diaconal training, some of which had been dispersed across the country, was centred on the Queen's Foundation in Birmingham.

Deacons are 'stationed' across the country. This means that the Methodist Diaconal Order is a widely dispersed community - from Shetland to the Channel Islands. However, this dispersal is balanced by deacons gathering annually at a three day Convocation, by the provision of area groups and a range of networking facilities now assisted by the Internet. Though being able to express a preference for the type of work they wish to do, deacons are 'stationed' by the Order for an average of about five years in places requesting their services. In recent years, the procedures for dealing with the selection, training and placement of deacons have become more closely integrated with those for presbyters.

Since its re-opening in 1986, the leadership of the Order has changed in character. The Warden became a deacon, so far all have been women, chosen by Convocation and approved by the Methodist Conference. A Deputy Warden (sometimes a man) has been in place for most of the period though for a time in the first decade of the twenty-first century a 'voluntary' team ministry approach was attempted. In 2014 a Leadership Group, made up of lay people, presbyters and deacons, was appointed by the Methodist Conference to support the Warden and Deputy Warden and facilitate support for members of the Order.

The Methodist Diaconal Order as a religious order today[1]

In what follows we identify a number of ways in which the Methodist Diaconal Order as a religious order manifests the kingdom community's gifts of life, liberation, love and learning. This enables the Order to be a model and inspiration for the Methodist Church as a whole. It also provides the Order with an immense resource in its development as an order of mission (Chapter 13).

The Methodist Diaconal Order and traditional religious orders

It should be noted at the outset that as 'a religious order' the Methodist Diaconal Order differs in many respects from the religious orders of the Roman Catholic Church or Church of England. Christine Walters, a former Warden of the Order, writes[2]:

> The Wesley Deaconess Order and its successor, the Methodist Diaconal Order, were not religious orders in the pattern of the 'Catholic' type of religious order. The last remaining shadow of any approximation was removed in 1963 when sisters were allowed to marry and stay in the Order, and thus 'chastity' flew out of the window! A kind of 'poverty' still remained with Wesley Deaconesses getting only an allowance and not a stipend until the 1990 Methodist Conference's decision (to pay deacons a stipend and one equal to that of a presbyter).

Nor was the Wesley Deaconess Order pledged to 'obedience' in the same sense as the traditional religious orders. Jennifer Lloyd (2010) writes: 'No sisters took vows but they were expected to serve for a considerable number of years... They were free to leave for any reason, including marriage' (p. 253). However, they were 'expected to take any assignment offered them' (p. 254). As Thomas Bowman put it 'There should be vocation but no vow...' Christine Walters adds[3]:

---

[1] The following section draws from Clark (2013) 'The hallmark of the Methodist Diaconal Order - its life as a religious order - and some implications the future of Methodism' in *Theology and Ministry - An Online Journal*. (Vol. 2) University of Durham: St John's College (www.durham.ac.uk/theologyandministry). It is reprinted here with the permission of that Journal.

[2] In correspondence with the author

[3] 1996 (Unpublished paper for the Methodist Diaconal Order's student conference)

There was also 'a sense of discipline but without the severity often attached to (other) religious orders (and) a sense of association, a bonding together of membership, yet without excluding a freedom to do many types of work and express ministry in many different ways.'

In the case of the Methodist Diaconal Order, therefore, we are looking at a religious order of a much less formal kind than that of the traditional religious orders. However, it was still founded on and retains a deep sense of commitment to serve church and kingdom, a very strong sense of mutual loyalty, and the readiness of members to sacrifice their own freedom of choice (and that of their families if married) in order to honour the promises made at their ordination.

An overview from the perspective of 'best practice'

Features of the life of the Methodist Diaconal Order which manifest the gifts of the kingdom community are described below in terms of 'best practice'. However, the Order would be the first to acknowledge how often it falls short of this ideal.[1]

Convocation – all the gifts of the kingdom community

One major event in the Methodist Diaconal Order's calendar can be seen as embodying all the gifts of the kingdom community: its annual Convocation. This is normally held over three days at the Hayes Conference Centre in Derbyshire. Convocation is the one occasion each year when all active deacons, students in training and many retired deacons gather together.

Convocation bears witness to the gift of *life* in a number of ways. Collective worship is creative and inspiring. It includes heartfelt hymn singing, live music and inspiring visual aids. Convocation is also an occasion for much fun and laughter, with at least one structured event arranged to foster collective enjoyment.

Convocation demonstrates the gift of *liberation*. All attending, including those recently ordained, candidates for ordination, those about to retire, guests from other churches and the partners of deacon's present, gain a sense of significance through being personally identified and welcomed. The many opportunities to share hopes and

---

[1] I suggest in articles not published in this book (Clark, May 2015, October 2015) that there are a number of initiatives that need to be considered by the Methodist Diaconal Order if it is to manifest the gifts of the kingdom community, especially that of learning, more fully.

fears about life and work with fellow deacons bring support and encouragement.

The gift of *love* is evident in the strong sense of caring and sharing which pervades Convocation. At the opening service each area group brings a candle to the front to affirm its solidarity with the Order. Deacons are encouraged to identify collectively with the concerns of the Order by being brought up to date with the latest news and issues relating to its life and work. There is lively engagement in many sessions and decisions are democratically taken. Common meals and meetings of year groups and friends strengthen a sense of solidarity. Arrangements are made to deliver greetings and gifts to elderly deacons unable to be present.

Convocation also furthers the gift of *learning*. There are plenary bible studies and lectures. A variety of workshops also play an important part here.

In sociological terms, Convocation is communally a very important 'symbolic event'. It is a gathering which exemplifies communal holiness or wholeness. Its impact continues for months afterwards. It is also an occasion which makes a deep and positive impression on guests and speakers who frequently express surprise at its vitality, warmth and dynamism.

There are numerous other features of the life of the Order, not as all-encompassing as Convocation, which manifest one or more of the gifts of the kingdom community. Some of these are briefly described below.

The gift of *life*

Methodist deacons generally experience a strong a sense of security, as far as is possible being assured of a job of work, a house, a stipend and a pension. They are also encouraged to find a rhythm to life (an aspect of the rule of life) which includes rest and recreation (*Methodist Diaconal Order ring binder*, 2002). Area groups, which meet at least three times a year, are occasions for creative worship, shared meals, lively discussion and a good deal of laughter.

The gift of *liberation*

The Methodist Diaconal Order has surmounted earlier gender divisions and is now open to men as well as women. The former, though a minority, are regarded as full members of the Order.

The Order values all its members. Student deacons and retired deacons are seen as integral to the life and work of the Order and involved as far as possible in its decision making. Retired deacons continue to be members of area groups, are included in the Daily Prayer List (see below), and are called upon to express their opinion on current issues and concerns facing the Order.

The Daily Prayer List (2015-2016) is a key publication reinforcing the value of every member of the Order. It emphasises that 'each counts and all matter' by ensuring that, on one day every four months, the personal, family or work concerns of each deacon are shared and prayed for by the whole Order. The manual includes a head-and-shoulders photo of nearly every deacon, an initiative which aids the memory and identification of those who are widely dispersed and may meet only at Convocation.

Through its web-site the Order enables its active, if not as easily its retired members to keep in touch by sharing personal news and views. Via this form of networking, deacons can make their concerns known, be supported and receive the reflections, guidance and encouragement of their fellow deacons.

Many deacons experience the gift of liberation through the work in which they are involved. This is one of the positive outcomes of the increasing diversity of ministries mentioned above. The matching of roles with a deacon's interests, skills and attributes, together with the care with which deacons are 'stationed', enables them to experience a good deal of personal fulfilment in their work. The fact that the Order is itinerant means that interest and thus commitment can be sustained over many years, or renewed if all has not gone well in a previous appointment.

The gift of *love*

The Methodist Diaconal Order is exceptional in the pastoral care it offers to its members. Its Pastoral Care Co-ordinator and Pastoral Care Committee have a wide brief ranging from matters to do with diaconal appointments to personal and family issues. The Co-ordinator comments: 'How we express our care for each other within the Order can be a measure of what we hope and desire for all God's creation' (*Convocation Handbook*, 2011, p. 58).

The pastoral care of deacons is also undertaken through the work of area groups which spend a good deal of time monitoring the well-being of their members. Pastoral visits to deacons living in the same region, cards and emails offering support or greetings on birthdays or similar events are legion. *The Daily Prayer List* referred to above ensures a personal and prayerful response to the longer term needs of colleagues.

Regular communication helps to engender a sense of solidarity. The web-site and the regular *Order Paper* carry a message from the Warden, news about members of the Order, *Twenty to Ten* prayer needs (see below) and a section on business matters.

The Order's 'Mother House', as *What is a Deacon?* calls it (7.8.1), and pastoral centre, whether in Ilkley or Birmingham, has always been, in sociological terms, 'a symbolic place' which gives a communal heart to a widely dispersed membership.[1] 'It provides the spiritual and physical focus for this dispersed religious community, and is regarded as a spiritual home', states *What is a Deacon?* (6.6). Until recently the Centre has been used not only for administration and business meetings but, with residential accommodation available, as a place of hospitality and informal encounter. At the centre, a *Twenty to Ten* time is set aside each morning to offer prayer for the Order. The Centre houses the Order's prayer candle and its prayer diary (*In the Navy...* 2011-2012, pp. 6-7). Prayer spaces have also been available to visitors.

The gift of *learning*

Though numbers are relatively small, every effort is made to ensure that student deacons can share their training with other student deacons.[2] Following ordination deacons undertake probationary studies. In-service training is more ad hoc and largely left to the initiative of the deacon concerned. Informal learning goes on through Convocation, area groups and retreats.

The Order arranges occasional consultations and conferences. For example, in 2011, a consultation with Church of England deacons was held at the diaconal centre (*Convocation Handbook*, 2011, pp. 87-103), the Order's Faith and Work Group set up a consultation there for

---

[1] The Birmingham Diaconal Centre has now been sold and the Order's headquarters moved to London.

[2] Diaconal pre-ordination training is now based at the Queen's Foundation in Birmingham.

deacons involved in chaplaincy, and a large conference, 'Making Connections: Exploring Good Practice in Diaconal Ministry' was organized in Durham by the Wesley Study Centre. Such occasions build on a long heritage of ecumenical and international involvement with deacons of other churches and important contributions that the Order has made over the years in conversations concerning the theology and practice of diaconal ministry.

Communal leadership

Since the Order re-opened, the Warden has become 'first among equals'. From 2008 to 2012 the then Warden pioneered the practice of working closely with a team of five.[1] Each team member carried responsibility for one aspect of the work of the Order: pastoral care, vocations, communication, or budgets and resources. 'This has been a very successful development and much appreciated by the members of the Order,' comments Jackie Fowler (2010, p. 146). The leadership team sought to relate closely to a number of diaconal committees whose members have been democratically elected by the Order. Area Group Co-ordinators also play an important part in leadership (*Convocation Handbook*, 2011, pp. 108-109).

The Warden of the Order, elected for a six year period, gives particular attention to the roles of animator (life), enabler (liberation) and intermediary (love). She travels widely to ensure that deacons are trained effectively, stationed appropriately and supported pastorally. She represents the Order to the Methodist Church, as well as the Methodist Church to the Order. In this capacity she becomes a significant 'symbolic figure' with responsibility for enhancing diaconal collegiality amongst a widely scattered constituency.

Ordination and a rule of life

Deacons make a serious commitment to the Methodist Diaconal Order. Following a communally empowering ordination retreat, deacons are ordained at a service separate from that of presbyters (*What is a Deacon?* 5.1). They are presented with the badge of the Order, a Celtic cross, a symbol which underlines the fact that the life and work of the Order are shaped more by the communal forms and

---

[1] Largely because of financial constraints, the leadership team has now reverted to that of a Warden and Deputy Warden

practices of the Celtic Church than the institutionalised structures of the Christendom model of church (Finney, 1996, pp. 50-74).

Members of the Methodist Diaconal Order also 'make a public, lifelong commitment, renewed annually at Convocation, to following a rule of life and living as members of a religious community' (*What is a Deacon?* 6.2 and pp. 27-28). The rule of life embraces a personal devotional discipline, which includes daily prayer for members of the Order, and a readiness to use the services of a spiritual director. The rule involves commitment to engage in the communal gatherings of the Order, such as attendance at Convocation and area groups. However, the Order insists that its 'rule does not bind (deacons) in a way that stifles and disables, but is a means by which they might be liberated to find a sense of wholeness in the rhythm of life'. It is significant that 'there is no element of compulsion in it, but the hope that... it will become a framework for the enrichment of their own life, the life of the Order and the people of God amongst whom they live' (*In the Navy...* 2011-2012, p. 2).

A communal culture

Because the Methodist Diaconal Order gives practical expression to the gifts of the kingdom community, deacons are socialised into the culture of that community in a way similar to that in which the young person is socialised into the culture of the family. Deacons may not always be aware of the ways in which they are making the theology of the kingdom community their own, but the quality of their life as a religious order speaks for itself, not least to those outside the order.

13. *The Methodist Diaconal Order as an order of mission*

Preamble

The diaconal church is a vision of the church to come but not yet here. There are still significant developments which will have to occur if Methodism is to become more fully a diaconal church. As we noted at the end of Chapter 11, pre-eminent amongst these is the reclaiming of its historic calling to be a movement witnessing to the gospel of communal holiness.

This chapter[1] argues that it is through the Methodist Diaconal Order becoming an order of mission, nurtured by its ongoing life as a religious order, that Methodism has a unique opportunity to reclaim its historic calling. In this chapter we reflect on what needs to be done if the Methodist Church and the Methodist Diaconal Order together seize the day. Finally, we consider the implications for other denominations of such a radical development.

Methodism's response to the communal imperative

In Part 1 of this book, we observed that we live in a world needing to grow together as a community of communities. We also observed that in the West we have inherited a church still unable to break free from the mould of Christendom and thus gravely limited in its ability to offer a gospel relevant to the needs of our time. A key question facing every denomination, therefore, is how to break that mould and bring the diaconal church into being.

The Methodist Church, like every church, is wrestling with such challenges. As a church in which the social gospel has always been to the fore, it remains deeply committed to transforming a fragmented world into a global community of communities. It is also committed to renewing its own life in a way that can free it to engage in its historic mission more effectively. Yet its institutionalization hampers its attempts to stem its decline in influence and resources. In 2008, Martyn Atkins, then General Secretary of the Methodist Church,

---

[1] This chapter has not appeared in print before.

described Methodism's decreasing membership over recent decades as 'catastrophic'. A couple of years before (2006), David Hempton, a very perceptive American writer about Methodist history talked of 'the dying embers of British Methodism'.

Nevertheless, over recent years the Methodist Church has been as adventurous as any in pursuing 'fresh expressions' of church. Other initiatives have ranged from reorganization, such as the creation of larger circuits, to conversations with the Church of England about how to draw closer together. Even so, these and other endeavours have as yet indicated no clear way forward. It is our belief that if Methodism is to make a creative response to the communal imperative and find a new identity in the process, three fundamental changes will be required.

A gospel of communal holiness

First and foremost, Methodism needs to reclaim the gospel (good news) of *communal holiness*. In Chapter 11 we defined the latter as 'a divine gift which, embodying the kingdom community's gifts of life, liberation, love and learning, transforms humankind into whole persons, whole families, whole institutions, whole cities, whole societies and one world, and reveals the integrity of creation'. For the Methodist Church to find a purpose and identity which resonate with its past and provide it with a call to mission fully aligned with the needs of this day and age, we believe that the gospel of communal holiness needs to be re-affirmed, made accessible to its people and become the driving force for the deployment of its resources.

Re-creating Methodism as a movement - a diaconal order of mission

Secondly, and integral to its reclaiming the gospel of communal holiness, Methodism needs to prioritize the transformation of a major part of its life and work into the form of a *movement*.

As we observed in Chapter 11, Methodism cannot ignore the fact that over the years it has become increasingly institutionalized. However, in Methodism's case we have argued it has been able to retain a number of important characteristics of the diaconal church. Because of this the Methodist Church as an institution is still well placed to provide a springboard for the reinvention of a significant part of its life and work as a movement committed to making the gospel of communal holiness a reality in society and world.

The trigger for that radical but vital transformation could be the designation of the Methodism Diaconal Order an order of mission. What such a transformation would mean in practice is explored below. However, it is clear that it will call for a fundamental re-appraisal of some of the answers given to the question posed in the report *What is a Deacon?* (2004).

New forms of church leadership

In the third place, and in the context of the above changes, Methodism needs to review the division of labour currently shaping the responsibilities of its ordained *leadership*. As well as the Methodist Diaconal Order becoming an order of mission, presbyteral ministry should be designated an order of continuity. The latter should have the explicit task of transforming and sustaining Methodism as an institution.

At the same time both deacons and presbyters should be inspired and guided by the call to make manifest the gospel of communal holiness, and its offer of the gifts of life, liberation, love and learning, within church and world. This would necessitate not only the re-appraisal of *What is a Deacon?* but also an in-depth review of the *What is a Presbyter?* (2002).

Strengths of the Methodist Diaconal Order as an order of ministry

The transformation of the Methodist Diaconal Order into an order of mission would need to affirm and utilize its current strengths as an order of ministry. The latter could become assets not liabilities in such a transition.

Most deacons enter the Methodist Diaconal Order in mid-life and have children that are into their 'teen years or older. This means that many bring a good deal of practical experience of the working world and of family life to bear on their diaconal responsibilities. This stands them in good stead in the variety of appointments which they are likely to undertake during their time as active deacons. Most have some experience of the ethos and work of the Methodist Church, a small but increasing number being married to presbyters.

As an order of ministry, deacons already seek to model the good news of the kingdom community's gifts of life, liberation, love and learning within a divided and fragmented world. In particular, the Order's 'servant ministry reflects the Servant Christ whose mission involved crossing boundaries, making connections between alienated or fragmented groups, including those beyond the margins, overturning unjust structures, standing in solidarity with the vulnerable and helping them discover their voice,' states *What is a Deacon?* (5.7). It is notably through their ministries 'on the margins' (*Voice from the margins*, 2005) that deacons make manifest the gifts of the kingdom community to wider society. *What is a Deacon?* comments that 'it is the self-emptying, self-offering love of Christ that reaches beyond established boundaries, cares for the most vulnerable, seeks healing, justice, liberation and restoration, and so proclaims the Good News of God's Kingdom, which is the foundation of, and template for, diaconal ministry' (4.4).

Taking a more radical stance, the Order believes it is called 'to unsettle and challenge the church' (*Convocation Handbook*, 2011, p. 88). 'Deacons... represent to the Church its calling as servant (of the kingdom community) in the world' states *What is a Deacon?* (4.1). The Order's task is to remind 'the whole Methodist Church of its calling to be an open, welcoming community that reaches out beyond itself' (6.7.2). It is not surprising, therefore, that Helen Cameron describes the Methodist Diaconal Order as 'yeast in the dough of Methodism' (*Who do you say we are?* 2010-2011, p. 15).

Members of the Methodist Diaconal Order have a strong commitment to ecumenism. They frequently engage in partnerships with those of other denominations or none, both within and beyond the church. Their experience of addressing some formidable challenges within society gives them a clear awareness of the need for Christians to act as one people so that they can become an example for all those seeking to build one world.

Finally, a considerable strength of the Methodist Diaconal Order as an order of ministry is the networking that goes on between deacons through social media as well as more structured means of communication such as area groups and Convocation. Over time deacons come to know each other well and frequently share their experiences and insights.

From an order of ministry to an order of mission - theology and leadership

The strengths of the Methodist Diaconal Order as an order of ministry are considerable assets and should be integrated into its development as an order of mission. However, there are new and essential features of being an order of mission (see *Diagram 6*, Chapter 10) which need to be introduced if such a transition is to be definitive. The Methodist Church and Methodist Diaconal Order would need to share responsibility for implementing these changes.

The need for a communal theology and communal spirituality of mission

The Methodist Diaconal Order is at present not equipped with a theology of diaconal ministry sufficiently distinctive to enable it to develop much further as an order of mission. It is our conviction that the theology of the kingdom community, or of communal holiness (Chapter 11), described in this book could fill this gap and offer an important foundation for the life and work of the Methodist Diaconal Order as an order of mission. For any significant developments to take place the Methodist Church and the Methodist Diaconal Order will need to work together to bring such a communal theology to the fore and to integrate it into the life and work of the Connexion. The communal spirituality set out in Chapter 3 would further enable the Order to be enriched and empowered as an order of mission.

Equality of leadership

The Methodist Church and Methodist Diaconal Order require a new approach to ordination if the mould of Christendom is to be broken and Methodism re-equipped for mission in this day and age. Both presbyters and deacons need to be recognized as servant leaders. Here the emphasis is not only on servanthood but on leadership. A renewed diaconate should be playing a lead role in developing the mission of Methodism and in equipping lay people for their mission in daily life. To accomplish this task, deacons need to be well trained and their job description explicitly to cover this leadership role.

It should no longer be assumed, as is still common, that deacons are appointed as 'assistants' to presbyters. The current inequality of leadership status is in part due to the fact that the deacon, without special dispensation, is unable to preside at holy communion. It is this restriction that, in large part, produces the anomaly of a deacon never being able to stand for election as President of the Methodist Conference.

We have already argued (Chapter 10) that to remove this hierarchical model of leadership and to enable deacons to be recognized as the missional leaders of Methodism, they should be ordained to a ministry of word and sacrament, even if normatively it is the presbyter who presides at holy communion. We have also contended that the sacrament of the washing of feet should come much more to fore in the church's worship and be regarded as the deacons' particular responsibility.

From an order of ministry to an order of mission - mission agendas[1]

What is a Deacon?, the most recent attempt by the Methodist Conference to define diaconal ministry, is very ambiguous. One section of that report (para. 5) states very clearly that 'the *core* emphasis'[2] of diaconal ministry is 'witness through service' (para. 5). However, elsewhere (para 5.4) the report states that 'the *primary* purpose'[3] of diaconal ministry is 'to help all Christians discover, develop and express their own servant ministry. Deacons therefore engage in educational and nurturing activities to enable people to see God's activity in daily life and world, and encourage them in expressing their faith in relevant ways'.

This confusion of priorities is no minor issue. A ministry of service and an educational and enabling ministry are very different forms of ministry. Whichever is given precedence will not only have an impact on how deacons interpret their role and use their time and energy but, just as important, on the expectations of those who employ them.

In practice, it is the multiplicity of ministries of service which dominates the scene. This leaves little time or space for deacons to equip the laity for their hugely challenging ministries in secular life. Furthermore, the assumption that diaconal ministry is pre-eminently 'witness through service', a calling which should be the vocation of

---

[1] Practical examples of these mission agendas are referenced in Appendix 2.
[2] Our italics
[3] Ibid

every Christian, makes it hard to distinguish how the role of deacon, as currently played out within Methodism, is any different from that of lay people and lay workers.

On the other hand, if the first responsibility of a renewed diaconate as an order of mission is to equip the laity to become kingdom community builders in society and world, it is the deacon's educational and enabling role which must come to the fore. In principle at least, it would appear that the Methodist Diaconal Order itself accepts this understanding of diaconal ministry. Its mission statement reads: '(The Methodist Diaconal Order is) a mission focused, pioneering religious community committed to *enabling* outreach, evangelism and service in God's world.' Unfortunately, however, the verb 'enabling' is all too often ignored. Thus many deacons assume that diaconal ministry is about they themselves doing the serving and, only when there is time to spare, their taking a lead role in facilitating other servant ministries.

Sue Jackson, a former Warden of the Order, acknowledged the challenge to current assumptions that the emergence of the Methodist Diaconal Order as an enabling order of mission poses. She writes (2008, p. 162):

> I believe we are dealing with the need for a Copernican shift in people's understanding of diaconal leadership. All of us have to move from focusing on deacons as the prime agents of diaconal ministry to lay people as the crucial servants, assisted by deacons. This is as much a matter of attitudinal change in deacons themselves as in the church generally.

To rein back the Methodist diaconate from its multitude of pro-active ministries of service will be a long haul. Yet if the Methodist Diaconal Order is to take the lead in helping Methodism to reclaim its heritage as a communal holiness movement, an educational and enabling ministry must move to the top of the agenda.

Nevertheless, whilst insisting on the educational and enabling role of deacons within an order of mission as primary, we acknowledge that there will be some times and places where other roles and skills will be required. Because the church is now weak or no longer represented in many spheres of the public realm, the deacon will sometimes be required to act as a kingdom community builder in a more pro-active and direct way. In such situations it is likely that the servant leadership roles of visionary, animator (catalyst) or intermediary will come to the fore and need to take on a pioneering quality.

Responsibilities of deacons as an order of mission

In what follows, we distinguish a number of areas of responsibility in which deacons as an order of mission will be involved. Examples of what these responsibilities might mean in practice are given in Appendix 2.

1. Working within or alongside the local church

(a) Working within the local church to equip the laity for mission in daily life - the deacon as educator and enabler

As an order of mission, deacons are called to work within the local church to equip its members for mission in daily life, notably within the world of work.[1] This means equipping the laity, through worship, pastoral care and especially education, for building kingdom communities. It will also involve deacons in finding ways in which the congregation as a whole can be well informed about, encourage and support the diverse ministries of their members undertaken beyond the local church.

(b) Engaging the local church in mission through the life and work of its area - the deacon as visionary, animator and intermediary (pioneer)

As an order of mission, deacons are called to assist the local church to engage in kingdom community building initiatives with organizations and groups in the business, statutory and voluntary sectors, Christian or otherwise, situated in the area in which the church is located. Here deacons may be engaged in a pioneering role.

2. Working beyond the local church and its area

(a) Working beyond the local church to equip the dispersed church for mission in daily life - the deacon as educator and enabler

As an order of mission, deacons are called to work alongside lay people engaged in their ministries in daily life. This form of intervention requires the deacon to be knowledgeable about and in touch with the daily responsibilities of members of the dispersed

---

[1] For a comprehensive review of what this role might entail in relation to mission in the world of work see Clark (2014) *The Kingdom at Work Project.*

church. It may well entail the deacon meeting and mentoring lay people, as individuals or in groups, within or near their places of work. Some deacons will undertake this mission agenda in the role of chaplain.

(b) Working alongside Christian organizations and agencies - the deacon as intermediary, enabler and educator

As an order of mission, deacons are called to assist Christian organizations and agencies, involved in activities such as youth and community work, education, residential care, nursing and various forms of voluntary work, in initiating and developing kingdom community building initiatives and in sharing their experiences, expertise and resources in the process.

3. Working beyond the dispersed church

Working alongside secular institutions and agencies to build communities which manifest kingdom values - the deacon as visionary, animator and intermediary (pioneer)

As an order of mission, deacons are called to engage in kingdom community building where the church is absent or very sparsely represented. This is a situation in which deacons will, initially at least, have to engage in intervention on their own. In this undertaking, deacons will have special need of the active support of the Order as a supportive religious community. Again such situations will have a pioneering emphasis.

Team ministries

Even though they will form distinctive orders, deacons and presbyters will need to work as closely as possible with each other. Both are responsible for the worship life, education and pastoral support of the laity, one representing an order of continuity and the other an order of mission. Furthermore no one person has the range of skills to fulfil all the responsibilities outlined above. Thus team ministries, with deacons, presbyters and lay people as members, will remain the norm within the diaconal church. [1]

---

[1] It was Methodism which some decades ago pioneered this form of ministry. See Mason (et al) (1967) *News from Notting Hill: The Formation of a Group Ministry*.

Support and training for an order of mission

The Methodist Diaconal Order as a 'mission focused' religious order

One of the unique assets of the Methodist Diaconal Order is that, as well as being an order of ministry, it is a religious order. The demands on the Methodist Diaconal Order as an order of mission would be impossible to meet if it were not for the fact that its life as a religious order was able to inform, empower and sustain deacons in their mission agendas. Chapter 12 has already explored these communal assets. They provide a rich resource for deacons as an order of mission.

Training

All that has been said above will necessitate a thorough re-appraisal of diaconal training. Not only does the Methodist deacon need to be introduced to the traditional ordination curriculum but also to the theology and spirituality underpinning the gifts of the kingdom community. The deacon also requires specialist skills, especially those of educator, enabler, and intermediary.

Currently diaconal training in the Methodist Church is so closely aligned with presbyteral training that there is neither the time nor the scope to address the distinctive function of the diaconate. If the Methodist Diaconal Order is to lead the way as an order of mission then it is essential that the training of deacons be given as much care and attention as that of presbyters. This means tutors being equipped to offer a distinctive and full diaconal curriculum, including the skills training required.[1] It will mean that those offering for the Order are aware of what will be required of them, academically as well as practically.

It will also mean that training is regarded as a life-long undertaking and that ongoing diaconal studies receive active encouragement and adequate resources. Because the Methodist Diaconal Order as a religious order bears many of the hall-marks of a learning community it has itself a great deal to add to more formal

---

[1] See the Appendix 1 for an example of a revised diaconal curriculum.

diaconal training. However, I have suggested elsewhere ways in which this aspect of the Order's life might be further enhanced.[1]

In addition to a rigorous review into the training of deacons, the Methodist Church should commission and fund research into the best way of developing the work of the Methodist Diaconal Order as an order of mission.

Issues of transition

In recent times, publications advocating new ways forward for Methodism have come thick and fast, many of which are already gathering dust on the shelves.[2] However, it is our conviction that the way forward suggested in this book is congruent with the original calling and character of Methodism. If that is the case what issues need to be tackled to facilitate the Methodist Diaconal Order's transformation into an order of mission?

Moving from a presbyteral to diaconal form of ministry

The Methodist Church has made it relatively easy for deacons to become presbyters and many have done so. Methodism now needs to make the transition from presbyter to deacon just as feasible and commonplace. The equalization of stipends and housing provision has made this move economically feasible. However, as noted above, the ruling that Methodist deacons cannot preside at holy communion without a special dispensation remains more typical of a Christendom model of church, with its hierarchal order of ministry, than a diaconal model of church. This anomaly needs to be addressed with some urgency if the Methodist Church is to become a movement to

---

[1] Clark (October, 2105) *The Methodist Diaconal Order as a Learning Community* (available from david@clark58.eclipse.co.uk).

[2] Epitomized by the publication, in 1947, of W.E. Sangster's *Methodism – Her Unfinished Task*. In more recent years, other publications have sought to identify the hall-marks of Methodism and their potential contribution to its renewal: see Pickford, D. (1985); Craske, J. and Marsh, C. (1999); Carter, D. (2002); Marsh, C., Beck, B., Shier-Jones, A. (2005); Curran, L. and Shier-Jones, A. (2009); Clark, D (2010). A number of Methodist Conference reports have also made their contribution to this debate, notably *Called to Love and Praise: A Methodist Conference Statement on the Church* (1999); *Leadership in the Methodist Church* (2002); *The Nature of Oversight* (2005) and the *What is a ...?* series of reports (2002–2006).

communicate the gospel of communal holiness and its diaconate an order of mission to enable Methodism to fulfil that calling.

Expanding the Methodist Diaconal Order

The Methodist Diaconal Order has recruited well since its re-opening in 1986 even if it remains a relatively small body within the Methodist Church. Unfortunately in recent years it seems that the Methodist Church has been more concerned with rationalizing its resources than with developing its diaconal order. The Methodist Diaconal Order has seen severe financial constraints placed upon it, the closure of its 'Mother House' in Birmingham and its headquarters moved to Methodist Church House in London. Such matters as selection and training have been increasingly integrated with that of presbyters. Some of these developments send out the message that Methodism has failed to grasp the potential of one of the few bodies within the Connexion that offers real promise for the redirection of its life and work.

Rather than slowly undermining the identity of the Methodist Diaconal Order and weakening its potential as a catalyst for renewal, we believe that Methodism should be going all out to designate and develop the Order as an order of mission. Where would recruits come from?

Our conviction is that all Methodists at present clearly engaged in facilitating the building of kingdom communities through the church dispersed in the world should be invited to become members of the Methodist Diaconal Order. This cohort of people would include presbyters, some of whom are at the moment in chaplaincy posts or in secular employment. Unfortunately a number of presbyters who, in private, express a genuine wish to become members of the Methodist Diaconal Order are held back by the fact that such a transition would mean them no longer being able to preside at the sacrament of holy communion.

The Methodist Church has in recent years introduced a diverse host of posts in an attempt to revive the mission of Methodism. These range from certain lay worker appointments, through those who are designated 'mission enablers', and others with a different title but a similar role, to a new cohort of 'learning and development officers'. Methodism has also started to train pioneer ministers, though these are often presbyters. All in such posts have a vocation for mission and are undoubtedly exercising an important ministry. Nevertheless, those trying to fulfil these often disparate and disconnected roles are scattered widely across the Connexion and cannot hope to possess the strong collective sense of purpose and communal bonding offered by a new order of mission, empowered by also being a religious order.

We believe that those currently in these posts, as well as those to be appointed in the future, should be integrated into this new order of mission. As part of that process, they should be asked to consider offering for the Methodist Diaconal Order, the core of this missionary order. Where this proves impossible, those in such posts should be invited to become members of a diaconal Third Order, one which would reflect features of Third Orders associated with the historic religious orders, such as the Franciscans. Those in a diaconal Third Order would be seen as an integral part of the Methodist Diaconal Order's life and work, but less formally involved than those who are full members.

This extremely important development would enable those in such posts to play a vital role in the development of a pioneering order of mission, give them a common missional purpose with the diaconate, provide them with the powerful communal support of a religious order and, in the process, give the Methodist Diaconal Order the human resources needed to help Methodism reclaim its calling as a communal holiness movement.

There are also many lay people within Methodism engaged in ministries which could further the life and work of a new order of mission. Those wishing to be involved should be encouraged to join a diaconal Third Order.

Men and women

At present the Methodist Diaconal Order, as the relatively recent successor of the all-female Wesley Deaconess Order, is largely made up of women. A better gender balance would enrich the life and work of the Order and better reflect the world in which a renewed diaconate as an order of mission would be working.

Funding

'Without a vision the people perish.' However, funding is always needed to make visions become a reality. Where might such funding come from when the contraction of Methodism is calling into question many attempts at renewal?

Those moving from existing posts into a diaconal order of mission would strengthen the Methodist Diaconal Order without much extra cost to the Connexion. Some large circuits now existing or coming into being have funds which could be used to employ a deacon as a member of an order of mission. A portion of the sale of many of Methodism's redundant churches could go to support such an order. There may well be Christian organizations working within society willing to fund a deacon as a mission enabler. Similarly there could be a number of trusts willing to fund a deacon to work at community building in relation to the development of secular (and religious) organizations. It is not beyond the bounds of imagination that the 'launch' of an order of mission within Methodism might well attract additional giving from the Methodist people. Finally, as described below, a partnership with the Church of England to establish an ecumenical order of mission should warrant some funding from that quarter.

The ecumenical imperative

Just as important as responding to the communal imperative is the need to respond to the ecumenical imperative. The two imperatives are in reality two sides of the same coin - the quest to bring into being one world and one church. Thus the development of the Methodist Diaconal Order as an order of mission needs at every step to take on board the potential of entering into partnership with those of other denominations, not least the diaconate in other churches, who are seeking in their own way to promote the gospel of communal holiness.

Nevertheless, Methodism's affinity with the Church of England, and its attempts over recent decades to initiate closer co-operation with the latter, mean that its first priority may well be to see how the emergence of the Methodist Diaconal Order as an order of mission and presbyters as an order of continuity might dove-tail with developments on the Anglican scene.

This initiative would necessitate approaching the conversations between Methodists and Anglicans from a perspective quite different from that which has so far led to the very limited impact of well-intentioned covenants. It would be an approach which sought to integrate continuity and mission in an imaginative yet realistic way within both churches. What is needed is for Methodists and Anglicans to grasp the nettle of resolving the wasteful duplication of buildings and human resources calling into question the future of both denominations. The ecumenical movement urgently needs to get real. All parties have to stop pretending that the current squandering of resources can continue ad infinitum. An ecumenical division of plant and labour is the only realistic way forward.

For historical and organizational reasons, it is the Church of England that must take the main responsibility for the continuity of a church rooted in community of place. The parish system, for all its weaknesses, still has a vital role in this context and Anglican priests (presbyters) are in pole position to take on the responsibilities of an order of continuity. Methodism's contribution to the sustainability of the local (or parish) church is to work with the Church of England in particular to sort out how the combined resources of both denominations, especially that of presbyteral leadership, can be better deployed.

However, the essential offering of Methodism to an ecumenical division of labour would be the development and expansion of its diaconate as an order of mission. Angela Shier-Jones (2009) argues that 'the model of the parish priest, ministering primarily to a single geographical bounded community of people who regularly attend "church" has increasingly been superimposed on the significantly different role of the Methodist circuit minister' (p. 47). She adds that in fulfilling that role historically, it was always deemed right and proper that ministers apportioned more time to 'pioneering' than to local church 'pastoring' (p. 47). It is the Methodist Diaconal Order, with its numbers supplemented by Anglicans playing a similar diaconal role, which could form the foundation of a new ecumenical order of mission.

An ecumenical division of resources along the lines indicated above should not be dismissed as ignoring the theological differences between the two denominations which have put paid to so much shared endeavor over the past half century. These doctrinal road blocks will have to be negotiated sooner or later - but later may well be too late for both churches. The mould of Christendom has to be broken. The immediate challenge is to begin creating mini-models of an order of mission in practice based on an ecumenical deployment of human resources, on however limited a scale, somehow and somewhere in the country. This is most likely to happen where ecumenical collaboration is already ahead of its time.

Appendix 1

Learning outcomes

These learning outcomes for the formation and training of Methodist deacons were prepared at the instigation of the Methodist Diaconal Candidates and Probationers Oversight Committee (DCPOC). The full document was published in November 2008. The recommendations were the result of a long period of discussion and debate which had led to the drafting and re-drafting of the document until it reached its present form. The draft was circulated to nine Methodist institutions involved in the training of deacons at that time. Their comments were taken into account when drawing up the final version. However due to major administrative changes in the life of the Order, further discussion and development of the document was shelved.[1]

The extract below is a small section of the full document. The latter included a longer form of training outcomes, with key academic sources noted, and three other sections entitled 'The ministry of the deacon in today's world' and 'The implementation of the new learning outcomes' and a bibliography. The document is now somewhat dated as no key articles or papers published after 2008 are mentioned, there is currently only one Methodist institution training deacons and the arrangements for probationer or post-ordination diaconal training have changed.

The extract is reproduced here because the training outcomes suggested for Methodist deacons reflect in many ways the theology and ecclesiology contained in this book

-----

[1] A digital version of the full document is available from the David Clark at david@clark58.eclipse.co.uk

Short form of the learning outcomes

Principal learning outcome and primary diaconal calling

The understanding, skills and commitment to equip the people of God in the world to build communities that manifest the communal nature of Trinity and kingdom

Associated learning outcomes

1. Understanding

World focused learning outcomes

1.1 An understanding of the power of *community* and its primacy for the well-being and sustainability of human civilisation

1.2 An understanding of *Trinity* and *kingdom* as the supreme manifestations of community

1.3 An understanding of *mission* as the building of communities that manifest the communal nature of Trinity and kingdom

1.4 An understanding of the importance of *dialogue* as a means of mission

1.5 An understanding of the foundations of *Christian ethics*

Church focused learning outcomes

1.6 An understanding of *the church as servant* of the kingdom

1.7 An understanding of *the church as a learning community*

1.8 An understanding of *the people of God* as *the church dispersed* in the world

1.9 An understanding of the deacon as *servant leader*

1.10 An understanding of *the Methodist Diaconal Order as a model* of community and servant ministry for church and world

2. Skills

The role of community enabler and educator

Core skills

2.1 Demonstrate *enabling* skills

2.2 Demonstrate *educational* skills

Complementary skills

2.3 Demonstrate skills of *relationship building*

2.4 Demonstrate skills of *communication*

2.5 Demonstrate the skills of a *change agent*

2.6 Demonstrate the skills of an *intermediary*
2.7 Demonstrate the skills of a *worship leader*
2.8 Demonstrate skills of *collaboration and team building*
2.9 Demonstrate an ability to develop a personal *spirituality*
2.10 Demonstrate the skills of *self-management*

Optional special skills associated with the core skills
Mentoring
Counselling
Group work
Neighbourhood work
Youth work
Management and organisation

3. Positioning

['Positioning' means that deacons have understood and committed themselves to their ministry within the contexts identified below.]

Essential positioning

3.1 Show that they have positioned themselves as members of an order of ministry within the Methodist Church
3.2 Show that they have positioned themselves as representatives of the Methodist Church
3.3 Show that they have positioned themselves as deacons in relation to presbyters and lay people
3.4 Show that they have positioned themselves as members of the Methodist Diaconal Order

Other important positioning

3.5 Show that they have positioned themselves as deacons within the context of the diaconal forms and practices of *other churches* worldwide
3.6 Show that they have positioned themselves in relation to *other faiths*
3.7 Show that they have positioned themselves as *professionals* within a secular society

4. Practice

['Practice' refers to the ability of deacons to put their ministry into practice and to reflect on that experience in a way that enables them to develop their ministry further.]

4.1 The ability to relate the outcomes of their learning (understanding, skills and positioning) to inform and develop their practice

4.2 The ability to reflect on their practice to inform and develop the outcomes of their learning (understanding, skills and positioning)

Appendix 2

Examples of mission agendas in practice

Appendix 2 documents some practical examples of the sort of mission agendas that deacons might be engaged with if the Methodist Diaconal Order were designated an order of mission. At the obvious risk of constructing the role of deacon in one's own image, I draw many of these examples from my own experience as an ordained minister in the Methodist Church. They are described very briefly for two reasons. First, to give the reader a full understanding of the particular mission agendas identified would make for a very long Appendix. Secondly, the agendas are already described in considerable detail elsewhere. What appears below, therefore, are simply pointers to a range of possible mission agendas which might be pursued by members of a diaconal order of mission. What matters most in all these cases is that, in whatever role the deacon operates, the guiding stance is that of servant leadership and the primary purpose is that of building kingdom communities within church and world.

I recognize that it would be no easy task for others to replicate many of the mission agendas described. Every intervention is shaped by the situation in which the deacon finds themselves and the particular interests and skills of the deacon concerned. Some deacons are specialists whilst others are generalists, some are more at home with a limited and more local brief, others enjoy working at a city or regional level. However, they remain examples of what has proved possible and worthwhile.

A personal perspective

From 1962 until 2005 I served as a Methodist presbyter. From 1962 until 1973 I was a circuit minister, first in Sheffield and then in inner London. In 1973, I received permission to become what in Methodism is referred to as 'a sector minister' (in the Church of England, called 'a minister in secular employment') and was appointed as a senior lecturer on the staff of Westhill College, Birmingham. The latter was a college of higher education within the Selly Oak Federation of colleges, its courses being validated by the University of Birmingham. Until I finished in 1995, my task was the training of youth and community workers, social workers and, later on, those working in the field of community education.

In part because men were not able to enter the Methodist Diaconal Order until after it re-opened in 1986, and in part because at the time I did not think that becoming a Methodist deacon would have been of any added-value to my ministry, I remained a presbyter. However, increasing contact with the Order after retirement, together with the personal encouragement of its then Warden, Sue Jackson, prompted me to seek (re)ordination as a deacon in 2005.

Throughout my ministry, in paid employment as well as in retirement, I have been involved in a range of projects concerned with furthering the mission of the church in today's world. All have been of an ecumenical nature. On reflection, I am convinced that all of them have been far more typical of what a diaconal order of mission should be about than of normative presbyteral practice. Hence many of the projects described below are what I regard as typical of those in which deacons as an order of mission would be involved even though when they were undertaken I was officially designated a presbyter.

Since entering the Order in 2005, I set up the Diaconal Faith and Work Group which for five years from 2006 tried to inform and support deacons seeking to further the mission of the church in the world of work. In 2009 the group published a series of papers on that theme and referenced below. Out of the group also sprang *The Kingdom at Work Project*, fully documented in the book of that title (Clark, 2014)

Diaconal mission agendas in practice[1]

1. Working within or alongside the local church

(a) *Working within the local church to equip the laity for mission in daily life - the deacon as educator and enabler*

As an order of mission, deacons are called to work within the local church to equip its members for mission in daily life, notably within the world of work.[2] This means equipping the laity, through worship,

---

[1] This list of diaconal mission agendas is the same as that set out earlier in this chapter.

[2] For a comprehensive review of what this role might entail in relation to mission in the world of work see Clark (2014) *The Kingdom at Work Project*.

pastoral care and especially education, for building kingdom communities. It will also involve deacons in finding ways in which the congregation as a whole can be well informed about, encourage and support the diverse ministries of their members undertaken beyond the local church.

The Bakewell Methodist Church@Work Project began in 2007 and has run until the present time. It involved me as the deacon on the spot working in partnership with the resident presbyter. To support lay people at work I held small group meetings to discuss how people's faith could be expressed through their work. In a number of worship services lay people were invited to speak about their faith and work and their concerns were included in the intercessions. People were asked to supply symbols of their work, paid or voluntary, to make up a collage in the church foyer. A booklet, reprinted at regular intervals, was produced informing the whole congregation in what work, paid or voluntary, church members were involved and providing prayers to support them in their work.

Key reference: Clark (2014) *The Kingdom at Work Project* (pp. 350-358).

The Methodist Diaconal Faith and Work Group has produced a number of worksheets, based on their own practice, describing initiatives deacons might take to further this mission agenda.

Methodist Diaconal Order (2009) *Worksheets* F2, F3, H and I1 - download from www.methodist.org.uk/businessworksheets

---

Comprehensive lists of a range of ways of supporting members of the congregation in their ministries at work are contained in a number of publications.

Key references: Clark (2005) *Breaking the Mould of Christendom* (pp. 284-289) and Clark (2014) *The Kingdom at Work Project* (pp. 339-344)

(b) Engaging the local church in mission through the life and work of its area - the deacon as visionary, animator and intermediary (pioneer)

As an order of mission, deacons are called to assist the local church to engage in kingdom community building initiatives with organizations and groups in the business, statutory and voluntary sectors, Christian or otherwise, situated in the area in which the church is located. Here deacons may be engaged in a pioneering role.

One example of this missional agenda comes from *The Bakewell@Work Project*. The initiatives to link the local church and the market town of Bakewell in Derbyshire included a 'harvest' celebration when the local businesses offered examples of their produce and services to decorate the church. A prayer booklet containing prayers for businesses and services in the town was published to be used in worship or privately. A display of the work of local schools entitled 'Learning for Life' was set up in the Methodist church foyer and teachers and young people were involved in a service of thanksgiving. For several years an A4 broadsheet produced three times a year jointly by the church and Bakewell traders was delivered by church distributors to all the businesses in the town. The contacts made often developed into pastoral opportunities.

Key reference: Clark (2015) *The Kingdom at Work Project* (pp. 353-358)

See also: Methodist Diaconal Order (2009) *Worksheets*. D and F5 - download from www.methodist.org.uk/businessworksheets

---

2. Working beyond the local church and its area

(a) *Working beyond the local church to equip the dispersed church for mission in daily life - the deacon as educator and enabler*

As an order of mission, deacons are called to work alongside lay people engaged in their ministries in daily life. This form of intervention requires the deacon to be knowledgeable about and in touch with the daily responsibilities of members of the dispersed church. It may well entail the deacon meeting and mentoring lay people, as individuals or in groups, within or near their places of work. Some deacons will undertake this mission agenda in the role of chaplain.

One example of this agenda was instigated in the Birmingham District of the Methodist Church. It was called *Methodists at Work* and drew lay people together from across the district on a regular basis to share their experiences and concerns about their workplace ministries. A Newsletter was produced and circulated to all members of the network. Each participant had a membership card which included the purpose of the network printed inside it, a set of commitments and a prayer.

Details from david@clark58.eclipse.co.uk

A number of independent Christian organizations and agencies, with whom deacons might be in a position to work, seek to promote workplace groups for Christians across a diversity of occupations. For example:

The London Institute for Contemporary Christianity - www.licc.org.uk/engaging-with-work
Christians at Work - www.christiansatwork.org.uk
Transform Work UK - www.transformworkuk.org

Some organizations draw Christians in management together to further their ministries at work. For example:

Christian Association of Business Executives (CABE) - *www.cabe-online.org*
London Institute for Contemporary Christianity (see above for web site)
Quaker and Business Group - www.qandb.org
Young Christian Workers - www.ycwimpact.com - draws together young Roman Catholics to reflect on their faith at work.

A number of Anglican dioceses also bring lay people at work together from time to time

---

(b) Working alongside Christian organizations and agencies - the deacon as intermediary, enabler and educator

As an order of mission, deacons are called to assist Christian organizations and agencies, involved in activities such as youth and community work, education, residential care, nursing and various forms of voluntary work, in initiating and developing kingdom community building initiatives and in sharing their experiences, expertise and resources in the process.

For nearly twenty years, from the early 1970s, I was involved in establishing a network of Christian lay communities, religious orders and other groups of all denominations across the UK. The groups and communities concerned were part of what was called *The Christian Community Movement*. They were involved in a diversity of initiatives including communal living, new forms of spirituality, stewardship of the environment, education, caring for those on the margins and promoting justice and peace. A national resource centre was established in 1980 in Birmingham. This published a magazine called *Community* and a *Directory* of groups and religious orders involved in the movement. The centre set up three national community congresses. The movement continued until the end of the 1990s

Key reference: Clark (2005) *Breaking the Mould of Christendom* (pp. 150-167).

See also: Clark (1977) *Basic Communities*. Clark (1984) *The Liberation of the Church*. Clark (1985) *On the Frontiers: From the beginning to 1985*. Clark (1987) *Yes to Life*.

From 1992 for nearly ten years, I directed *The Christians in Public Life Programme*. This involved establishing an ecumenical network of several hundred individuals and groups across the UK who were seeking to explore and develop the influence of Christian faith on public life. The network operated through a newsletter and a number of conferences Its main achievement was the publication of over 200 short position papers written by a wide diversity of Christians on various aspects of the engagement of the church with public life.

Key reference: Clark (2005) *Breaking the Mould of Christendom* (pp. 170-187).

See also: Clark (1997) *Changing World, Unchanging Church?*

From 1994 until 2001, I worked full-time setting up and overseeing Birmingham's *Human City Initiative*. This began as an ecumenical venture. However, from 1997, when the Initiative became *the Human*

City Institute, secular as well as religious groups and organizations were involved. The Institute's purpose was - 'To enable those who share a vision of Birmingham as a human city to work together with others to make that vision a reality'. The project published a *Bulletin* which went to over 3000 people across the city, held public 'hearings' and workshops, organized conferences, set up and networked 'human city sites' and engaged in research. It sponsored sister projects in Bradford and Swindon.

Key references: Clark (2005) *Breaking the Mould of Christendom* (pp. 188-209) and Clark (2012) *Building the Human City - the Origins and Future Potential of the Human City Institute (1995 - 2002) - download from: www.humancity.org.uk*

The Methodist Diaconal Order's Faith and Work Group initiated what is currently called The Kingdom at Work Project. This has become a national and ecumenical network of over 200 people involved in furthering mission in the workplace. The project has led to the publication of a comprehensive text on the subject (below) and to an occasional Bulletin which covers issues related to the church's engagement with the world of work.

Key reference: Clark (2014) *The Kingdom at Work Project*.

In the past, the Methodist Church has been instrumental in founding a number of social welfare organizations, such as Action for Children and MHA care homes, and, more recently, race relations projects such as Touchstone in Bradford, which have operated on a national or regional level. With larger and, increasingly, city-wide circuits coming into being, deacons would be in a pole position to support, link and work with these bodies to develop their mission potential more fully. A model of how a servant role might be developed working alongside these so-called Methodist 'communities of practice' is outlined in Clark (2010) *Reshaping the mission of Methodism* (pp. 210-220).

---

3. Working beyond the dispersed church

Working alongside secular institutions and agencies to build communities which manifest kingdom values - the deacon as visionary, animator and intermediary (pioneer)

As an order of mission, deacons are called to engage in kingdom community building where the church is absent or very sparsely represented. This is a situation in which deacons will, initially at least, have to engage in intervention on their own. In this undertaking, deacons will have special need of the active support of the Order as a supportive religious community. Again such situations will have a pioneering emphasis.

For some thirty years I worked as a sector minister and *lecturer in community and youth work, and later in community education*, at a college of higher education in Birmingham. The students I trained were all preparing to be involved in some aspect of community building in the secular world. Although their professional training did in no way allow proselytization, there were many legitimate opportunities to introduce kingdom community values into the courses for consideration and discussion.

Key reference: Clark (1996) *Transforming Education - The school as a learning community*.

See also: Clark (1992) 'Education for Community in the 1990s: A Christian Perspective' in Allen, G and Martin, I. (eds) *Education and Community – the Politics of Practice*

The Human City Institute referred to above could also come into this category.

Glossary

The communal dilemma	The problem human collectives face when needing to become increasingly open to one another without undermining or weakening their own sense of community or that of others
Communal holiness	A divine gift which, embodying the kingdom community's gifts of life, liberation, love and learning, transforms humankind into whole persons, whole families, whole institutions, whole cities, whole societies and one world, and reveals the integrity of creation.
Community educator	A person who educates others in the art of community building. A key aspect of servant leadership.
Connexion(al)	The term given by the Methodist Church referring to the entirety of its organizational life and work
Deacon, diaconal, diaconate	'Deacon' - an office or role within the church characterized by *e* the stance of servanthood 'Diaconal' - the features of an organization or institution which reflect the stance of servanthood 'Diaconate' - a collective consisting of deacons and/or deaconesses
Deacon - distinctive or permanent	The ministry of a deacon undertaken for life and not as a stage en route to being ordained a priest

Diaconal church	A church which seeks to be the servant of the kingdom community. Its mission is the building of communities transformed by (and which manifest) the kingdom community's gifts of life, liberation, love and learning.
Dispersed church	Church members when engaged in ministry and mission in the world
The 4Ls	The kingdom community's gifts of life, liberation, love and learning
The 4Ss	A sense of security, of significance, of solidarity and socialization – the key components of a sociological understanding of the concept of community
Gifts of the kingdom community –	The universal and inclusive gifts of life, liberation, love and learning
The gift of life	The gift of God as Creator
The gift of liberation	The gift of Christ as Liberator
The gift of love	The gift of the Holy Spirit as Unifier
The gift of learning	The gift of the Trinity as a learning community
Human collectives	A generic term to denote any form of human gathering from the small group to the large institution
Holy communion	A sacrament in other contexts referred to as the Eucharist or Mass
Kingdom community	The divine community which manifests the Trinity's universal and inclusive gifts of life, liberation, love and learning
Kingdom communities	Human collectives that manifest one or more of the kingdom

	community's gifts of, life, liberation, love and learning.
Local church	The church (people and plant) situated in a particular locality (such as a parish). Sometimes referred to as the gathered church if its members have to travel some distance to attend it.
Mission	The building of communities transformed by (and which manifest) the kingdom community's gifts of life, liberation, love and learning.
Pioneer minister	In the context of the 'servant leader', a ministry which combines the roles of 'visionary' and 'animator'.
Presbyter	A leadership role referred to in the early church but in a number of churches now superseded by that of 'priest'.
Servant leadership	A form of leadership which seeks to create human collectives that manifest the kingdom community's gifts of life, liberation, love and learning
Servant leadership - complementary roles	Visionary (envisions the 4Ls), strategist (earths the 4Ls, animator (advances the gift of life); enabler (advances the gift of liberation); intermediary (advances the gift of love); educator (advances the gift of learning)
Threefold ministry	The ministries of deacon, presbyter and bishop often taken as forming an hierarchical model of authority

ascending from the deacon through the presbyter (priest) to the bishop.

Word and sacrament

An aspect of ministry focused, most often in worship, on the exposition of the bible and the administration of the sacraments, especially that of holy communion

.

Bibliography

About our Father's Business (2010) Birmingham: St Peter's Saltley Trust and Diocese of Birmingham

Adair, J. (2000) *How to Find Your Vocation*. Norwich: The Canterbury Press

Adair, J. (2001) *The Leadership of Jesus and its Legacy Today*. Norwich: The Canterbury Press

Adair, J. and Nelson, J. (2004) *Creative Church Leadership*. Norwich: The Canterbury Press

Aitchison, R. (2003) *The Ministry of a Deacon*. London: Epworth Press

Atkinson, C. G. (2005) *The place of the deacon within the Methodist Church*. Paper presented to the Methodist Diaconal Order

Ambler, R. (2002) *Light to Live By - an exploration of Quaker spirituality*. London: Quaker Books

Andrew, R., 'An impoverished catholicity; theological considerations for a Methodist future' in Marsh, C., Beck, B., Shier-Jones, A. and Wareing, H. (eds) (2004) Unmasking Methodist Theology. London: Continuum

Argyris, C. and Schön, D. (1978) *Organizational Learning: A theory of action perspective*. Reading, MA: Addison-Wesley

Arias, M. (1984) *Announcing the Reign of God*. Philadelphia: Fortress

Atkins, M. (2007) *Resourcing Renewal: Shaping churches for the emerging future*. Peterborough: Inspire

Atkins, M. (2008) - in a video describing the Methodist Youth Participation Strategy

Atkins, M. (2010) *Discipleship... and the people called Methodists*. London: Methodist Publishing House

Bakewell@Work Prayer Booklet (2009). Bakewell: Bakewell Association of Christians

Bakhtin, M. M. (1984) *Problems of Dostoevsky's Poetics*, trans. by C. Emerson. Minneapolis: University of Minnesota Press

Baptism, Eucharist and Ministry (1982). Geneva: World Council of Churches, Faith and Order

Barkway, L. in *An Anthology of the Love of God - from the writings of Evelyn Underhill* (1953) London: Mowbray

Bauman, Z. (2001) *Community*. Cambridge: Polity.

Beck, U. (translated by Ritter, M.) (1992) *The Risk Society*. London: Sage

Berger, P. L. (1980) *The Heretical Imperative*. New York: Anchor Press/Doubleday

Berger, L. P., Berger, B. and Kellner, H. (1973) *The Homeless Mind*. Harmondsworth: Penguin

Berger, L. P. and Luckmann, T. (1984) *The Social Construction of Reality*. Harmondsworth: Penguin

Bethge, E. (1979) *Bonhoeffer*, London: Collins

Bevans, S. B. (1992) *Models of Contextual Theology*, Maryknoll, NY: Orbis Books

Bloom, A. (1988) *The Closing of the American Mind*. Harmondsworth: Penguin.

Boswell, J. (1990) *Community and the Economy: the Theory of Public Co-operation*. London: Routledge

Bradley, I. (1993) *The Celtic Way*. London: Darton, Longman and Todd

Borgegard, G., Fanuelsen, O. and Hall, C. (eds.) (1999) *The Ministry of the Deacon, 1. Anglican-Lutheran Perspectives*. Uppsala: Nordic Ecumenical Council.

Borgegard, G., Fanuelsen, O. and Hall, C. (eds.) (2000) *The Ministry of the Deacon, 2. Ecclesiological Explorations*. Uppsala: Nordic Ecumenical Council

Bosch, D. (1991) *Transforming Mission*. Maryknoll, NY: Orbis

Brodrick, J. (1940) *The Origin of the Jesuits*. London: Longmans

Brown, R. (2005) *The Ministry of the Deacon*. Norwich: Canterbury Press

Cadbury, D. (2010) *Chocolate Wars*. London: HarperPress

Called to Love and Praise: A Methodist Conference Statement on the Church (1999) Peterborough: Methodist Publishing House

Carter, D. (2002) *Love Bade Me Welcome. A British Methodist perspective on the Church*. London: Epworth Press

Chaplaincy (2004) Birmingham: Methodist Diaconal Order

Christians in Public Life Programme (CIPL) (various dates). Birmingham: Westhill College (a selection of these papers are published in Clark, D. (1997) *Changing World, Unchanging Church?* see below)

Clark, D. (August, 1973) 'The Concept of Community – a Re-examination' in *The Sociological Review* 3 (21) Keele: University of Keele

Clark, D. (1977) *Basic Communities*. London: SPCK

Clark, D. (1984) *The Liberation of the Church*. Westhill College, Birmingham: NACCCAN

Clark, D. (1985) *On the Frontiers: From the beginning to 1985*. Weshill College, Birmingham: NACCCAN

Clark, D. (1987) *Yes to Life*. London: Collins

Clark, D. (1988) *What Future for Methodism?* Birmingham: Harborne Group

Clark, D. (1993) *A Survey of Christians at Work*. Westhill College, Birmingham: CIPL

Clark, D. (1996) *Schools as Learning Communities*. London: Cassell

Clark, D. (1997) *Changing World, Unchanging Church?* London: Mowbray.

Clark, D. (1999) 'The Human City' in Burgess, S. J. (ed) *Coming of Age: Challenges and Opportunities in the 21st Century*. Boston Spa: Outset Services.

Clark, D. (2004) 'Mission in a Society without God' in *Crucible*. April – July 2004 Lowestoft: Tyndale Press

Clark, D. (2005; second printing 2014) *Breaking the Mould of Christendom: Kingdom community, diaconal church and the liberation of the laity*. Peterborough: Upfront Publishing

Clark, D. (ed) (2008a) *The Diaconal Church - beyond the mould of Christendom*. Peterborough: Epworth Press

Clark, D. (2008b) *The Lord's Prayer* (unpublished)

Clark, D. (2010) *Reshaping the mission of Methodism - a diaconal church approach*. Oldham: Church in the Market Place (pp. 167-191)

Clark, D. (2012) *Building the Human City - the Origins and Future Potential of the Human City Institute (1995 - 2002)*. Birmingham: Human City Institute (available from HCI, 239 Holliday Street, Birmingham B1 1SJ or *download from www.humancity.org.uk*)

Clark, D. (2013) 'The hallmark of the Methodist Diaconal Order - its life as a religious order - and some implications the future of Methodism' in *Theology and Ministry - An Online Journal*. (Vol. 2)

University of Durham: St John's College - www.durham.ac.uk/theologyandministry

Clark, D. (2014) *The Kingdom at Work Project - a communal approach to mission in the workplace*. Peterborough: Upfront Publishing

Clark, D. (May, 2015) *Convocation 2015 - reflections of a 'newcomer'* - available on the Methodist Diaconal Order's web site (Order Paper for October 2015) - www.methodistdiaconalorder.org.uk

Clark, D. (October, 2015) *The Methodist Diaconal Order as a learning community*. (unpublished paper - david@clark58.eclipse.co.uk)

Clutterbuck, R. 'Theology as Interaction: Ecumenism and the World Church' in Marsh, C., Beck, B., Shier-Jones, A. and Wareing, H. (eds) (2004) *Unmasking Methodist Theology*. London: Continuum

Collins, J. N. (1990) *Diakonia: Re-interpreting the Ancient Sources*. Oxford: Oxford University Press

Collins, J. N. (1992) *Are All Christian Ministers?* Newtown, Australia: E. J. Dwyer

Collins, J. N. (2002) *Deacons and the Church*. Leominster: Gracewing

Collins, J.N. (2014) *Diakonia Studies: Critical issues in ministry*. Oxford: Oxford University Press

Conference Statement on Ordination (1974)

Convocation Handbook (May, 2011) Birmingham: The Methodist Diaconal Order

Crain, M. A. and Seymour, J. L. (2001) *A Deacon's Heart*. Nashville: Abingdon Press

Craske, J. and Marsh, C. (1999) *Methodism and the Future*. London: Cassell

Craske, J. 'The threads with which we weave: Towards a holy church' in Craske, J. And Marsh, C. (eds) (1999a) *Methodism and the Future*. London: Cassell

Croft, S. (1999) *Ministry in Three Dimensions*. London: Darton, Longman and Todd

Cunningham, D. S. (1998) *These Three Are One: The Practice of Trinitarian* Theology Oxford: Blackwell

Curran, L. and Shier-Jones, A. (2009) *Methodist Present Potential*. Peterborough: Epworth

Curran, L. 'A Shared Faith' (2009a) in Curran, L. and Shier-Jones, A. *Methodist Present Potential*. Peterborough: Epworth

Daily Prayer List (2011-2012). Birmingham: The Methodist Diaconal Order

Dare to be a deacon (2009-2010) London: Methodist Publishing

Davey, A. (2001) *Urban Christianity and Global Order*. London: SPCK

Davie, G. (2002) *Europe: The Exceptional Case*. London: Darton, Longman and Todd.

Davis, C. (1994) *Religion and the Making of Society*. Cambridge: Cambridge University Press

Dawes. S. (2003) 'The Spirituality of "Scriptural Holiness"'. Scriptural Holiness Project: Methodist Church web site - www.mwthodist.org.uk

Deeks, D. (2006) *Mapping a Way Forward: Regrouping for Mission*

de Waal, E. (1996) *The Celtic Way of Prayer*. London: Hodder and Stoughton

de Waal, E. (ed) (2001 revised edition) *The Celtic Vision*. Liguori, Missouri: Liguori/Triumph

Diaconal Reflections: How we experience our diaconal calling in our diversity (1998) (a paper produced for DIAKONIA - see below)

Diaconal Students' and Probationers' Handbook (2010) Birmingham: Methodist Diaconal Order

The Diaconate as Ecumenical Opportunity (1996) Hanover Report of the Anglican-Lutheran International Commission. Anglican Communion Publications

DIAKONIA. The World Federation of Diaconal Associations and Communities (for legal purposes domiciled in the Netherlands) - www.diakonia-world.org

Diakonia – Challenge and Response (1996) The Netherlands: World Federation of Diaconal Associations and Communities

The Distinctive Diaconate (2003). Salisbury: Diocese of Salisbury

Dollard, K., Marrett-Crosby, A. and Wright, T. (2002) *Doing business with Benedict – the Rule of Saint Benedict and business management: a conversation*. London: Continuum

Drucker, P. F. (1993) *Post-Capitalist Society*. Oxford: Butterworth-Heinemann.

Dulles, A. (1976) *Models of the Church*. London: Gill and Macmillan

Durkheim, E. (translated by Spaulding, J.A. and Simpson, G.) (1951) *Suicide: A Study in Sociology*. New York: The Free Press

Ecclestone, A. (1975) *Yes to God*, London: Darton, Longman and Todd

Ecclestone, A. (compiled by Cotter, J.) (1999) *Firing the Clay – Articles and Addresses*. Sheffield: Cairns Publications

Echelin, P. E. (1971) *The Deacon in the Church: Past and Future*. New York: Alba House. *Epworth Review* 24.2

Elliott, C. (1985) *Praying the Kingdom*. London: Darton, Longman and Todd)

Finney, J. (1996) *Recovering the Past – Celtic and Roman Mission*. London: Darton, Longman and Todd

Fitzgerald, W. (1903) *The Roots of Methodism* (London: Epworth)

The Formation and Training of Deacons (November, 2008). Birmingham: The Methodist Diaconal Order. From david@clark58.eclipse.co.uk

Forster, D. 'A world faith' in Curran, L. and Shier-Jones, A. (eds) (2009) *Methodist Present Potential*. Peterborough: Epworth Press

For such a time as this. A renewed diaconate in the Church of England (2001).London: Church House Publishing

Fowler, J. 'The contribution of the Methodist Diaconal Order to the ministry and mission of the future church' in Clark, D. (ed) (2010) *Reshaping the mission of Methodism*. Oldham: Church in the Market Place

Fox, M. (1994) *The Reinvention of Work*. San Francisco: Harper: San Francisco

Fox, R. (2011) *Coaching Church Leaders –An Introduction to Coaching*. MODEM Occasional Paper No. 4 - www.modem-uk.org

Fresh Expressions of the Methodist Diaconal Order (2006) London: Methodist Church Communication Office

From the Diakonia of Christ to the Diakonia of the Apostles (2003). International Theological Commission. London: Catholic Truth Society

Galbraith, J. K. (1992) *The Culture of Contentment*. Harmondsworth: Penguin

Gibbs, M. and Morton, T. R. (1964) *God's Frozen People*. London: Fontana/Collins

Gibbs, M. and Morton, T. R. (1971) *God's Lively People*. London: Fontana/Collins

Gilbert, A. D. (1976) *Religion and Society in Industrial England*. London: Longman

Gilbert, A. D. (1980) *The Making of Post-Christian Britain*, London: Longman

Glasner, P. E. (1977) *The Sociology of Secularisation*, London: Routledge and Kegan Paul

Glover, J. (1999) *Humanity*. London: Jonathan Cape

Gore, A. (2013) *The Future*. London: W. H. Allen

Graham, E. D. (2002) *Saved to Serve. The Story of the Wesley Deaconess Order. 1890-1978*. Peterborough: Methodist Publishing House

Grey. M. (1989) *Redeeming the Dream*. London: SPCK

Grey, M. (1993) *The Wisdom of Fools?* London: SPCK

Gunton, C. E. (1993) *The One, the Three and the Many*. Cambridge: Cambridge University Press

Hall, C. (ed) (1992) *The Deacon's Ministry*. Leominster: Gracewing

Handy, C. (1990) *The Age of Unreason*. London: Arrow Books

Havel, V. (20 September, 1990) *Guardian*. London: Guardian Newspaper

Hawkins, P. (Autumn 1991) 'The Spiritual Dimension of the Learning Organization', *Management Education and Development*, **22** (3)

Hempton, D. (2006) - in an email to the author

Hobson, T. (2003) *Against Establishment*, London: Darton, Longman and Todd

Holland, J. and Henriot, P. (1983) *Social Analysis – Linking Faith and Justice*, Maryknoll, NY: Orbis Books

Holloway, R. (1990) *The Divine Risk*, London: Darton, Longman and Todd

Howe, S. (2002) *Empire*, Oxford: Oxford University Press

Hughes, G. (1985) *God of Surprises*. London: Darton, Longman and Todd

Hull, J. M. (1975) *School Worship – an Obituary*. London: SCM Press

Hull, J. M. (1985) *What Prevents Christian Adults from Learning?* London: SCM Press

Hull, J. M. (1993) *The Hockerill Lecture. 1993*. London: Hockerill Educational Foundation

Hymns and Psalms (1983). London: Methodist Publishing House

Ignatieff, M. (1993) *Blood and Belonging*. London: Chatto and Windus

In the Navy... (2011-2012) London: Methodist Publishing

Isin, E. F. and Wood, P. F. (1999) *Citizenship and Identity*. London: Sage

Jackson, S. 'The Methodist Diaconal Order: a sign of the diaconal church' in Clark, D. (ed) (2008) *The Diaconal Church: Beyond the Mould of Christendom*. Peterborough: Epworth Press

Jenkins, D. (1976) *The Contradiction of Christianity*. London: SCM Press

Jenkins, P. (2003) *The Next Christendom*. Oxford: Oxford University Press

Jenner, J., 'The Society of Friends as a learning community: the Quaker experience' in Clark, D. (ed) (2008) *The Diaconal Church - beyond the mould of Christendom*. Peterborough: Epworth Press

Jones, M. 'Growing in Grace and Holiness' in Marsh, C. et al. (2004) *Unmasking Methodist Theology*. London: Continuum

Ker, I. (2001) *The New Movements*. London: Catholic Truth Society

Korten, D. C. (1996) *When Corporations Rule the World*. Connecticut: Kumarian Press

Kraemer, H. (1958; 2005 edition) *A Theology of the Laity*. Vancouver: Regent College Publishing

Lakeland, P. (2003) *The Liberation of the Laity*. London: Continuum

Lambert, L. (1999) *Called to Serve*. Manual for the Diaconate. Evangelical Lutheran Church in America, 8765 West Higgins Road, Chicago IL 60631, USA

Brother Lawrence (2008) *The Practice of the Presence of God*. Radford VA: Wilde Publications

Lay Workers' Terms and Conditions (2007) Methodist Conference

Lloyd, J. M. (2010) *Women and the Shaping of British Methodism: Persistent Preachers, 1807-1907*. Manchester and New York: Manchester University Press

McFayden, A. I. (1990) *The call to personhood - a Christian theory of the individual in social relationships*. Cambridge: Cambridge University Press

MacIntyre, A. (1985) (second edition) *After Virtue: a study in moral theory*. London: Duckworth

MacIver, R. M. (1924) *Community*. London: Macmillan

MacIver, R.M. and Page, C.H. (1950) *Society*. London: Macmillan

McLeod, H. and Ustorf, W. (eds) (2003) *The Decline of Christendom in Western Europe, 1750-2000*. Cambridge: Cambridge University Press

Mcluhan, M. (1973) *Understanding Media*. London: Abacus

McManners, J. (ed) (1990) *The Oxford Illustrated History of Christianity*. Oxford: Oxford University Press

McMaster, J. (2002) 'Wesley on Social Holiness'. Scriptural Holiness Project: see Methodist Church web site - www.methodist.org.uk

Marsh, C., Beck, B., Shier-Jones, A. and Wareing, H. (eds) (2004) *Unmasking Methodist Theology*. London: Continuum

Martin, I. (1987) 'Community education; towards a theoretical analysis' in Allen, G.,

Bastiani, J., Martin, I., and Richards, K. (eds.), *Community Education: an Agenda for Educational Reform*. Milton Keynes: Open University Press

Mason, D., Ainger.,G. and Denny, N. (1967) *News from Notting Hill: The Formation of a Group Ministry*. London: Epworth Press

Mason, P. (2012) *Why it's Kicking off Everywhere*. London: Verso

Mead, L. B. (1991) *The One and Future Church*. New York: The Alban Institute.

Merton, R.K. (1957) 'Patterns of Influence: Local and Cosmopolitan Influentials' in *Social Theory and Social Structure* (revised edition). New York: The Free Press

Methodist Diaconal Order ring binder (2002) Birmingham: Methodist Diaconal Order

Methodist Diaconal Order (MDO) (2009) *Worksheets*. Methodist Diaconal Order's Faith and Work Group - www.methodist.org.uk/businessworksheets

The Ministry of the People of God. Methodist Conference (1988)

The Ministry of the People of God in the World. Methodist Conference (1990)

mission-shaped church (2004). London: Church House Publishing

The Nature of Oversight: Leadership, Management and Governance in the Methodist Church in Great Britain (2005) Methodist Conference

Newbigin, L. (1980) *Your Kingdom Come*. Leeds: John Paul the Preacher's Press

Newbibin, L. (1983) *The Other Side of 1984*. Geneva: WCC

Newbigin, L. (1989) *The Gospel in a Pluralist Society*, London: SPCK

The New Dictionary of Pastoral Studies, 2002, London: SPCK

Nichols, A. (1999) *Christendom Awake*, Edinburgh: T. and T. Clark

Orton, A. and Stockdale, T. (2014) *Making Connections - Exploring Methodist Deacons'*

Perspectives on Contemporary Diaconal Ministry. Durham: Sacristy Press

Our Calling (2000) Methodist Conference

Palmer, P. (1987) *A Place Called Community*. Pennsylvannia: Pendle Hill

Pattison, S. (1997) *The Faith of the Managers*. London: Cassell

Pickford, D. (ed) (1985) *The Future of Methodism - approaching end or new beginning?* Westhill College, Birmingham: NACCCAN

Piketty, T. (translated by Goldhammer, A.) (2014) *Capital in the Twenty-First Century*. MA, USA: Harvard University Press

Porter, A. (2004) *Religion versus Empire: British Protestant missionaries and overseas expansion, 1700-1914*. Manchester: Manchester University Press

Priorities for the Methodist Church (2004) Methodist Conference

Quaker Faith and Practice (QFP) (third edition) (2005) London: Religious Society of Friends

Riesman, D. (1950) *The Lonely Crowd*. New York: Doubleday Anchor.

Rowe, T. (1997) 'The reformation of the diaconal order' in *Epworth Review* 24.2

Rudge, P. F. (1968) *Ministry and Management*, London: Tavistock Publications

Sacks, J. (2011) *The Great Partnership - God, Science and the Search for Meaning*. London: Hodder

Sandercock, L. (1998) *Towards Cosmopolis*. John Wiley and Sons: Chichester

Schön, D. A. (1991) *The Reflective Practitioner*, New York: Basic Books

Schumacher, E. F. (1973) *Small Is Beautiful: A Study of Economics as if People Mattered*. London: Blond and Briggs

Senge, P.M. (1990) *The Fifth Discipline*. New York: Currency and Doubleday

Shier-Jones, A. 'Conferring as a Theological Method' in Marsh, C. et al. (2004) *Unmasking Methodist Theology*. London: Continuum

Shier-Jones, A. (2005) *A Work in Progress*. London: Epworth

Shier-Jones, A. 'Pioneering Circuit Ministry' in *Epworth Review* (July 2009) Vol. 36. No. 3. London: Methodist Publishing

Shreeve, E. and Luscombe, P. (2002) *What is a Minister?* Peterborough: EpworthPress

Simpson, G. (1937) *Conflict and Community*. New York: Liberal Press

Singing the Faith (2011) London: Hymns Ancient & Modern

Snyder, H. A. (1991) *Models of the Kingdom*. Eugene, Oregon: Wipf and Stock

Snyder, H. A. 'Holiness of heart and life in a postmodern world' in Greenway, J.B. and Green, J.B. (2007) *Grace and Holiness in a Changing World*. Nashville: Abingdon Press

Spiritual Direction for Ministers in Secular Employment. CHRISM 11 (2011) - www.chrism.org.uk

The Spiritual Exercises of Saint Ignatius Loyola. Hughes, G. and Ivens, M. (translator) (2004) Leominster: Gracewing

Spufford, F. (2012) *Unapologetic*. London: Faber and Faber

Stamp, G. (January 1992) *Stealing the Churches' Clothes*, CIPL Position paper

Staton, M. W. (2000) *Biblical and Early Church Sources for Diaconal Ministry* (unpublished paper)

Staton, M. W. (2001) *The Development of the Diaconal Ministry in the Methodist Church: A Historical and Theological Study*. Ph.D. thesis (unpublished): University of Leeds

Stephenson, T. B. (1890) *Concerning Sisterhoods*. London: Charles H. Kelly

Taylor, C. (2007) *A Secular* Age. Cambridge, MA: Harvard University Press

Taylor, J. (1979) *The Go-Between God*. Oxford: Oxford University Press

Team Focus: Project 1 (2007) London: Methodist Church

'Theological and biblical reflection on *diakonia*: a survey of discussions within the WCC' in *The Ecumenical Review*, 46 (1994)

Tolle, E. (2001) *The Power of Now*. London: Hodder and Stoughton

Tolle, E. (2002) *Practising the Power of Now*. London: Hodder and Stoughton

Tolle, E. (2005) *A New Earth*. London: Penguin Books

Turner, J.M. (2005) *Wesleyan Methodism*. London: Epworth Press

Underhill, E. (1934) *The School of Charity*. London: Longmans, Green and Co.

Underhill. E (1937) *The Spiritual Life*. London: Hodder and Stoughton

Underhill, E. (1953) *An Anthology of the Love of God*. London: Mowbray

Voices from the margins (2005) London: Methodist Church Communication Office

Wakefield, G. S. (1999) *Methodist Spirituality*. Peterborough: Epworth

Walters, C. (1996) 'To the Circuits: the Methodist Diaconal Order' in *Epworth Review* 23:1

Ward, G. (2009) *The Politics of Discipleship*. Grand Rapids, MI: Baker Academic

A way of life (2007) London: Methodist Church Communication Office

Wenger, E. (1998) *Communities of Practice*. Cambridge: Cambridge University Press

Wenger, E. (2002) *Cultivating Communities of Practice*. Boston, Massachusetts: Harvard Business School Press

What is a Deacon? (2004) Methodist Conference

What is a Presbyter? (2002) Methodist Conference

Who do you say we are? (2010-2011) London: Methodist Publishing

Whyte, W. H. (1956) *The Organization Man*. Harmondsworth: Penguin

Wilkinson, D. 'The Activity of God in Methodist Perspective' in Marsh, C. et al. (2004)

Unmasking Methodist Theology. London: Continuum

Windsor Statement of the United Kingdom Ecumenical Diaconal Consultation. (1997, October 1-3) Birmingham: Methodist Diaconal Order. (Issued following a consultation between the Church of Scotland, the Scottish Episcopal Church, the British Methodist Church, the Roman Catholic Church and the Church of England. The consultation included conversations with a United Reformed Church CRCW and a Deacon in training in the Orthodox Church.)

Williams, C. (1960) *John Wesley's Theology Today*. London: Epworth Press

Wuthnow, R. (1994) *Sharing the Journey – Support Groups and America's New Quest for Community*. New York: The Free Press